UDDERLY SPLENDID

Happy Collecting!

JOHN TUTTON

A Pictorial Guide to the Pyrograzed
OR Painted Milkbottle
History and Price Information

John Tutton
1967 Ridgeway Rd.
Front Royal, VA 22630
jtutton@rmaonline.net

The Bible contains the true meaning of Freedom. This is the freedom from sin which will keep us from heaven. This milkbottle pictures a lighthouse with the shining light which I show to represent Jesus which is the Light of the world and is the only way of salvation. Let's remember John 3:16--For God so loved the world that He gave His only begotten Son that whosoever believes in Him should not perish, but have eternal life.

I am dedicating this book to all the dairy farmers through the years who have worked so hard farming and getting little monitary reward. The dairy farmer enjoyed his cows and working the land on his farm. His cows were his pride as well as the buildings on the farm. Here we honor him, as with out the milk, we the milkbottle collector ,would not be able to have the beautiful glass containers. We thank you.

Farm in Virginia

Farm in Western New York

Milkbottle collecting continues to be very popular. The main purpose of this book is to increase the size of the history part of the book and to change dairy photos. Also reproductions continue to influence new collectors ,this section will help them isolate the problem. The reproduction problem will continue to plague collectors but the more information published will at least put all collectors on common ground. The term reproduction means to make a copy of a real milkbottle or make a fantasy type milkbottle which all collectors would want to add to their collection. These bottles are made to fool the public.

The prices listed in this book are for quarts, clean, no case wear or stain. Smaller Sizes are usually lower in price. The prices listed in this book are real and not the typical price guide exaggerated prices. The prices are being paid by collectors either at bottle shows or the internet. If you sell to dealers, expect to receive one half of prices quoted.

There seems to be three levels of prices. Auction, local collectors and general collectors. The general collector will pay a fair price at all times. Local collectors will pay top dollar for specific milkbottles from their towns or areas which the general collector could care less about. Auction prices are driven by the spur of the moment and usually not by people who know prices of milkbottles. Many milkbottles can be purchased much cheaper at bottle shows than auctions.

People often question where have these beautiful milkbottles have been for 40-50 years. Milkbottles are often found under houses where they were put instead of on the porch for the milkman. Others are found in basements with oil, buttons ,or who knows what in them. The pyro milkbottle is rarely dug as the mineral in the soil reacts to the painted label and it rubs off. A few milkbottles are found that were never used by the dairies, long out of business.

Do you have a milkbottle from the town where you grew up. I have milkbottles from all the towns we have lived and it seems now, collect milkbottles from the places I would like to live. Milk bottle collectors are the nicest people in the world and I hope you join us.

Authors Farm during the 50's-and early 60'
Maple Row Ayrshire Farm
Cherry Creek, New York

List of collectors who send photos:

Elaine Rankin
Alberta Oonk
Al Miller
Jack Slootweg
Joe Los
Paul Irby
Paul Doucette
Paul Santuccdi
Walter Fitler
Bob H endershot
Tom Wageling
Edward Getz
Mike King
Albert Morin,jr.
David Copeland
Ernie Probst
Doug Eiker
Kenneth Eiker
Margaret Zimmerman
Steve Wallace
Tom Hendrichs
David Kuntz
Marie and Dale Peacock
Kester Poust
John Patterson
Charles Iager
Bob and Stacy Bernett
Claude Wambold
Robert Hoppe
Dean Shipley
Floyd Smallwood
Earl Nydan
John Jakett
Larry Berndt
Jim Fagan
Stan & Junes's Heirlooms
John Hine
John Waz
Leroy & Kathryn Korth
Mary Lou Andes
Robert Smith
Mrs.Shirley Shorter
Fred Seagle
Donald Campbell
Don Church
Ronald Sibcy
Bill Kisner
Richard Smith
Robert Miller
Russ Yap
Thomas Rippeon
John Adams
Donald Hoover
Tom Williams
Keith Petty
Larry Caddell
Bill Duey
Carl Onufer
Tony Knipp
Mike Leib
Craig Bingman
Larry E.Berndt
Paul Hodsdon
Ron Kremer
Dan and Cathy Krassinger
J.Frank Zeager
Ed Davenport
Ralph Riovo
Roy Demory
Greg Printz
Donna Webber
Terry Alwine
John Mau
Gordon Overdorf

US0001

Glass containers whose sole purpose was to contain milk are the bottles that will be presented in this book. To be a collectable milkbottle, bottles must either have embossed (raised glass lettering) or pyro (painted on letters) names of diaries applied to them. Sears and Wards catalogs, as well as many others sold milkbottles in all sizes without dairy names. They were generic, cheap and readily available.

The earliest record of the use of glass milkbottles has been lost. Milkbottles that predate patented milkbottles exist. One is pictured (US0001) and is from Ireland, has an iron pontil and has an interesting enameled picture of a cow and pasture.

The New York Dairy Company founded by Alex Campbell is credited with using the first factory produced milkbottle. (US0002) The earliest known patent for a milkbottle or jar is the Lester Milk Jar. The patent date was Jan.29, 1878 and less than 5 examples are known. An earlier patent date is found on a milkbottle tin top but is related to the tin top rather than the bottle. This type closure was also used on soda pop bottles. This date is Jan.5, 1875.

US0002

Other interesting milkbottles from this early era are as follows: Mackworth Pure Jersey Cream, a crockery type jar from Maine (US0003), Manorfield Stock Farm, Manor, Pa, a glass wide mouth jar (US0004) and the Tuthill'sDairy, Unionville, N.Y.

The first patent relating to milkbottles is dated March 23,1880 and is for a glass milkbottle with a small glass lid with a tin cap. A very hard to find milkbottle. The next patent date is for a milkbottle with a dome type tin top and is dated Sept.24, 1884. The patented dome tin top is pictured on the Willowbrook milkbottle. (US0005)

The Original Thatcher is one of the most desirable milkbottles to be collected and the most confused with a reproduction. Please note photo (US0006) which shows the reproduction on the right and the Original Thatcher on the left. The patent date of April 27,1886 is for the clamp and while not covering the milk jar itself, is worded as to convey that the jar is a wide mouth bottle, free from retaining cavities or crevices of the typical vessels of the time. It should be noted here that there is several variation of the Original Thatcher milkbottle.

US0003

US0004

US0005

US0006

US0006A

The earliest jar has the regular man milking the cow but the slug plate on back is embossed-H.D.T & Co. Pottsdam, N.Y. The variation include the Common Sense milk jar as noted from ad in the John Pearce catalog dated 1894 (US0006a) and photo (US0007). Original Thatcher's with a slug plate with a dairy name is very rare and highly prized. Photo (US0008) is an example.

During this period of time, different types of bottles were used to hold milk with dairy names embossed on them so we classify them as milkbottles. These include the pop bottle type with wire clamp used by the Chicago Sterilized Milk Co., Sweet Clover and others. (US0009) Fruit jars were also used, only one company sold jars with dairy names embossed on them. The Cohansey Glass Manufacturing Co. made this milk jar and the Echo Farm and Deerfoot Farms used them. (US0010)

US0007

US0008

The patent for the common tin top was issued in April 17,1888 to G.L.Carll. He assigned the patent to Mr. Whiteman who made many of the nice old milkbottles. T.B.Howe made an unusual closer for a milkbottle which is a snap type tin top, wired at one end and the wire snaps over a special made lip. A very hard variation to find. (US0011)

In the Whitall Tatum & Co. annual price list of 1892, they list a milk jar patented Sept.11, 1888, called the Crystal Milk Jar. This milk jar takes a flat glass lid with a separate spring clamp. (US0012) This company made the first Original

US0009

US0010

US0011

US0012

US0013

A. H. REID, PHILADELPHIA. 59

THE COMMON SENSE MILK BOTTLE.

This Milk Bottle is giving the best of satisfaction, as it combines ECONOMY OF TIME, LABOR AND EXPENSE OF MATERIALS.

It discards the use of glass or metal tops, wire bails, or other fastenings which render the ordinary milk jar so difficult to keep clean and in good order, and reduces the cost of manufacture and breakage to the smallest degree possible, and requires no washer. The old style attached cover interferes to a considerable extent with washing the jars.

This Jar, having no cover, either attached or detached, is cleansed thoroughly and with dispatch, having only a slight shoulder within the neck of the jar, which serves to hold the cap or cover in position when adjusted, and is all glass without separate parts.

The cap or cover is made of heavy wood fibre prepared so as to resist the moisture from within and without, and when pressed into the neck of the Jar to the shoulder with the thumb or finger it forms a tightly-fitting cover. The operation of capping is quickly and easily accomplished, and when completed is perfectly tight, and can be handled in any position and transported without danger of leakage. The disc can be removed when the milk is required for use by inserting the blade of a pen-knife or any other sharp instrument and lifting the cap out. The cap can again be used and will seal the Jar reasonably tight, but their nominal cost allows the dealer to discard them after using them once.

Large dealers or milk depots can stamp the cap with date, etc., giving the producer a number that will enable them to keep a thorough record of milk and trace the same to the producer when the milk proves unsatisfactory.

PRICE-LIST.

Quart Milk Bottles	per doz.,	$1.00;	per gross,	$10.00
Pint "	"	.90;	"	8.60
Half-pint "	"	.80;	"	7.00
Caps	per 1000,	.65;	per 10,000 lots	6.00

US0014

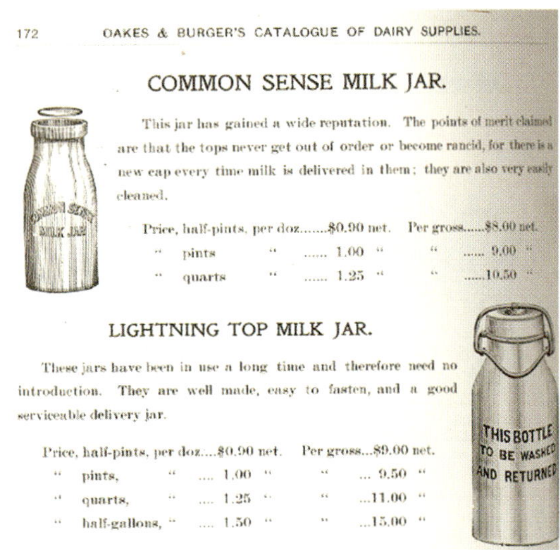

172 OAKES & BURGER'S CATALOGUE OF DAIRY SUPPLIES.

COMMON SENSE MILK JAR.

This jar has gained a wide reputation. The points of merit claimed are that the tops never get out of order or become rancid, for there is a new cap every time milk is delivered in them; they are also very easily cleaned.

Price, half-pints,	per doz.	$0.90 net.	Per gross......$8.00 net.
" pints	"	1.00 "	" ...... 9.00 "
" quarts	"	1.25 "	" ......10.50 "

LIGHTNING TOP MILK JAR.

These jars have been in use a long time and therefore need no introduction. They are well made, easy to fasten, and a good serviceable delivery jar.

Price, half-pints,	per doz.	$0.90 net.	Per gross...$9.00 net.
" pints,	"	1.00 "	" ... 9.50 "
" quarts,	"	1.25 "	" ...11.00 "
" half-gallons,	"	1.50 "	" ...15.00 "

US0015

Thatcher milkbottles for Dr.Thatcher and decided to make their own milkbottles to sell to their customers. These jars are quite rare and most desirable. It should be noted here that Thatcher and Barnhart patented the lid only so this company could use the milkbottle and change the glass lid. The jars as well as the Original Thatcher jars are found in pints and quarts. Photo (US0013) is this jar.

US0016

The next important date relating to milkbottles is Sept.17.1889. A patent was issued to H.P. and S.L. Barnhart for a means of capping and sealing milkbottles. These men were in the employ of Dr. Thatcher, so the company was given credit for the invention of the common sense milkbottle and milkbottle cap. This invention was and is still used today. As stated in the patent, the ordinary milkbottle now in use are usually supplied with glass or metal covers adapted to be attached or detached from the bottleneck. These need a paper or rubber or other packing to be inserted between the cover and bottle and be secured with a bail or fastener. These are objectionable. Metal tops and fasteners soon collect a coat of stale milk impossible to be removed and which soon renders them highly objectionable as new packing has to be supplied each time a bottle is used, the same adds to the expense. Glass stoppers are more ever liable if not adjusted with packing, to come in contact with glass and, of course, serious breakage is caused on return trips. To this end, this invention consists in the construction of the bottle mouth as adapted to receive and retain a wafer-like disc or cap, called in later time, the milkbottle cap. This invention revolutionized the milkbottle industry and the crude types of milkbottles were slowly replaced. Most glassworks were using this patent by 1895 and I do not know if they paid royalties to Thatcher. The common sense milkbottles were highly advertised at the time. Sears, Roebuck & Co. ran ads for the common sense milk jar as well as the Champion Milk Cooler Co. Cortland, N.Y. and the A.H. Reid Co. Phila, Pa. As noted in ads (US0014)&(US0015) milkbottles that are collected as common sense milk jars are not embossed as per that ad but as pictured in photo (US0015). Please note photo (US0016), this milkbottle is more like the bottle pictured in (US0015).The Common Sense milkbottle is quite rare and valued between $400-$500. They are found also in pints and quarts.

F.K.Ward received three different patents for different variations of milkbottles. His third patent is the familar Wards Jar.(US0017)This is a hand finished blown bottles which takes a heavy glass lid. The glass lid has lots of embossing plus a cows head, a very nice jar and is considered rare.

US0017

During this time, that is before cap seated milkbottles were in general use, we find a number of different base embossed milkbottles, not related to any patents. These base embossed milkbottles do not have cap seats. I will list two who used the word Maker, which I assume they actually made the bottles, the rest were wholesalers or jobbers, the two are: Powell & Lockwood Makers, 112 Chambers St., NYC and J.B. Brooke 86 Fulton St.N.Y. Other base embossed milkbottles usually with cap seats are as follows: Fisher, Smith & co. Buffalo, N.Y., R.G.Wright & Co. Buffalo, N.Y., Russell & Whatson, Buffalo, N.Y., W.G.Orr & Co. Washington, D.C., Belle Pre Bottle Co., Alex. Va, Climax Atlantic Bottle Co. N.Y. Stoddard Mfg. Co. Ruthland, Vt.

A.V.Whiteman patented a milk jar on Feb.18th, 1890. This patent is for his famous Cream Line bottle, which shows the quality of the milk or the percent of cream.(US0018) As Mr. Whiteman puts it, the purchaser of the milk is not obliged to submit the milk to any test or to perform any operation with respect to it. He has not ever to pour it into any tester or to introduce any tester into the milk. It will only be necessary for him to allow the jar to stand and when the cream shall have separated from the milk, the jar itself will indicate to him the quality of the milk. I have seen this bottles with regular tin tops, dome caps and with the common cap seat. Also they come in pints and quarts with the pint being the rarest.

US0018

A.G.Smalley is noted for his patent of 1898.(US0019) The patent is for a handled device for bottles or jars consisting of an upper band attached to the neck, middle band in the middle of the bottle with a handle connecting both by a soldered joint. The bottle is shaped like a regular milkbottle, but many different paper labels have been found on them. (US0020)(US0021) Note the copy of the Smalley glass milk jar ad.(US0022) These bottles were sold at most hardware stores by 1900 and were used for all types of liquids. They come in five standard sizes, these being gallon, 1/2 gallon, quart, pint and 1/2pint. The quart is the most common and will be embossed on the base with initials, full name and patent date. Smalley quarts in color exist, one being Photo No. (US0023) and the other is a deep purple.

US0019

US0020

US0021

Heavy White Flint Glass

No. 2 NEW SMALLEY PATENT GLASS MILK JAR

With Smalley Tin Handle and Tin Top Cover Attached.

RETAIL.

½ Pints, each	10c.	3 Pts. each	20c.
Pints, "	12c.	½ Gals. each	25c.
Quarts, "	15c.	1 Gals. "	40c.

WHOLESALE. Net per Dozen.

	½ Pts.	Pts.	Qts.	3 Pts.	½ Gals.	1 Gals.
Less than ½ gross	$1.00	$1.25	$1.40	$1.65	$1.75	$2.75

Reduction in Wholesale Net Prices. Net per Gross.

	½ Pts.	Pts.	Qts.	3 Pts.	½ Gals.	1 Gals.
½ and less than 5 gross	$9.00	$11.00	$13.00	$17.00	$18.00	$29.00
5 " " 10 "	8.75	10.75	12.75	16.75	17.75	28.00
10 " " 25 "	8.50	10.50	12.50	16.50	17.50	27.00
25 gross and over	8.25	10.25	12.25	16.25	17.25	26.00

WITHOUT TIN TOPS, $1.00 PER GROSS LESS.

No. 1 Pulp Caps may also be used on the above. All sizes packed in open crates of six dozen of one size in a crate, except ½ Gals., and 1 Gals., which are in 3 dozen open crates.

Heavy White Flint Glass

No. 5 PATENT GLASS MILK JAR

With Duffy Handle and Tin Top Cover Attached.

What is a pitcher without a handle? What is a tin milk can without a handle? Why not use our glass milk jar with tin handle? Costs but little more than those without handles.

RETAIL.

½ Pints, each	8c.	Quarts, each	13c.
Pints, "	10c.	½ Gals. "	18c

WHOLESALE. Net per Dozen.

	½ Pts.	Pts.	Qts.	½ Gal.
Less than ½ gross	$0.80	$1.05	$1.20	$1.55

Wholesale Net Prices. Net per Gross.

	½ Pts.	Pts.	Qts.	½ Gals.
½ and less than 5 gross	$7.00	$9.00	$11.00	$16.00
5 and less than 10 gross	6.75	8.75	10.75	15.75
10 and less than 25 gross	6.50	8.50	10.50	15.50
25 gross and over	6.25	8.25	10.25	15.25

No. 1 Pulp Caps may also be used on the above. All sizes packed in open crates of six dozen of one size in a crate.

US0022

US0023

US0024

It is interesting to note that the square milkbottle, thought to be modern, was patented on Nov.15.1898. These early square milkbottles have no cap seats and are hand finished. Very few collections have even one so I would consider them rare. (US0024).

Amber milkbottles were used before 1900. It would seem during this time, they were used only for buttermilk as most of the amber bottles have hand finished lips and were embossed buttermilk. One example not fitting the previous statement is Dr. Brushís Milk for Infants. This rare amber bottle is found in pints and quarts and does not have cap seats. Early amber milkbottles are found in one half pints, pint, quarts and one half gallons with the quarts being the most common and one half pints and one half gallons being rare. Note Photos (US0025) & (US0026).

US0025

US0026

The turn of the century saw the increase of dairies delivering milk in glass bottles as more people moved off the farm into cities. Many glass works seeing the demand for glass milkbottle began producing milkbottles. Producing milkbottles by hand blowing was very time consuming but with the introduction of the Owens Semi-Automatic bottle machine, milkbottles could be made cheap and fast. It is interesting to note here that Thatcher Manufacturing Co. learned about the fully automatic Owens bottle machine which could be operated by anybody and quickly acquired the exclusive rights to produce milkbottle on said machine. As stated in information from the company, this was the beginning of big business for Thatcher and the real opening of the bottled milk era for the consumer. Use of the glass milkbottle in 1905 did not exceed 14.5 million bottles per year but with in 10 year, 288 million milkbottles were being produced. Other glass companies still used the Owens semi automatic bottle machine until the Hartford-Empire automatic bottle -making machine was perfected. Please note photos (US0027)(US0028)

US0027

US0028

US0029

US0030

US0031

US0032

It is also interesting to note what was used to make glass milkbottle and the type of molds used. Please note photo (US0029). This shows the mold room at Thatchers in Elmira, NY about 1927, which show a skilled worker cutting a dairy name into mold, and rows and rows of molds. The molds were property of the glass works so were kept at the glass houses. Photos (US0030)(US0031)(US0032) shows mold room, cleaning molds and the molds of the Lockport Glass Co Lockport, NY.(US0033)

The crown lip milkbottle was used during the early part of the century. This patent was issued in 1891 and was used mostly for beer and pop bottles. The Crown Cork & Seal Co. of Baltimore, Md. held this patent. Early milkbottles are found with the early crown lip as shown in photo (US0034). Note the wording from the ad (US0035) which states the Dacro Crown is a hermetic seal. It automatically locks under the glass rim of the bottle. It is scientifically a perfect closure. This type of closure was updated later to the regular dacro which does not have the pop bottle type crown lip.

US0034

US0033

THE

DACRO

METAL CAP

Here at last is the perfect package of Milk or Cream, pure and sweet pasteurized IN the bottle! Made possible by a mechanically perfect closure.

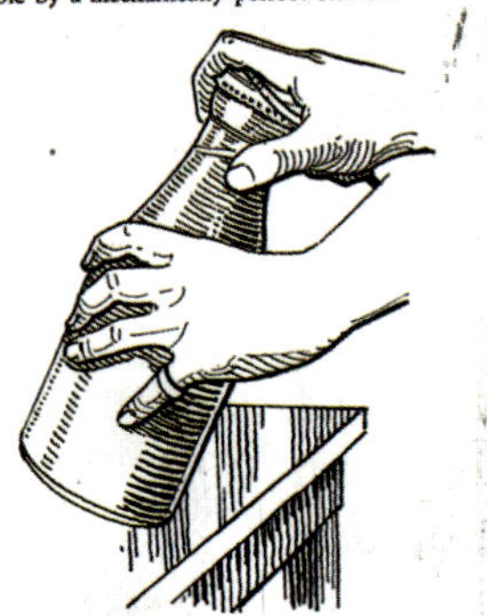

Pure, sweet MILK—delivered under hermetic seal to the home. Handy openers supplied at small cost.

The Dacro Metal Crown — This remarkable cap is made on exactly the same principle as the famous Crown Cork which revolutionized the bottled beverage industry. The Dacro Crown is a hermetic seal. It automatically locks under the glass rim of the bottle. It is scientifically a perfect closure. Sealed with the Dacro Crown, Milk or Cream can be pasteurized in the bottle, an exclusive advantage of this seal. The Dacro Crown covers and protects the pouring lip. It KEEPS clean milk clean! No danger of contamination or tampering with pure contents. And the Dacro Crown can be replaced for temporary covering and seal after opening bottle.

PASTEURIZE YOUR MILK IN-THE-BOTTLE

THE
Crown Cork & Seal Co.
BALTIMORE, U. S. A.

Inventors and originators of the famous "Crown Cork"

US0035

US0036

Weis Fibre Containers
DIPT IN PARAFFINE USED ONLY ONCE

SERVE
your Milk, Cream, Buttermilk, Cottage Cheese and similar products in Weis fiber containers.

Leading health authorities endorse the Weis Fibre Containers. They will hold liquid products for days—even for weeks.

The Weis always brings satisfaction to consumers and larger profits to producers.

Prices Greatly Reduced!

Send for samples and tell us your problem. We'll gladly respond

The Weis
FIBRE CONTAINER CORP.
26 FIRST ST. MONROE, MICH.

US0037

Paper cones and square paper milkbottles were introduced as a one time used container thus more sanitary. The Square paper and waxed container was patented July 18,1911 and is pictured in Photo (US0036). As stated on container-This sanitary container is made of Pure Spruce Wood Fibre. After the container is completely formed, it is immersed, dipped in hot refined paraffin. Thus the inside and outside, including all corners and edges are coated with refined paraffin. Contents are not affected in any way. Paraffined Fibre is opaque and is a non-conductor of heat. Never refill or reuse this container. (US0037) The cone-type milkbottle, called the Purity Bottle, was made by purity Paper Vessels of Baltimore, Md. (This bottle was patented on august 18,1914. (US0038) Other manufacturers were quick to try different paper bottles and note ads (US0039) &(US0040)& waxed bottle (US0041)

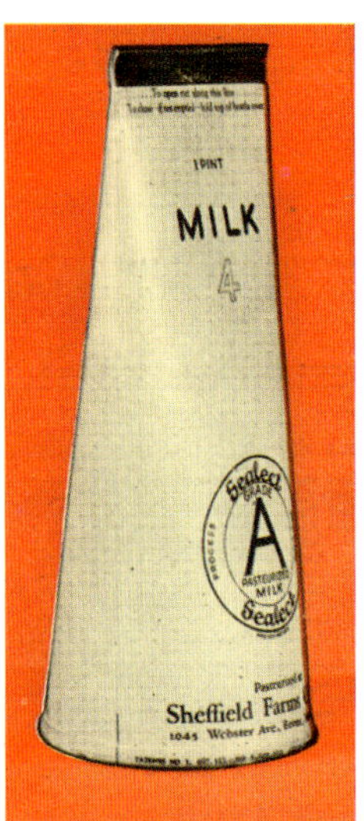

US0040

US0041

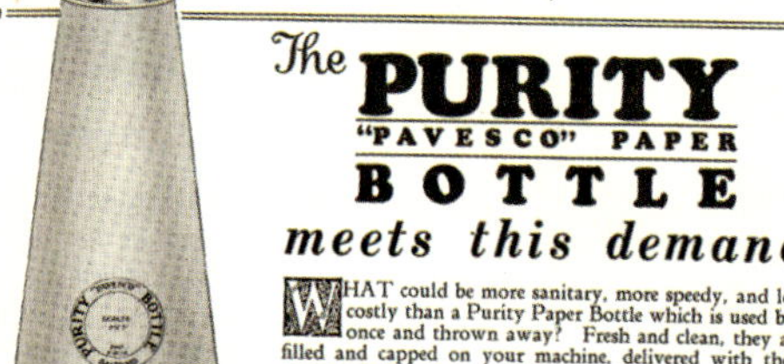

The **PURITY**
"PAVESCO" PAPER
BOTTLE
meets this demand

WHAT could be more sanitary, more speedy, and less costly than a Purity Paper Bottle which is used but once and thrown away? Fresh and clean, they are filled and capped on your machine, delivered with their contents in first-class condition, and destroyed. There are no bottle losses—no bottle collections. The Purity Bottle rounds out the cycle of modern production. You manufacture with modern machines to insure high quality and high profits. You advertise and sell according to modern requirements because competition demands it. Now you can beat competition by delivering your products in Purity Sanitary Paper Bottles. Please your customers, your drivers, and add to your profits with Purity Bottles.

for Ice Cream and Cottage Cheese

LOCKED TOP and BOTTOM

Purity Paper Cans are excellent for ice cream and cottage cheese. They are strong and durable—fine protection for your product, and their neat, attractive appearance proves a great help in sales. Write for free samples of the Purity Paper Cans and the Purity "Pavesco" Paper Bottles.

THE PURITY PAPER VESSELS COMPANY
BALTIMORE, MARYLAND

US0038

Why You Should Use SAN-I-DEAL Paper Bottles

They are MORE PROFITABLE for the Dairyman — They are MORE SANITARY for the Consumer

No Washing / No Breaking — No Lost Bottles / No Extra Load — No Danger from Contagion / No More Returning Empties — No Paying for Losses / No More Short Measure

Here is a bottle shaped paper container with sufficient strength to be used under various types of automatic fillers, and at the lowest price asked for any paper container on the market.

Can be used for MILK, OYSTERS and ALL LIQUID and DRY FOODS

ABSOLUTELY THE LAST WORD IN A PAPER BOTTLE

NO POST CARD INQUIRIES ANSWERED" — WRITE FOR SAMPLES AND PRICES TO

THE PURPUS FIBER PRODUCTS CO. 1808-10 Brown St. **Dayton, Ohio**

US0039

US0042

IF you are located in Chicago, St. Louis, New Orleans or west to the Pacific Coast, we are in excellent position and condition to serve you with high grade milk bottles—none better. Our customers always say of our bottles.

"They Satisfy"

LIBERTY GLASS CO.
SAPULPA, OKLAHOMA

Chicago Representative

2515½ N. Clark St. R. J. CRADDOCK Phone Diversey 3798

US0043

US0044

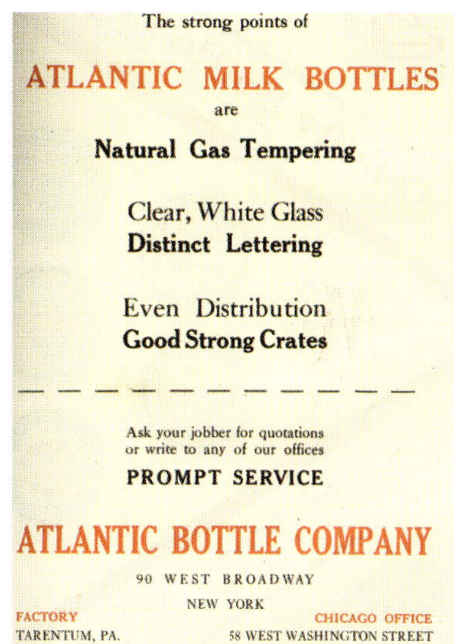

US0045

US0046

US0047

Early manufacturers of glass milkbottles have been noted in my earlier books but I never had ads from either magazines or company literature to help indentify them.. Please note the following ads,which help identify milkbottles: (US0042), (US0043),(US0044), (US0045), (US0046),(US0047), (US0047a), (US0047b).

US0047a

US0047b

Tlhe invention of the Creamtop milkbottle was of great importance to the milkbottle industry. The milkbottles, used in the first part of the century, were tall bodied, short-necked bottles. Thatcher Mfg. noted the housewife wanted to see the cream, so they devoloped the Cream Line Bottle. This bottle had a longer neck, thereby showing off the cream to the greatest advantage. On March 3,1925, Norman Henderson of Albany, N.Y. was awarded a patent for the Creamtop Milkbottle. (US0048) The purpose of the milkbottle was to have a bottle with a cream portion and a milk portion separated from each other by a passage, which could be sealed off by a separator or so called creamtop spoon. (US0049)(US0050)

US0048

Babytop and Cop the Cream type creamtops are continually added to milkbottle collections. These special milkbottles are found embossed, pyro or painted label, all sizes and both round and square. The square babytops and cop the cream do not have the value as do the older round types. I expect at this time, the round types command 2-3 times the prices as the square types. It is amazing the new dairies being found that used this type of milkbottle. The round pyro babytops and cop the cream are commanding top prices around the country at this time.

US0049

US0050

On Sept.22, 1925, an unusual patent was issued. This milkbottle had a slot for a metal or fiber token. As stated in the patent, it is common practice to serve milk to guests in a restaurant and the like in the original container, usually a milkbottle. The milkbottle generally has a cap indicating the origin of the milk and the grade. The bottle usually comes to the customer with the cap removed so that the customer has no means of knowing the grade of milk being received or where the milk originated. The pocket or slot, which is on the side, (US0051), could be readily visible to the customer and there, within, is the invention. Not many dairies used this type of bottle and only a few have survived. If the dairy used a metal token or silver dollar, kids broke the bottles to get the token or money, therefore few have survived (US0052.)

US0047a

US0052

More live dairymen who want to put out "the best bottle of milk in town" are adopting the Duplex Milk Seal every day—

Investigate it!

NATIONAL SEAL CO., Inc.
BROOKLYN

The only real re-seal in the trade

To open a Duplex-Sealed milk or cream bottle, turn the seal a quarter turn to the left. To re-seal turn to right.

WHEN WRITING TO ADVERTISERS PLEASE MENTION THE MILK DEALER.

US0053

June, 1925 THE MILK DEALER 93

BLAKE-HART
Square-Milk-Bottle

Increases capacity of refrigerators and wagon load. Reduces breakage. A stronger—better bottle in every respect. Fills, caps and washes in any standard continuous equipment. An advertising asset. Investigate.

Ask your regular bottle manufacturer or jobber.

Blake-Hart Products Co.
P. O. Box 902
SACRAMENTO, CALIFORNIA

Mr. W. W. Bradford, Sales Manager, will be at Pennsylvania Hotel, New York, from June 15th to July 1st, to give full details and make sales arrangements for eastern territory.

US0056

US0054

US0057

The New and Improved
STRATE SIDE BOTTLE

A DISTINCTIVE PACKAGE
that Trademarks Your Product

A GLASS bottle, designed by a practical milk dealer to provide the highest degree of sanitation and reduce his bottle loss, the Strate Side Bottle offers you the same opportunity. Manufactured by large bottle companies it costs the same as your present bottle. To introduce it into your plant no change in your equipment is necessary, and it can be capped with any standard cap or hood. It is not necessary even to junk your present bottles under the change-over plan we use.

The small royalty cost for the exclusive use of this bottle in your locality will be largely offset by a reduction in your bottle loss.

Write for samples and rates.

The Strate Side Bottle Company
1916 Liberty Bank Building • • Buffalo, New York

US0058

US0055

The National Seal Co., Brooklyn, N.Y. invented the Duplex Milk Seal which is pictured in the ad from The Milk Dealer 10/25. (US0053) You might have come across a milkbottle with screw threads and the ad shows how it was used. Please note Photo number (US0054), (US0055) which shows a milkbottle with the correct steel ring and waxed cap from Creamline Dairy Bethany, Ct.

The first patent for square milkbottles found little success. In 1927, Mr. Blake and Mr. Hart were granted a patent for a square milkbottle. Note ad from The Milk Dealer 6/25 (US0056) for the Blake Hart milkbottle and note on the bottle Pat. Appd. For. (US0057) The square milkbottle are quite heavy unlike the modern type square milkbottles. Very few dairies used this type of milkbottle.

Henry Kart also received a design patent for a special shape milkbottle. The date was May 28.1929 for a tapered-sided milkbottle more like a round paper cone milkbottle (US0058). Henry

US0059

Kart had a diary in Buffalo, NY and used his bottle in this dairy. Another dairy, which used this bottle, was the Alta Crest Farms Spencer, Mass. The green glass milkbottle from this dairy is highly sought after because of the color, shape and because of the cow's head embossed on it. (US0059)

I know of more than 23 dairies that used the green milkbottle. They were made by Reed Glass Works (US0060)(US0061) and Owen Illinois Glass works. Dairymen tell me that they were used at Christmas time for eggnog.

Amber milkbottles were also used during this period of time and quite a few dairies across the country used them. They were used for buttermilk as noted by this milkbottle (US0062) but not all milkbottles used the buttermilk wording on their bottles. I would expect more than 150 dairies used the old type amber milkbottle.

US0060

G.E. West patented a unique milkbottle in 1930 that is highly sought after. This is the cream separator bottle with the indented side. As stated in the patent papers, the novel milkbottle is so constructed as to hold back the milk whilst the cream in the bottle is being poured off. These bottles are found in all sizes and both embossed and pyroglazed. (US0063)(US0064)

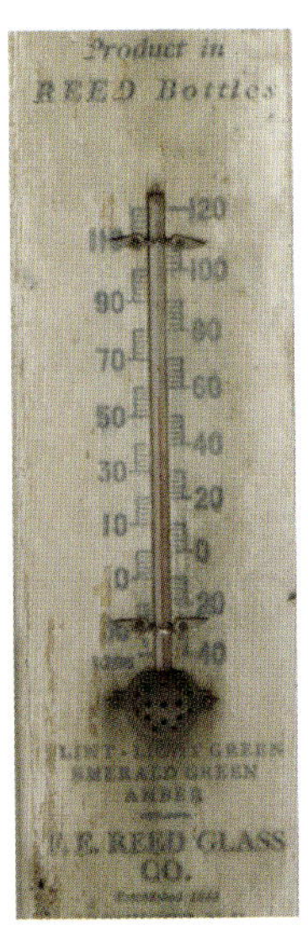

US0061

US0062

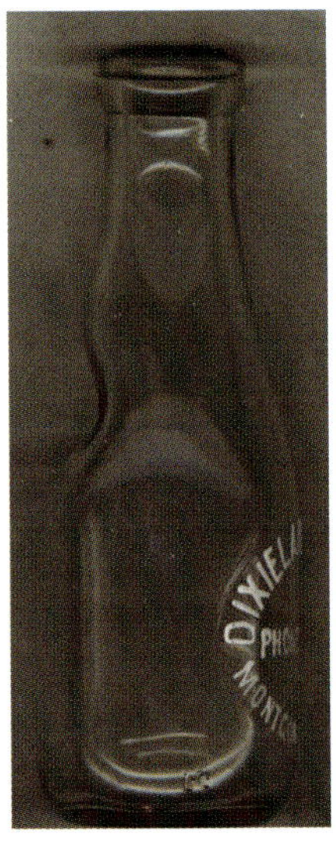

US0063

US0064

US0065

The HOLD-FAST Grip

BRANCH OFFICES

Berney Bond Atlantic Milk Bottles are the only milk bottles made offering the patented Hold-fast Grip finish. This exclusive feature is appreciated by your customers. The patented corrugations insure a firm grip; lend individuality to your package, and make your bottle easily identified. Bottles with this exclusive Hold-fast Grip feature may be furnished in all standard sizes and in many pleasing styles. Write us for samples.

BERNEY BOND—ATLANTIC BOTTLES

Milk Bottle Division

OWENS-ILLINOIS GLASS COMPANY · *Toledo, Ohio*

US0066

In order to give a more complete history of the glass works which made milkbottles, during this time frame of late 1920ís and early 1930's,We can note a news release of the following: Berney Bond Glass Co of Clarion, Pa and Winslow Glass Co of Columbus, Ohio have joined forces to the end that they may effect a wider field of usefulness. This new Unit will have 5 manufacturing units, two at Clarion, Pa, two at Columbus, Oh and another at Hazelhurst, Pa. Note ad for Berney Bond Glass Co. (US0065) listing the factories as stated above. The new name for this company was Berney Bond Glass Co.Note ad (US0066) which now states that Owens Illinois Glass Company has a milkbottle division consisting of Berney Bond and Atlantic Bottles. The date of this ad is July 1931. (US0067) ad is very interesting, adding to the information about the Owens Co. and the Illinois Co. joining together in 1929.

A SYMBOL
of vast significance and importance
to all users of Bottles

In 1929 two rugged old giants of the glass industry clasped hands. Both stood upon adjacent peaks of accomplishment. Behind each lay long years of service in developing management and production to a point where the bottles that bore either name were accepted as BEST by the customers who used them. The familiar "O" of the Owens Company in its square frame and the well-known Illinois "I" in its diamond-shaped frame were symbols that stood for an enormous background of human thought and skill, for problems met and solved, for tasks well done.

The Illinois Company had been in operation since 1873; the Owens Company since 1903. When these two great companies joined forces they fell into step toward still greater accomplishment and still better service. . . . As the Owens-Illinois Glass Company they extended their efforts beyond their products to render valuable assistance to their customers.

Today the "O" and the "I" are combined in the symbolized word Onized. This term is already widely used in the midst of hurried American business life to denote with staccato brevity a standard of quality and service that would require pages of specifications to set forth in detail.

With this one word the customer designates bottles the entire production of which shall be under the most rigid control from the choice of their raw materials to their final checking and approval when released. It means that the ablest engineering and glass making talent in the country is constantly alert in grasping every means for betterment of the product.

The single, compact word,—Onized, commands the activities of plants and offices from coast to coast. It opens the doors to the facilities of a Research Laboratory and Design service maintained wholly for the solution of customers' problems. . . . It is the password admitting the customer to the advantages of a factory system so marvelously flexible, yet so thoroughly standardized in equipment that instant and perfect fulfilment of every requirement is available in any part of the country.

Onized extends its vigilant, all-embracing assurance of quality and service even beyond the vast range of enterprises in which bottles are used. Through the Industrial Materials Division, Onized represents progress toward other fields where glass may bring improved processes, new conveniences and lower costs.

Onized means, in brief, trained men, experienced operation, quality products. It stands for eternal progress, and, greatest of all, for a spirit of helpfulness toward every user of the Owens-Illinois Glass Company's products.

OWENS-ILLINOIS
MILK BOTTLE DIVISION
Berney-Bond Atlantic Bottles

US0067

Many discussion have been held about the first use of the painted label milkbottles and while the following ads will help, not all glass milkbottles have used the print medium to tell us when they started using painted label milkbottles. In a news release in The Milk Dealer magazine, dated May 1933, Applied Color Process enables dairies to give distinction to milkbottles. The Ownes-Illinois glass Co. has developed in its plant at Huntington, W.Va., a method for fusing monograms and distinctive lettering directly into the glass by a process employing coloring enamels that remain a permanent part of the bottle. Four colors, red, blue, green and orange were offered that resisted the cleaning of milkbottles. Photo(US0068) shows the three bottles that were in the new release. In June,1933, a full page ad from Owens Illinois(US0069) using almost the same wording, using the same milkbottles is found. It is hard to say if they developed this process as stated but soon after all the glass works were offering a painted label milkbottle. I expect this applied color label (ACL) process was introduced at the 1933 worlds fair as noted in their large ad.

APPLIED COLOR PROCESS ENABLES DAIRIES TO GIVE DISTINCTION TO MILK BOTTLES

With dairymen every day giving proof of the possibilities of merchandising, the milk container which has so long been "just nother milk bottle" is now coming in for special attention as a package with individuality.

The Owens-Illinois Glass Co. has developed in its plant at Huntington, W. Va., a method for fusing monograms and distinctive lettering directly into the glass by a process employing coloring enamels that remain a permanent part of the bottle. Four colors, red, blue, green and orange, are offered that will resist the action of the alkali solution in washing tanks. The lettering and design in color, being fused with the bottle, cannot be scratched or marred in handling even through the many washings of the bottle.

The white milk in the filled bottle makes an excellent background for the monogram or other lettering printed on the outside of the bottle, and enables the dairyman to mark his package so that it is strikingly individual and a continual advertisement for his products. The colored designs and lettering makes it easy to distinguish the bottle in sorting, and, if desired, various colors can be employed to identify different grades of milk.

* * *

US0068

US0069

US0070

US0072

Illistration no..(US0070) is a full-page ad from the July 1933 The Milk Dealer. shows an ad-(US0071) from March 1935, Milk Plant Monthly, Reed glass works offering colored lettering although not many Reed milkbottles are found with painted labels on them. The first ad I could find from Owens-Illinois greatest competitor, Thatcher Glass Works was in the Milk Plant Monthly dated Sept.1936. Note the fancy ad (US0072) with them stating they have 8 fused colors and stating the name of their painted labeling as Pyroglaze.

US0071

Universal glass Products Co Parkersburg, W.Va. ad in the Milk Dealer dated April 1938 pictured their version of painted label milkbottles which was called "Fire-Fused" (US0073)

US0073

An interesting article is noted in the Jan 1939 issue of The Milk Dealer. It explains an effective means of advertising using painted label milkbottles in Columbus, Ohio. We have all seen the poems on the C.M.D.A. milkbottles from Columbus, Ohio. The lettering is embossed on the shoulder of the bottle and poem is pyro-glazed in the middle. The idea of the poems was to create a nursery rhyme treasure hunt to promote milk. Mispelled words were on only a few milkbotles in circulation and the finder of the misspelled word bottle received $1.00. 60,000 milkbottles of each of 6 nursery rhymes bottles and 200 of the misspelled nursery rhyme were purchased. They were all put into use and as soon as returned, put back into use. I have yet to find one of the misspelled word rhyme bottles. I expect they just wore out, as this was

US0074

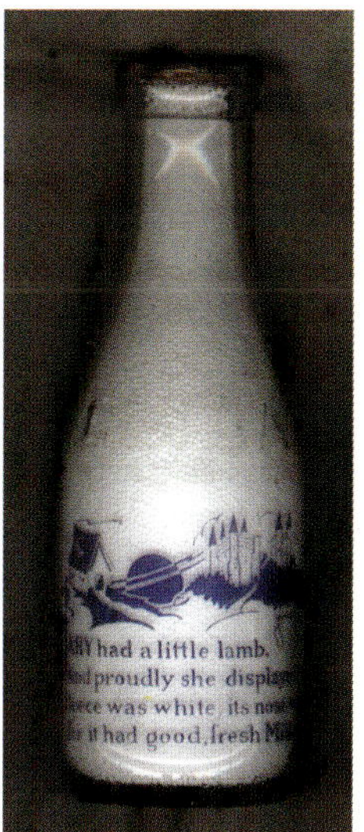

US0075

Meyer Dairy Uses Bottles to Publicize Awards

Winner of first prize on their milk and cream at the Ohio State Fair, the Meyer Dairy Products Company, Cleveland, is telling about it in applied color lettering on its milk and cream bottles. The ACL design created

for the Meyer Company by the Owens-Illinois Glass Company, Toledo, includes a prize-ribbon motif carrying the message, "First Prize . . . Both Milk and Cream . . . Ohio State Fair . . . 1938." Other slogans

US0078

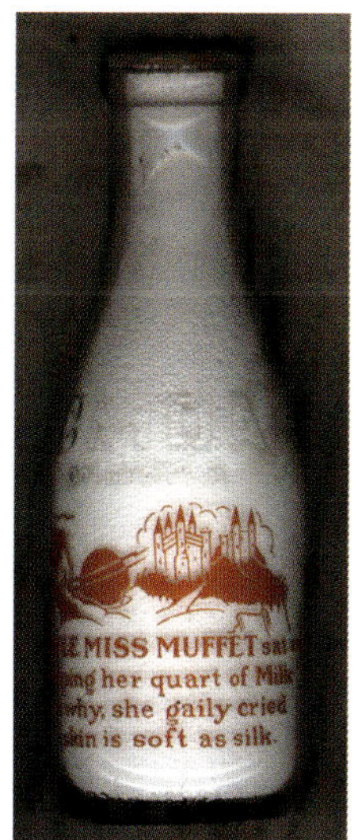

US0076

Slogans on Bottles Win Good Will for Dairies

SINCE milk bottles are objects that come frequently to the attention of school children, many dairies have used colored lettering to aid in the training of children for their protection against traffic dangers.

Roberts Dairy, Omaha, Neb., with branches in Sioux City, Ia., and Lincoln, Neb., adopted such safety slogans on its milk bottles in co-operation with the Omaha Safety Council. Miss Grace Roberts, manager of the dairy, is also secretary of the Safety Council and an enthusiastic believer in the value of these slogans not only in promoting safety but also in promoting due good will for the dairy.

She cites as a typical example of results her solicitation of the account of a newcomer in the city. During the interview her prospective customer remarked, "Sure, we are going to buy Roberts milk . . . because we like what they are doing in the way of teaching the children to be careful, as well as grown-ups."

Other dairies make their safety appeal wholly to adults. Wm. Parry & Sons, Inc., Sunshine Dairies, Utica, N. Y., for example, have, since the opening of school last Fall, used bottles bearing the slogan "Protect Our Children."

In Charleston, W. Va., earlier in the year, the Valley Bell Dairy Co., Inc., won high commendation and much good will for, their vigorous cooperation in a city campaign for traffic safety. As members of the Kanawha Valley Safety Council they voluntarily placed in service 500,000

(Continued on page 80)

(Photos courtesy Owens-Illinois Glass Co.)

US0077

a very successful stunt. It is interesting to note the article stated that a lot of the poem bottles were kept at home, as the children liked the poems. Note photos of some of the poem bottles.(US0074), (US0075), (US0076)

The companies making and selling milkbottle, first thought the use of pyro-glazing was for dairy names only and promoted this use. Note article from Jan.1939 issue of The Milk Dealer that now is promoting the use of slogans of good will.(US0077)

The same issue of The Milk Dealer has article about a milkbottle collector William Conner of Laramie, Wyo. who started collecting when he noticed a large number of out-of-state bottles that made their appearance during the tourist season. He now has over 800 bottles from 38 states and five foreign countries, including one from China. I wonder where that collection is today.

Note article from Milk Plant Monthly Jan.1939 stating the use of ACL designs for Meyer Dairy Cleveland, Oh.(US0078)

Modern top cream top milkbottles used the ACL or pyro-glazed bottles to

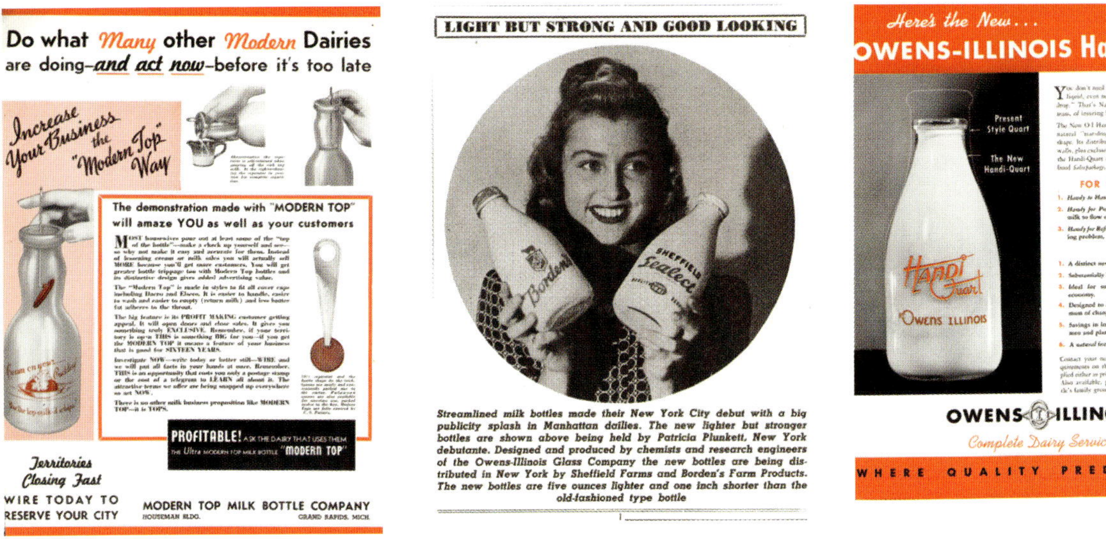

US0079 US0080 US0081

great sucess. Note the full-page ad (US0079). Also note the separator or stopper used to hold skim milk in the bottle while cream is poured off.

The Milk Plant Monthly dating Sept.1940 introduced the squat milkbottle. Milkbottle collectors do not seem to like this short, squatty milkbottles but the housewife did and many dairies chose this style over the tall type(US0080)(US0081)

Milk Plant Monthly dating March 1942 had a great full page ad from Owens-Illinois. Great pyro pictures-do you have them all in your collection?(US0082) Also a full page ad with Liberty Glass Co advertising their painted label called Lustro Color, also note they show the squat milkbottle

US0082 US0083

US0084

US0086

US0085

with a great war slogan.(US0083) This magazine also had a 4-page ad for Thatcher Glass Works but will only show the back page which shows both tall and squat pyro milkbottles. (US0084)

World War II had a big effect on the milk business and glass milkbottles. The milkbottle made a great billboard as noted in both ads (US0085), (US0086) This ad is taken from Milk Plant Monthly dated May 1943. Also in this magazine is the Thatcher Glass Works which pictures an army jeep.(US0087) note under war slogans the only army jeep on a milkbottle.

US0087

pencil rubbing of the lettering of each size ordered.

Pyroglaze--Colored Lettering.

This is put on both sides of the bottles - either on the body or shoulders - but only on lots of 5 gross or more.

The extra cost per gross to be added to the prices above is as follows:

	5 gross	10 gross	car loads
QUARTS	$3.25	$2.30	$1.65
PINTS	3.25	2.20	1.55
½ PINTS	3.25	2.15	1.50

Furnished in red, blue, black, orange, brown or yellow.

Old English, Script, or plain letters, and fancy designs if desired; and different lettering on the two sides if desired.

US0088

US0090

Thatcher Pyroglaze Milk Bottles

COLORED LETTERING ON BOTTLES HELPS ATTRACT CUSTOMERS AND BUILD SALES

Gives Dairy Products the Kind of Eye Appeal that Helps Sell Other Attractively Packaged Foods.

They Speak for Themselves: These new Thatcher Pyroglaze Bottles—with the lettering on the bottles in red, green, blue, black, orange or other striking colors—do a real sales and advertising job for you. When stores display them in their refrigerated cases, these brilliantly lettered bottles speak right out, command attention, and suggest the purchase of your products—just as colorful labels do for other foods. Wherever your Pyroglaze Bottles go, the clear colorful lettering advertises your products and gives them a "quality" appearance that stimulates sales.

Pyroglaze lettering, either one or two color work, may be applied to straight part or body of bottle, on shoulder of bottle or on straight part of neck of bottle approximately one-half inch below bottom of roll and on either one or both sides of bottle. Lettering on body or straight side of bottle is recommended.

Extreme height of Pyroglaze lettering on bottle must not exceed for—

Body Lettering:
- 3 inches on quarts.
- 2 inches on pints.
- 1⅝ inches on half pints and 10-ounce.
- 1½ inches on quarter pints.

For Shoulder Lettering:
- 1¾ inches on quarts.
- 1⅜ inches on pints.
- 1⅛ inches on half-pints and 10-ounce.

Quarter pints cannot be supplied with shoulder lettering.

Cottage cheese and sour cream jars may be lettered at prices the same as milk jars of corresponding capacity.

Colors: Black Blue Orange Yellow Pea Green Red Brown Maroon Dark Green

On **carload orders** any standard mould as now being used by customer will be duplicated in mould shape or finish. If changing to the new regular Milk Bottles, we will furnish the standard regular mould nearest possible to the shape you are now using. On less than carload orders Pyroglaze can be supplied on our standard mould shapes and standard finishes only. Ring, diamond, fluted, fluted to shoulder scroll, beaded, spiral and ribbon to shoulder neck bottles may be Pyroglazed on the body only. Full ribbed or full fluted bottles cannot be supplied, as Pyroglaze can only be applied on smooth surfaces. Banded bottles, either single or double banded, can be supplied with Pyroglaze lettering, on carload orders ONLY.

Special mould lettering on neck, shoulder or elsewhere as required will be supplied in conformity with our standard mould policy.

All capacity markings, shoulder or neck markings and state seals, where required, must be cut into the mould and can not be furnished in Pyroglaze.

We prefer **not to supply** less carload lots with bottom plate marking and if this is eliminated it will facilitate delivery to customer.

Sales Price. Differential to add for Pyroglaze:

Carloads and up **One Lettering:**	One color, body or Shoulder Qts. Pts. ½ Pts.	Two applications Body and Shoulder one or two colors Qts. Pts. ½ Pts.	Two colors, Body only or Shoulder only Qts. Pts. ½ Pts.
If assorted sizes, not less than 10 gross of any size	$....	$....	$.... ....
10 gross and up—one size and one lettering	$....	$....	$.... ....
Less than 10 gross on all sizes—5-gross minimum	$....	$....	$.... ....

One Color—Body or Shoulder—This classification covers one color designs placed on one or both body sides OR one or both shoulder sides of the bottle.

Two Color Designs—This classification applies where a combination of two colors are registered in the same design. If a close registration of the colors is required in the design, such two-color designs cannot be placed on opposite sides of the bottle. In such case, the design on one side must be either one of the two colors used on the opposite side, or, if two color lettering, should be in straight lines not requiring close registration.

Two Applications (one or two colors)—This classification covers one color designs placed on one or both body sides AND one or both shoulder sides. When entire design on one or both sides of body is of one color and entire design on one or both sides of shoulder is of different color the two location price classification shall apply.

Special—If two color, two application job is wanted, add to two-color price differential the difference between one and two application prices.

Carload Quantities—This classification applies to solid car shipments or orders or to contract carload orders to be taken in two shipments of 15,000 lbs. minimum within twelve months' time. Bottles must be lettered for one dairy but not to exceed four stencils may be supplied against such carload or contract order. Minimum quantity supplied against carload classification shall be not less than 10 gross of any size in one shipment.

Jiffy Milk Bottle Protector

Jiffy Milk Bottle Protector is **a heavy, waterproof, insulated** jacket to be put on the bottle when left on the doorstep. When returning the bottle the householder can put the jacket out on the empty bottle. It prevents **freezing in winter and souring in summer,** as well as **insuring** delivery of the milk to the consumer's kitchen in the same **sanitary condition** as when it leaves the dairy. No soot or other dirt can gather on the cap and no cat or dog can lick the top of the bottle. In industrial districts the empty bottle is likewise protected from soot and smoke which is difficult to remove.

See page 163

US0089

Thatcher Glass Works ads on pyro-glazed milkbottles are reproduced here.(US0088)(US0089)

The tall pyro quart has been the milkbottle of choice for the collector now for about 15 years. This was a result of the discovery of those tiny white pellet put into a pyro milkbottle and resulting effect of setting off the pyro or painted label to great advantage. Then the squatty milkbottle was collected but looked down upon by the top collectors. Now the square milkbottle is being collected and enjoyed by hundreds of collectors. I expect some of the new collectors are only collecting by family name or childhood home town. I will provide a short history of the pyro or painted square milkbottle and have included many photos of nicer square quarts with pictures.

The first mention of the modern square milkbottle appeared in the August,1944 issue of The Milk Plant Monthly. A long article about the square milkbottle and the resulting space and weight saving. Sanitary Farm Dairies of Cedar Rapids, Iowa called on Owens-Illinois Glass company for a square milkbottle. It was a success and well received by housewives. Owens-Illinois called the square quart-Handi-Squares. It was also noted that the square sides of the new styled milkbottle lend itself well to the application of color lettering and design.

The Sept.1944 issue of the Milk Plant Monthly pictures a full page ad(US0090) from Thatcher

Reading from left to right, Bob Moore, Production Manager at Borden's Racine, Wisconsin, plant, Charles Lundberg, General Sales Manager at Borden's Racine plant, and Norton B. Jackson, Advertising Manager, Thatcher Manufacturing Company, checking the new T-Square installation at Borden's Racine plant.

MILK PLANT MONTHLY, *September, 1944*

US0091

US0093

US0092

Glass Works introducing their square milkbottle called the T-square.This issue also has an article about Thatcher and the use of the new square milkbottle by the Borden Milk & Ice Cream Co. of Racine, Wis.(US0091) It is interesting to note how Thatcher checked to see how the house wife would react to the new T-square milkbottle. As stated in the article, different dairies bottled a few bottles of milk in square milkbottles and set them with the regular round bottles. A questionaire was left with the bottles for the housewife to fill out and return with the empty bottle. The questionaires asked if the housewife liked the square bottle better than the round and should the dairy change the style of milkbottles. It was noted that the housewife demanded the square bottle to be delivered to their homes. October, 1944 issue of the Milk Plant Monthly ad(US0092) shows how quickly other glass works changed gears and began to produce square milkbottles. Liberty Glass Co. special name for square milkbottles was the Econotainer.(US0093) pictures another ad from Liberty Glass Co showing the three styles of milkbottles used by dairies. All three styles were used until about 1960 and now only the square milkbottle is made. The only glass works making milkbottles at this time that I know of is Stanpac Smithville, Ont. Canada.

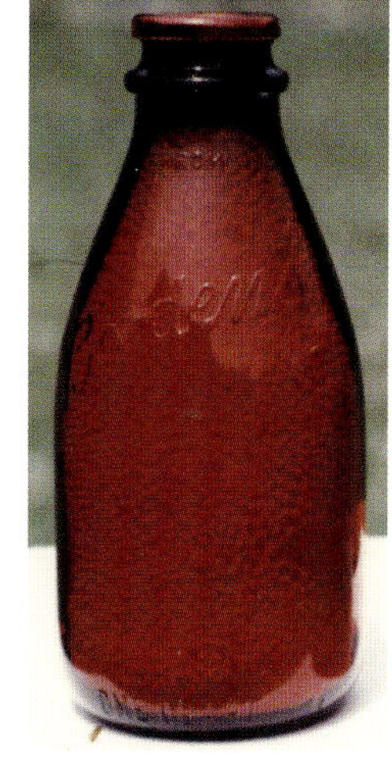

US0094

The last milkbottle to be mentioned here will be the ruby red Bordens milkbottle. Anchor Hocking Glass Corp. of Lancaster, Ohio made these bottles in an attempt to get the Borden Co. to use them as a special advertising campaign. The Borden Company did not like the ruby red milkbottle so were never used. This bottle is quite rare and commands a good price.(US0094).

Two Color Milkbottles

USCL01
Uncommon
Guernsey Dairy
Boise,Idaho
V-$100+

USCL02
Uncommon
Mountain Meadow
Hotchkiss,Co.
V-$100+

USCL03
Uncommon
Bordens
Grove City,Pa
V-$75

USCL04
Uncommon
Driftwood Dairy ------- Embassy Dairy
Driftwood,Ca ------- Washington,DC
V-$75+ each

USCL05
Uncommon
Pine Grove Farm
Binghamton,N.Y.
V-$75

USCL06
Uncommon

V-$50 each

USCL07
Uncommon
Blaisdell Bros.

V-$50

USCL08
Uncommon
Maple Lane

V-$50

USCL09
Rare
Calendar advertizing
Owens Illinois-Thatcher
V-$150+

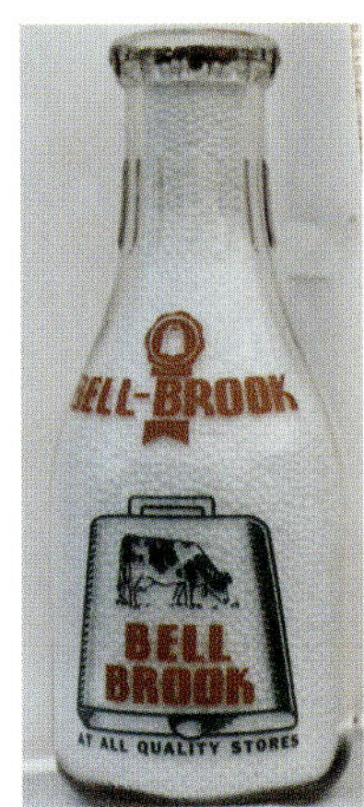

USCL10
Uncommon
Bell Brook
Calif.
V-$50+

USCL11
Uncommon
Baker's Dairy

V-$50

USCL12
Uncommon
W.H.Lee

V-$50

USCL13
RARE
DiSanto Dairy
Clyde,N.Y.
V-$150+

USCL14
Rare
Ideal Farm
Kane,Pa
V-$90+

USCL15
Rare
Adohr Dairy
L.A.Calif.
V-$250+

USCL16
Uncommon
Fuer's Dairy
Burlley,Idaho
V-$75+

USCL17
reverse #16
Fuer's Dairy
Burley,Idaho
V-$00

USCL18
Rare
Alamito Dairy
Omaha,Ne
V-$150+

USCL19
Uncommon
Chambers Dairy
Punxsutawney,Pa
V-$70+

USCL20
reverse#19
Chambers Dairy

V-$00

USCL21
Uncommon
Gateway Dairy

V-$50

USCL22
Rare
Green Medo Dairy
Baker,Or
V-$150

USCL23
reverse#21
Green Medo Dairy

V-$00

USCL24
Uncommon
Univ of Wyoming

V-$50

USCL25
Uncommon
Kirklawn Dairy
Topeka,Ks
V-$75+

USCL26
Uncommon
Kentucky Acres
Crestwood,Ky
V-$75

Two Color Milkbottles

USCL27
Uncommon
Meyer Dairy
Cleveland,Ohio
V-$75+

USCL28
Uncommon
reverse#27

V-$00

USCL29
Uncommon
Alamito Dairy
Amaha,Ne
V-$150+

USCL30
RARE
Del Rico
Santa Fe,N.M.
V-$unkown

USCL31
reverse#30
Del Rico

V-$00

USCL32
Uncommon
Maple City Dairy
Paw Paw,Mi
V-$150+

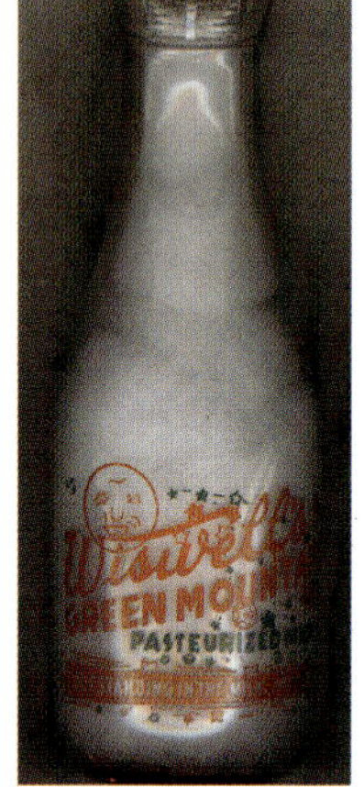

USCL33
Rare
Wiswell Dairy
Lamar.Co
V-$150+

USCL34
reverse#33
Wiswell Dairy

V-$00

USCL35
Uncommon
Midacre Farm
Littleton,N.H.
V-$75

USCL36
Uncommon
Penninsula Dairy
Newport News,Va.
V-$100

USCL37
Uncommon
Brookdale Farm

V-$75

USCL38
reverse#37
Brookdale Farm

V-$00

USCL39
Uncommon
Oakland Dairy

V-$70+

USCL40
RARE
Dunloggon

V-$?

USCL41
Rare
Dunloggon

V-$250+

USCL42
rare
Thatcher Manf.
Souvenir
V-$250+

USCL43
reverse#42
Thatcher Manf.

V-$00

UCSCL44
rare
Abbotts Dairy
Phila,Pa
V-$100+

USCL45
reverse#44
Abbotts Dairy

V-$00

USCL46
Uncommon
Angeles
L.A.,Calif
V-$50+

USCL47
Rare
Echo Hollow Dairy
Eugene,Or
V-$150+

USCL48
Uncommon
Fritzinger Dairy
Lehighton,Pa
V-$75+

USCL49
Uncommon
Parthemore & Sons
N.Cumberland,Pa.
V-$75+

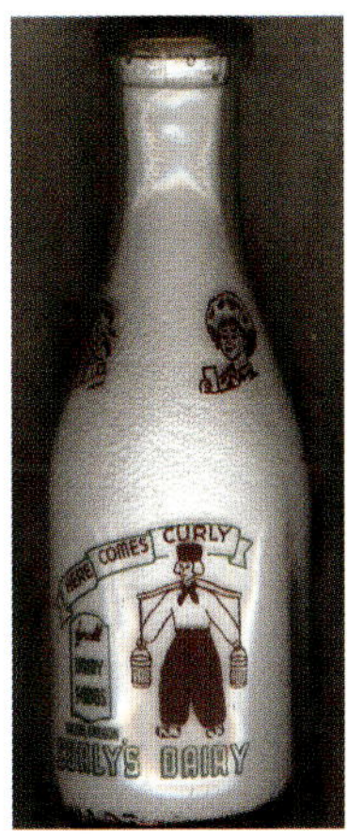

USCL50
Uncommon
Curles Dairy
Salem,Or
V-$75+

USCL51
reverse#50
Curles Dairy

V-$00

Two color samples from Thatcher Mfg Co Pyro glaze Catalog 1944

USST01
Jersey Dairy
Bessemer.Al
V75+50

USST02
Seward Dairy
Seward,Ak.
V-$$100+

USST03
University of Ark.

V-$250+

USST04
San Xauier Bae
Tucson,Az.
V-$100+

USST05
Bluebird dairy
Riverside,Ca
V-$100+

USST06
Careyland
Aurora,Co
V-$50+

USST07
Miller's Dairy
Bloomfield,Ct.
V$75+

USST08
Kennedy's Dairy
Milford,De
V-$150

USST09
H.M.Stone
Augustine,Fl.
V-$50+

USST10
Haskell's Milk
Savannah,Ga.
V-$50+

USST11
Dairymen's Assn.
Honolulu,Hi.
V-$75+

USST12
Hyde's Dairy
Rupert,Id
V-$50+

USST13
Sprague's
Lockport,Il
V-$75+

USST14
Mellody Lane
Hobort,In
V-$75+

USST15
Hamm's
Denmark,Ia
V-$75+

USST16
Mike Sheehan's
Oswatomie,Ks.
V-$50

USST17
Maple Grove Dairy
Shellyville,Ky
V-$75+

USST18
Residence Dairy
Houma,La.
V-$150+

USST19
Otis Dairy
Bridgeton,Me.
V-$100+

USST20
Sycamore Farm
Rockland,Md.
V-$50+

USST21
Brown Swiss Milk
Sterling,Ma.
V-$150+

USST22
Maple City Dairy
Paw Paw,Mi.
V-$150+

USST23
Land O'Lakes
Mankato,Mn.
V-$250+

USST24
Sardis Creamery
Sardis,Ms.
V-$150+

USST25
Melody Farm
Chesterfield,Mo.
V-$70+

USST26
B&C Dairy
Havre,Mt.
V-$50

USST27
Cloverleaf Dairy
McCook,Ne.
V-$50

USST28
Windmill Dairy
Minden,Nv.
V-$50+

USST29
Midacre Farm
Littleton,N.H.
V-$100+

USST30
Forest Dairy
North
Arlington,N.J.
V-$75+

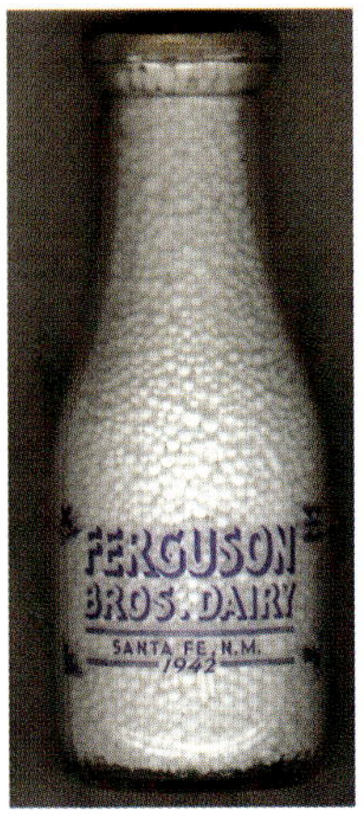

USST31
Ferguson Bros.
Santa Fe,N.M.
V-$50

USST32
D'Allaird Dairy
Troy,N.Y.
V-$50+

USST33
Green Acres Dairy
Kannapolis,N.C.
V-$50+

USST34
Rugby Dairy
Rugby,N.D.
V-$150+

USST35
Big Elm Dairy
Middlefield,O.
V-$50+

USST36
Nowata Dairy
Nowata,Ok.
V-$50

USST37
Rogers Ranch
Medford,Or.
V-$150+

USST38
Pine Grove Dairy
Chambersburg,Pa.
V-$75+

USST39
Consumers Dairy
Westerly,R.I.
V-$50

USST40
Chapmen's Dairy
Greenville,S.C.
V-$50

USST41
Keating
Yankton,S.D.
V-$50

USST43
Lusk&O'Bryan
Mt.Pleasant,Tn.
V-$75+

USST44
Golden Jersey Cry.
Dinburg,Tx.
V-$75+

USST45
Clark-Dale-Dairy
Panguitch,Ut.
V-$75+

USST46
Old Homestead
Windsor,Vt.
V-$125+

USST46
Peninsula Dairy
Newport News.Va.
V-$100+

USST47
Evergreen Dairy
Ellensburg,Wa.
V-$75+

USST48
St.Clair Dairy
Buckhaven,W.V.
V$75+

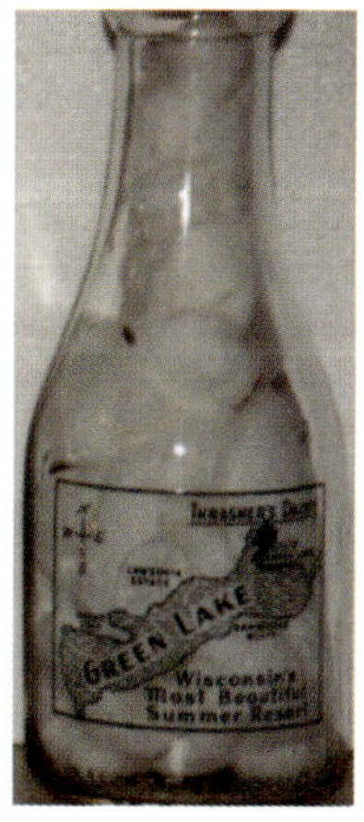

USST49
Thrasher Dairy
Green Lake,Wi.
V-$50+

USST50
Model Dairy
Cheyenne,Wy.
V-$50

USST51
Embassy Dairy
Washington,D.C.
V-$150+

Ads from Milk Plant Monthly Magazine

Animals

USAN01
Rare
Bear Lake
Bear Lake,Mi.
V-$150+

USAN02
Uncommon

V-$50

USAN03
Uncommon
Blue Bird Dairy
Riverside,Ca.
V-$50+

USAN04
Rare
Oso Flaco Dairy
California
V-$150+

USAN05
Rare
Elkmont Farm
Johnsonburg,Pa
V-$100

USAN06
Uncommon
Polar Bear
Denver,Co.
V-$50+

USAN07
Rare
Baer's
Meeker.,Co.
V-$150+

USAN8

Reverse
#UASAN07

USAN09
Semi-Rare
East End Dairy
Harrisburg,Pa
V-$75+

USAN10
Semi-Rare
Frear
Dover,De.
V-$75+

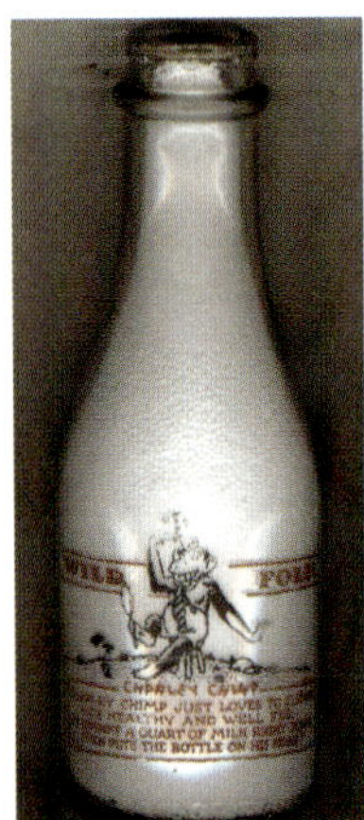

USAN11
Semi-Rare
Frear-60
Dover,De.
V-$75+

USAN12
Semi-Rare
Frear-75
Dover,De.
V-$75+

USAN13
Semi-Rare
Farmers Fairfield
Reading,Pa.
V-$75+

USAN14
Semi-Rare
McVeigh Dairy
Chicago,Il.
V-$75+

USAN15
Uncommon
Read'sGoat Dairy

V-$75+

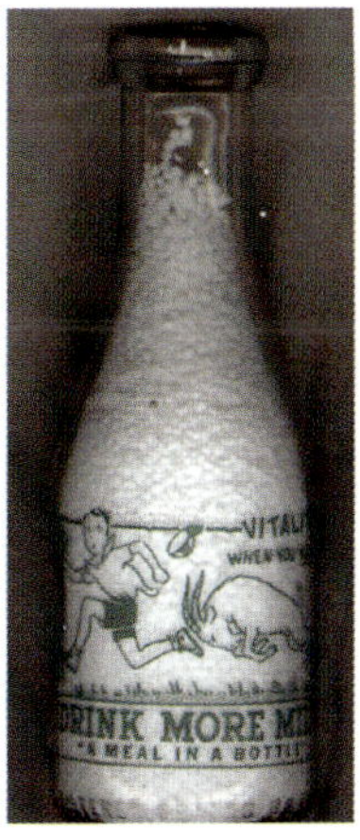

USAN16
Uncommon

V-$75+

USAN17a
Uncommon
Home Dairy
Lancaster,Oh.
V-$50+

USAN17b
Uncommon
Frear-77
Dover,De.
V-$50+

USAN18
Rare

V-$150+

USAN19
Semi-Rare
Panther Ledge
Hackettstown,N.J.
V-$250+

USAN20
Rare
Bear Creek Dairy
E.Mauch Chunk,P.
V-$250+

USAN21
Semi-Rare
Deer Creek Dairy
Marion,In.
V-$100+

USAN22
Uncommon
Morgan Farm

V-$50+

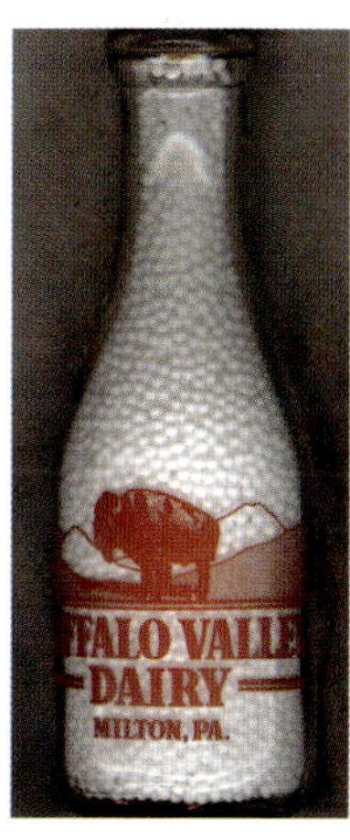

USAN23
Semi-Rare
Buffalo Valley
Milton,Pa.
V-$150+

USAN24
Semi-Rare
Seak's Dairy
Red Lion,Pa.
V-$100-

USAN25
Uncommon
Kaufman's Dairy
Schulkill Haven,Pa.
V-$50+

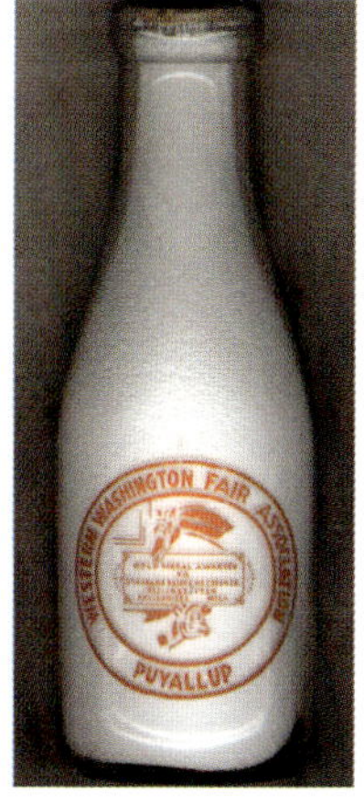

USAN26
Uncommon
Standard Dairy
Longview,Tx.
V-$50+

USAN27
Uncommon
Quality & Service
Red Lion,Pa.
V-$75+

Baby Tops

USBT01
Semi-Rare
Coweset Farm

V-$75+

USBT02
Semi-Rare
Rando Milk
Endicott,N.Y.
V-$75+

UDSBT03
Semi-Rare
Webb Brook Farm

V75+50

USBT04
Rare
Frozen Gold
Shebygan,Wi.
V-$?

USBT05
Semi-Rare
Associated Dairies
Los Angeles,Ca.
V-$250+

USBT06
Uncommon
J.J.Brown Dairy
Troy,N.Y.
V-$75+

USBT07
Uncommon
Fox Dairy
Fostoria,O.
V-$75+

USBT08
Uncommon
North Jersey
Irvington,N.J.
V-$50

USBT09
Semi-Rare
Wait's
Belvidere,Il.
V-$150

USBT10
Uncommon
Springfield
Savanah,Ga.
V-$100+

USBT11
common
Pecora's
Hazleton,Pa.
V-$50

USBT12
Semi-Rare
Sunnyhurst Dairy
Reading,Ma.
V-$150

The BABY TOP MILK BOTTLE

Parade is

Growing So Rapidly

you should investigate at once

◇ ◇ ◇

Beautiful

Distinctive

Exclusive

THE CREAM WHIPS — SALES BUILDER — LOWER BOTTLE COSTS — UNIVERSAL APPEAL — IT HAS EVERYTHING

YOU can be "TOPS" with BABY TOP

PECORA BABY TOP PRODUCTS COMPANY

34 EAST BROAD STREET — *Phone: Hazleton 2448* — WEST HAZLETON, PA.

USBT13
Uncommon
Dressel Dairy
Granite City,Il.
V-$100+

USBT14
Uncommon
United Farm
Albany,N.Y.
V-$100+

USBT15
common
Upton's Farm
Bridgewater,Ma.
V-$50

USBT16
Semi-Rare
Swayer Farms
Gilford,N.H.
V-$150+

USBT17
Semi-Rare
Edgewood Dairy
Beloit,Wi.
V-$100+

USBT18
Uncommon
Lemke'sDeluxe
Wausau,Wi.
V-$75+

USBT19
Uncommon
Embassy Dairy
Washington,D.C.
V-$50+

USBT20
Uncommon
Page's
Pittsburg,Pa.
V-$50+

USBT21
common
Sunshine Dairy

V-$35+

AND MILK DEALERS ARE ENTHUSIASTIC ABOUT THIS

Rapid-Fire Sales Builder

In less than 4 months time, Baby Top Milk Bottles are bringing in new customers for over 18 states. Eventually these sales-stimulating bottles will sweep the country. Somebody in your community will soon be using them. Get the jump on competition—increase your business the Baby Top Way.

Baby Top Milk Bottles give you continuous daily advertising at negligible cost. Each bottle is a distinctive advertisement—a miniature billboard that can't be missed. Baby Top Milk Bottles are piling up amazing records of sales success. *They're the "it" bottle of the industry.* On the route they prove that bottled milk can have personality and lasting remembrance value.

Take this new, low cost, direct, sure-fire way of stirring up sales and creating real merchandising excitement in your trading territory. Write for complete details now.

BABY TOP MILK BOTTLE

FULLY COVERED BY U. S. BASIC PATENT DESIGN No. 98609. (ALSO PATENTED IN CANADA).

PECORA BABY TOP PRODUCTS CO., 34 EAST BROAD STREET WEST HAZLETON, PENN.

MILK PLANT MONTHLY, *June, 1938* 53

Thatcher Mfg.Co Pyro Designs 1944

USBN01
common
Kornely Farm

V-$20-

USBN02
Uncommon
Country Milk

V-$20+

USBN03
common
Belleview Dairy
Syracuse,N.Y.
V-$20+

USBN04
common
Past. Dairy

V-$10+

USBN05
Uncommon
Oak Grove
Oak Grove,Il.
V-$20+

USBN06
Uncommon
Wilton Farm
Baltimore,Md.
V-$25+

USBN07
Uncommon
Guernsey Farm

V-$20

USBN08
special
Kolpen Dairy
Roselle,N.J.
V-$20+

USBN09
Uncommon
Foremost Herd

V-$20+

USBN10
special
Stedland Jersey

V-$20+

USBN11
special
Triangle Farm

V-$20+

USBN12
special
Broeske Dairy
North Wales,Pa.
V-$50+

USBN13

Reverse#12

USBN14
special
Hill & Dale Farm
Oldwick,N.J.
V-$50+

USBN15
special
Swenson Bros.
Lexington,Ma.
V-$20+

USBN16
special
Kensley Ranch

V-$20+

USBN17
Uncommon
Lincoln Woods

V-$35+

USBN18
special
Formost Mellow

V-$50+

USBN19
Uncommon
Platteville Dairy

V-$50

USBN20
special
Cold Spring Farm
Mass.
V-$50+

USBN21
special
Mullen'sDairy
Caldwell,Id.
V-$100+

USBN22
special
Maplewood Farm

V-$75+

USBN23
special
Hill Den
Dixon,Il.
V-$50+

USBN24
special
Cambridge Dairy
Denver,Co.
V-$30+

USBN25
special
McFarland's Dairy
Watertown,Wi.
V-$75+

USBN26
special
White Dotle
Vincentown,N.J.
V-$50+

USBN27
special
Mitchell's Dairy
Charlottte,Mi.
V-$75+

Amish Dairy Farm, Western New York State

USBN28
special

V-$30+

USBN29
special
Joe Rosser & Son

V-$50

USBN30
special
Guernsey Farm
Boulder,Co.
V-$50+

USBN31
special
Pleasant View
Ukiah,Ca.
V-$50+

USBN32
special
Julius Dairy
York,Pa
V-$50+

USBN33
special
Poplar Hill

V-$20

USBN34
Uncommon
Elm Dairy Farm

V-$30+

USBN35
special
Mountain View
Sonora,Ca.
V-$75+

USBN36
special
Bryncoed Farm
Harrisburg,Pa.
V-$50+

USBN37
Uncommon
Riverview
Needsville,Pa.
V-$75+

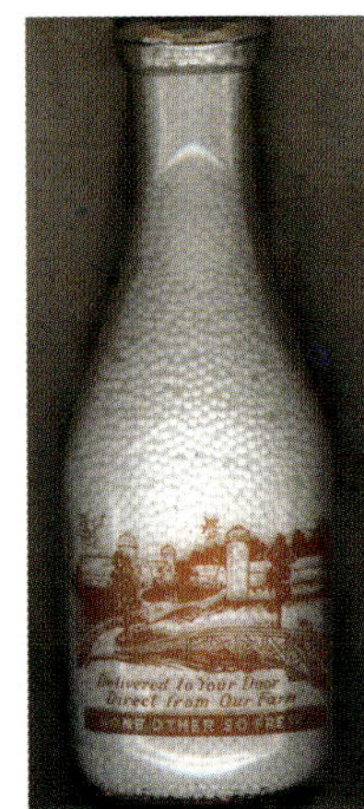

USBN38
special
Dunloggin Farm
Baltimore,Md
V-$100+

USBN39
Uncommon
D.MacKenzie
Waterford,Ct.
V-$50+

USBN40
Uncommon
Stony Crest Farm
Milford,Me.
V-$50+

USBN41
Uncommon
Spring Brook Farm
Newington Jct. Ct
V-$50

Stone Barn, Central New York State

USBN42
Uncommon
Caswell's Farm
Maine
V-$50

USBN43
special
Maid O Cream
LaGrange,Or.
V-$100-

USBN44
special
Castelli Bros.
Conn.
V-$50

USBN45
Uncommon

V-$50

USBN46
Uncommon
Blossom Hill
Lebanon,N.J.
V-$50+

Dairy Farm Barn, Western New York

USBN47
Uncommon
Shean's Jersey
Ranier.Or.
V-$50+

USBN48
special
Ganahl Dairy

V-$100

USBN49
Uncommon
Rhinhart

V-$50+

College

USUN01
Rare
State School
Dairy
V-$50+

USUN01a
Semi-Rare
Univ. Farm
Sewanee,Tn.
V-$50+

USUN02
Uncommon
N.Y. Agr.Tec Inst.
Canton,N.Y.
V-$50

USUN02a
Semi-Rare
Watkinson School

V-$50+

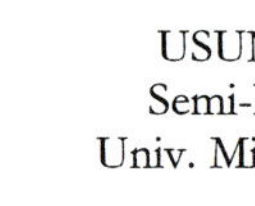

USUN03
Semi-Rare
Univ. Minnesota

V-$50

USUN03a
Uncommon
Dartmouth Dairy
Hanover,N.H
V-$50

USUN04
Rare
Conn. State
College
V-$100+

USUN05
Rare
St.Bona's Farm
Salamanca.N.Y.+
V-$150

USUN06
Uncommon
Univ. of Georgia
Ga.
V-$75+

USUN07
Rare
Carson Valley Sch.
Flourtown,Pa.
V-$150+

USUN08
Uncommon
St.Paul School
Concord,N.H.
V-$50+

USUN09
Semi-Rare
S.Missionary College
Collegedale,Tn.
V-$50+

USUN10
Uncommon
Univ. Wisconsin

V-$50+

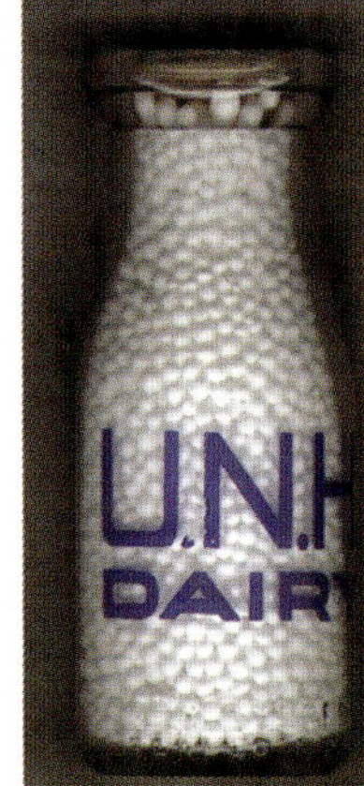

USUN11
common
Univ. of N.H.

V-$50

USUN12
Uncommon
Elmira College
Elmira,N.Y.
V-$50

USUN13
Semi_Rare
Cal Poly
San Luis Obispo
V-$100+

USCC02
Uncommon
Berverly Farms
Mass.
V-$15

USCC3a
Uncommon
Hillcrest Dairy
Bentleyville,Pa.
V-$15+

USCC3b
common
Farmers Delight
Pa.
V-$10

USCC3c
common
Wm.Colteryahn
Pa.
V-$10

USCC01
Uncommon
Owens Dairy
Englewood,Co.
V-$15+

USCC04
Uncommon
United Dairy
Ambridge,Pa.
V-$15+

USCC05
Rare
Clarion Club
Party 1939
V-$

USCC05a
Rare
Merry Christmas

V-$

USCC06
Rare
side of #5a

V-$

USCC07
Rare
side of #5a

V-$

USCC08
Uncommon
Bell Dairy
Norwalk,Oh.
V-$50

USCC09
Uncommon
Reed Sunshine Dairy
Painsville,Oh.
V-$50

USCC10
Uncommon
Strieter Bros.
Cleveland,Oh.
V-$50

USCC11
Uncommon
White Tower
Buffalo,N.Y.
V-$20

USCC12
Uncommon
Heifer Brand

V-$20

Cottage Cheese Jars

USCC13
Uncommon
Mayflower cry.
Boston,Ma.
V-$10

USCC14
common
Sealtest
V-$10

USCC14a
Uncommon
Deerfoot farm
Southbough,Ma.
V-$20

USCC15
Uncommon
Crane Dairy
Clinton,N.Y.
V-$20

USCC15a
Uncommon
Cream Crest
Skokie,Il.
V-$20

USCC15b
Uncommon
Farmers Dairy
Ft.Dodge,Ia.
V-$30

USCC16
Uncommon
Riverside Dairy
Belman,N.J.
V-$20

USCC16a
Uncommon
White Cry.
Charlestown,Ma.
V-$20

USCC16b
Uncommon
Dairy Dell
V-$10

USCC16c
Uncommon
Solois Dairy
Pawtucket.R.I.
V-$20

USCC17
Uncommon
Penn Maid
Phila.Pa.
V-$10

USCC17a
Uncommon
Sagal Farm
Branford,Ct.
V-$20

USCC18
Uncommon
Little Dutch Mill
Rochester,Mn.
V-$20

USCC18a
common
Gulf Hill
Mass.
V-$10

USCC18b
Uncommon
Idlenot Farm
Springfield,Vt.
V-$30

USCC19
Uncommon
Riverside Dairy
Woodville,Oh.
V-$20

USCC19a
common
Otto's Milk
Pg.Pa.
V-$10

USCC19b
Uncommon
Villa Park Dairy
Trenton,N.J.
V-$20

USCC20
Uncommon
Chapman

V-$10

USCC20a
Uncommon
Allvine Dairy
Kansas City,Ks.
V-$20

USCC20b
Uncommon
Lighthouse

V-$30

USCC21
Uncommon
Barton's Dairy
Pinto,Md.
V-$30

USCC21a
Uncommon
Weldonian Dairy
Wellsville,N.Y.
V-$20

USCC21b
Uncommon
Family Cry.

V-$10

USCC22
Uncommon
Foothill Dairy

V-$20

USCC22a
Uncommon
Queenboro Farm

V-$20

USCC22b
Uncommon
Anson's Dairy
Wadhams,N.Y.
V-$20

USCC23
Uncommon
Rose & Brady's
Auburn,N.Y.
V-$20

USCC23a
Uncommon
Bright Star
Meluoukee,Wi.
V-$10

USCC23b
Uncommon
GDC
Sour Cream
V-$10

USCC24
common
National cry.
Boston,Ma.
V-$10

USCC24a
Uncommon
Brookside Farm-
Haverstraw,N.Y.
V-$10

USCC24b
Uncommon
Delamore Farm
Wilm.De.
V-$30

USCC25
Uncommon
Gillespie Dairy
Gillespie,Il
V-$30

USCC25a
Uncommon
Sunny Slope
Spring City,Pa.
V-$20

USCC25b
Uncommon
Hamelin Dairy
Utica,N.Y.
V-$10

USCR01
Uncommon
Meadow Gold Milk

V-$20

USCR02
Uncommon
New London Dairy
Ct.
V-$20

USCR03
Uncommon
Neidig's Dairy
Sunbury,Pa.
V-$20

USCR04
Uncommon
Mountain Dairy

V-$30

USCR05
Uncommon
Moore

V-$20

USCR06
common
Mello-O

V-$10

USCR07
Uncommon
McCue's Dairy

V-$20

USCR08
Uncommon
Strickler's
Huntingdon,Pa.
V-$20

USCR09
Not a creamer
Homagentt
Bristol,Tn.

USCR10
common
Freemans Dairy

V-$20

USCR11
Uncommon
Whitney's

V-$30

USCR11a
Uncommon
Whitney's

V-$30

USCR12
Uncommon
Riggins Inc.
square
V-$20

USCER12a
Uncommon
Riggins Inc.
3/4 ounce
V-$20

USCR12b
Uncommon
Riggins Inc.
1/2 ounce
V-$20

USCR13
Uncommon
Producer's Quality

V-$20

USCR14
Uncommon
Picket's Products
Sheridan,In.
V-$40

USCR15
common
Covalts

V-$20

USCR16
Uncommon
Pilley's Dairy

V-$20

USCR17
Uncommon
Producer's Cry.

V-$20

USCR18
Semi-Rare
Richard Dairy
Neward,De.
V-$50+

USCR19
Uncommon
Valley Farm Dairy

V-$20

USCR20
Uncommon
Blanding Dairy
St.Johns,Mi.
V-$50

USCR20a
Uncommon
reverse#20

V-$o0

USCR21
Uncommon
Lincoln Trail
Tell City,In.
V-$50

USCR22
Uncommon
Idlenot Dairy

V-$30

USCR23
Uncommon
Dart's Dairy
Manchester,Ct.
V-$30

USCR24
Uncommon
Link's
Randolph,N.Y.
V-$40

USCR25
Semi-Rare
Ramon's Foods
Florence,Al.
V-$50+

USCR26
Uncommon
Indiana Dairy
Indiana,Pa.
V-$40+

USCR27
Uncommon
Kyles Dairy
Mackeyville,Pa.
V-$30

USCR28
Uncommon
Norman's Kill
Albany,N.Y.
V-$30

USCR29
Semi-Rare
reverse#29a

V-$00

USCR29a
Semi_Rare
Girton Equip.
Millville,Pa.
V-$70+

USCR30
Uncommon
Potomac Farms
Md.
V-$20

USCR31
Rare
C.C.C.Cross
Fort worth,Tx.
V-$?

USCR31a

reverse#31

V-$00

USCR32
Uncommon
Royale Dairy
Keyser,W.V.
V-$30

USCR33
Rare
N.Mex Milk
Belen,N.M.
V-$

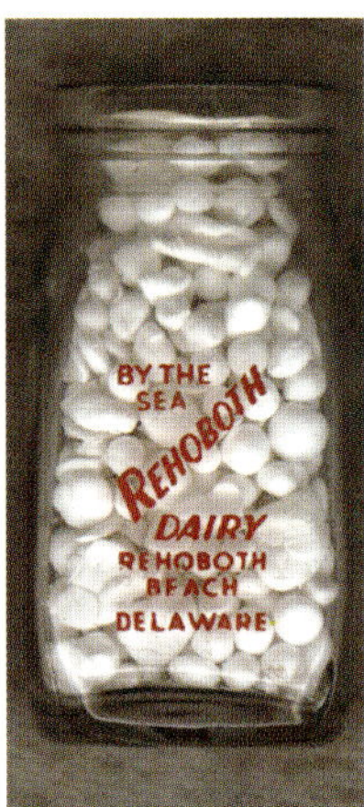

USCR34
Semi-Rare
Rehoboth Dairy
Rehoboth,De.
V-$50=

USCR34a
reverse#34
Rehoboth Dairy

V-$00

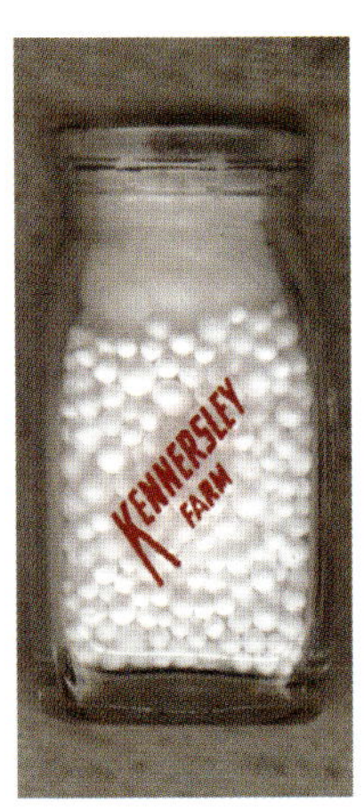

USCR35
Uncommon
Kennersley Farm
Md.
V-$30

USCR36
Uncommon
Marion Center Cry.
Indiana,Pa.
V-$20

USCR37
Uncommon
Greenhill
De.
V-$50+

USCR38
Uncommon
Cattlemen's Cafe
Oklahoma City,Ok.
V-$50+

USCR39
Uncommon
Sharpes Dairy
Jackson,Mi
V-$50

USCR39a
reverse#39
that good milk

V-$00

USCR40
Uncommon
Chicken in the Rough

V-$30

USCR40a
reverse#40

V-$00

USCR41
Semi-Rare
Johnson's Dairy
Coperstown,N.Y.
V-$75+

USCR41a
reverse$41

V-$00

USCR42
Uncommon
Twin Cedar Dairy
McClure,Pa.
V-$30

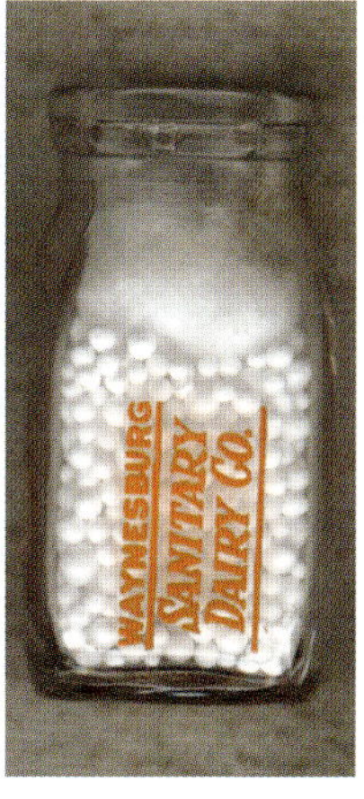

USCR43
Uncommon
Waynesburg Dairy
Waynesburg,Pa.
V-$30

USCR44
Uncommon
Kenmore Lanes
Kenmore,N.Y.
V-$50

USCR44a
reverse$44

V-$00

USCR45
Uncommon
Carrigan's
Niagara Falls,N.Y.
V-$30

USCR46
Uncommon
Rose Lawn Milk

V-$20

USCR47
Uncommon
White Way Dairy

V-$30

USCR48
Uncommon
R.J.Murphy &Sons

V-$30

USCR49
Uncommon
All Star Dairies

V-$20

USRPCR01
copy
Quality Dairy

V-$00

USRPCR02
copy
Muller's Dairy

V-$00

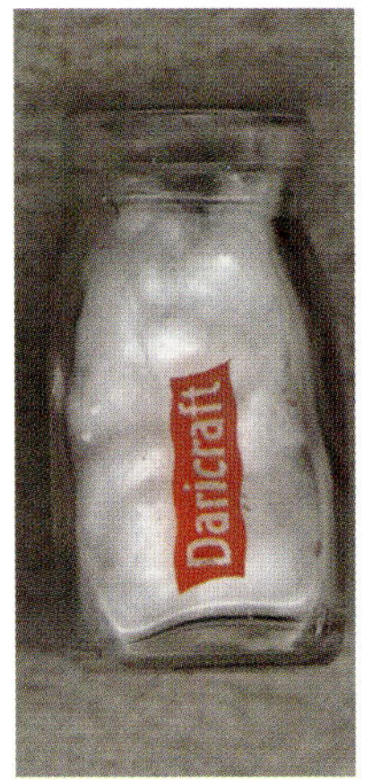

USRPCR03
copy
Daricraft

V-$00

USRPCR04
copy
Meadow Gold

V-$00

USRPCR05
copy
Quality Dairy

V-$00

USRPCR06
copy
Meadow Gold

V-$00

USRPCR07
Fake
Hollywood Diner
Dover,De.
V-$00

USRPCR08
Fake
Skenner Dairy
Jacksonville,Fl.
V-$00

USRPCR09
Fake
B&O

V-$00

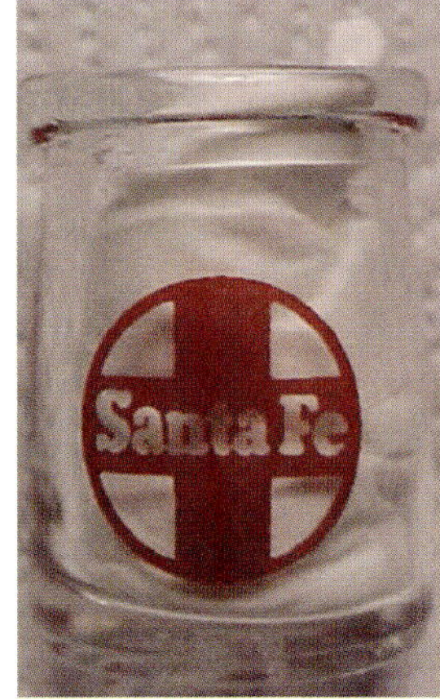

USRPCR10
Fake
Santa Fe

V-$00

USRPCR11
Fake
Royale Dairy
Hanover,Pa.
V-$00

USRPCR12
Fake
Blue Bell Farm
Russell,Pa.
V-$00

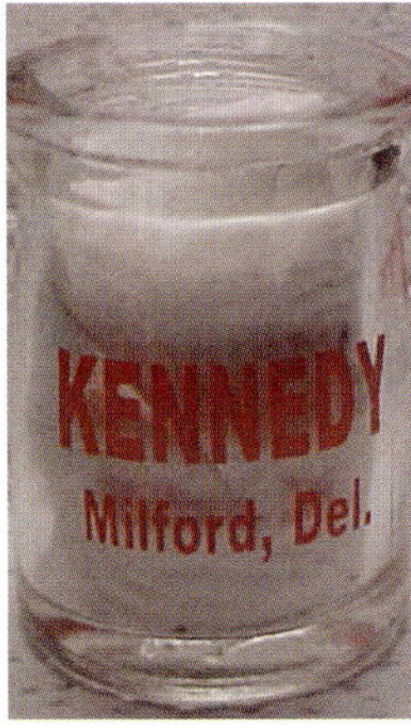

USRPCR13
Fake
Kennedy
Milford,De.
V-$00

USRPCR14
Fake
Northern Pacific
Railway
V-$00

USRPCR15
Fake
Lakeview Lodge
Big Moose,N.Y.
V-$00

USCX01
Uncommon
Fiske

V-$50

USCX01a
Uncommon
Remington

V-$50

USCX01b
Uncommon
Consumers
Westerly,R.I.
V-$50+

USCX02
reverse#01
0
V-$50

USCX02a
reverse#01a
Ayr Farms

V-$00

USCX02b
reverse#02b

V-$00

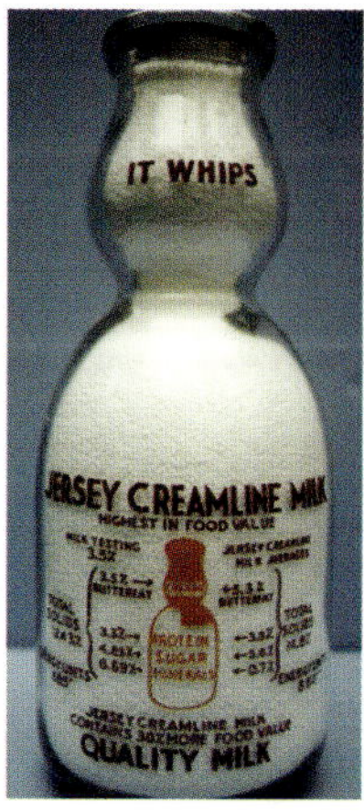

USCX03
Uncommon
Jersey Creamline

V-$50

USCX04
Uncommon
Model Dairy
Clintonville,Wi
V-$50+

USCX05
Uncommon
Mayflower Dairy
Vancuver,Wa.
V-$50

USCX06
Uncommon
Greenville Dairy
Greenville,Pa.
V-$50

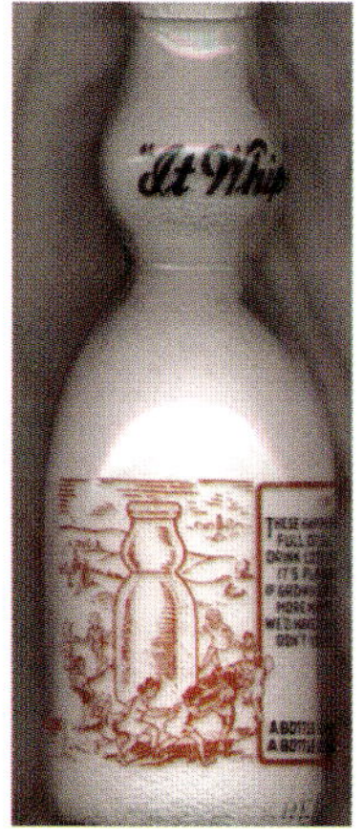

USCX07
Uncommon
Wauregan Dairy
Poem
V-$50

USCX08
Uncommon
Shamrock Dairy
Tucson,Az.
V-$50+

USCX09
Uncommon
Round Top Farm
Dammariscota,Me.
V-$50

USCX10
Uncommon
McAdams Dairy
Chelsea,Ma.
V-$50

USCX11
Uncommon
Shineman's Dairy
Canajoharie,N.Y.
V-$30

USCX12
Semi-Rare
Green Meadow
Rye,N.Y.
V-$75+

USCX12a
Semi-Rare
C.A.Dorr
Watertwon,N.Y.
V-$50+

USCX13
reverse#12

V-$00

USCX13a
reverse#13a

V-$00

USCX14
Uncommon
Week's Dairy
Laconia,N.H.
V-$30

USCX15
Uncommon
Chelsea Farms
Vineland,N.J.
V-$30

USCX16
Uncommon
Maple Tree Dairy
Fall River,Ma.
V-$50

USCX17
Uncommon
LaRose Dairy
So.Hadley Falls,Ma.
V-$50

USCX18
Uncommon
Central Special

V-$20

USCX19
Uncommon
Mt.Ararat Farm
Port Deposit,Md.
V-$30

USCX20
Uncommon
Union Dairy
Freeport,Il.
V-$30

USCX21
reverse#20

V-$00

USCX22
Semi-Rare
Muller's
Rockford,Il.
V-$75+

USCX23
Uncommon
Hudson Dairy
Jacksonville,Il.
V-$50

USCX24
Uncommon
Hoak's Dairy
Harrisburg,Pa.
V-$20

USCX25
Uncommon
Sunrise

V-$30

USCX26
Huge Display Creamtop
glass

V-$?

USSCX27
Uncommon
Geo.Thomas
Brattleboro.Vt.
V-$30

USCX28
Uncommon
Hileman Dairy
Altoona,Pa.
V-$30

USCX29
Uncommon
Gages Dairy
Ilion,N.Y.
V-$30

USCX30
Uncommon
Puritan Super
Cream
V-$30

USCX31
common
Cloverleaf Dairy
Stockton,Ca.
V-$20

USCX32
Uncommon
Trru-Li-Pure
Nashville,Tn.
V-$30

USCX33
Uncommon
Arctic Dairy

V-$20

USCX34
common
Queen City Dairy
Cumberland,Md.
V-$20

USCX35
Uncommon
St.Lawrence
Reading,Pa.
V-$30

USCX36
Uncommon
Miller Reed
Shippensburg,Pa.
V-$30

USCX37
Uncommon
Bellview Farm
Himrod,N.Y.
V-$30

USCX38
Uncommon
Gammel & Kimble

V-$20

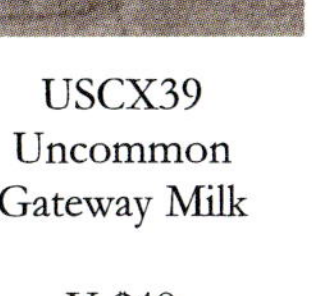

USCX39
Uncommon
Gateway Milk

V-$40

USCX40
Uncommon
Gnagey's Dairy
Meyersdale,Pa.
V-$30

USCX41
Uncommon
Marshall Dairy
Ithaca,N.Y.
V-$20

Full Page Ad

Milk Plant Monthly 1936

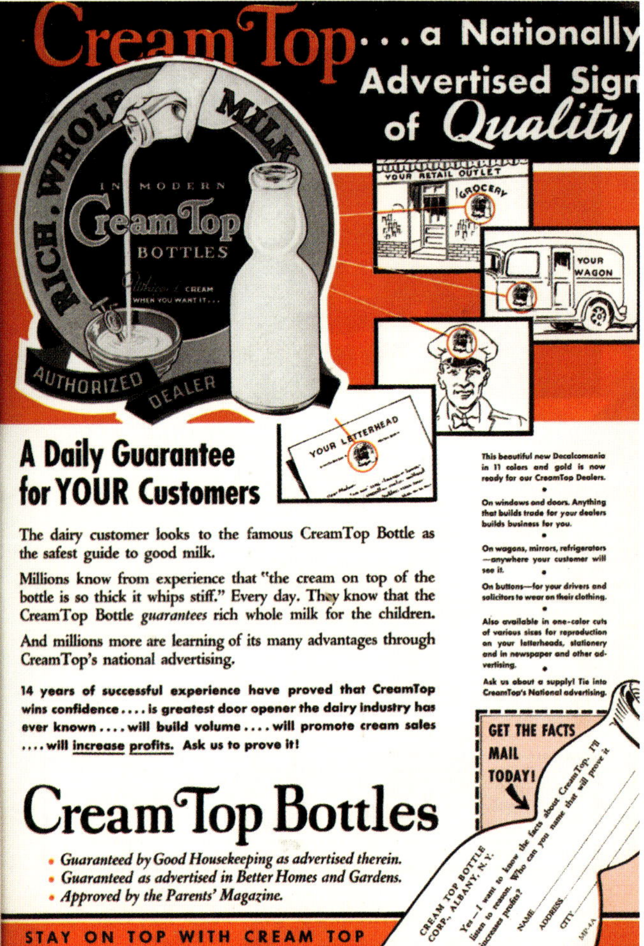

Full Page Ad

Milk Plant Monthly 1938

Results Count!

promises mean nothing...

The COP THE CREAM BOTTLE CO. was founded with two thoughts in mind.

First . . . being dairy owners themselves . . . the originators of this beautiful individual bottle felt it was their DUTY TO offer it to the milk industry because with it dairies can turn failure into success . . . success into real dollars and cents!

Secondly . . . we admit . . . a selfish thought . . . the desire to make the COP THE CREAM CO. the largest . . . most successful individual Bottle Co. in the country!

We can accomplish these two desires in only ONE way. . . .

That way is by ACTUAL RESULTS!

Give COP THE CREAM BOTTLES the opportunity to prove to you that they WILL INCREASE SALES and they WILL CUT YOUR BOTTLE COSTS!

YOUR SUCCESS IS OUR SUCCESS!

OUR GUARANTEE

To any milk dealer in the country . . . who after having used COP THE CREAM BOTTLES and the simple sales plan that we personally supervise . . . for a period of one year . . . and who has not obtained the actual results mentioned above . . . we will give him his next year's franchise ABSOLUTELY FREE!!

That's how confident WE are . . . let us PROVE it to YOU!

WRITE WIRE OR PHONE

NOTE: Our patent rights have been fully investigated and approved by: . . . PATENT PROTECTION CORP. NEW YORK CITY

PAT. NO. 108074 **TRADE MARK REG.**

COP The Cream Bottle Co.

OFFICE SIXTH and PEACE STREET - HAZLETON, PENNSYLVANIA

POST OFFICE BOX NO. 356 PHONE 1955

USCC01
Semi=Rare
Silver Hill Dairy
Portland,Or.
V-$150+

USCC02
Semi-Rare
Crombie Dairy
Joliet.Il.
V-$150+

USCC03
Semi-Rare
Pitstick Dairy
Ottowa.Il.
V-$150+

USCC04
Rare
Hy-Point Dairy
Wilmington,De.
V-$150+

USCC05
Semi-Rare
Roe Dairy

V-$150

USCC06
Uncommon
Leighty Milk
Connelleville,Pa.
V-$75+

USCC07
Semi-Rare
Watkins Dairy
Westminster,Vt.
V-$150+

USCC08
Semi-Rare
Hillside Milk
Whately,Ma.
V-$150+

USCC09
Semi-Rare
West Side Dairy
Albans,Vt.
V-$150+

USCC10
Semi-Rare
Morningcrest
Eau Claire,Wi.
V-$150

USCC11
Semi_Rare
Fountain Head
Hagerstown,Md.
V-$150+

USCC12
Rare
Sweet's Dairy
Fredonia,N.Y.
V-$150+

Full Page Ad, Milk Plant Monthly 1940

Another Booster for
COP THE CREAM BOTTLES
and the *NEW* Cream Copper!

The PAULUS DAIRY
Delivering in Allentown, Bethlehem and Easton, Pa.

Norman L. Paulus, founder and operator of one of the most modern and successful dairy plants in the east has added new sales appeal to his brand of milk. Now offered in COP THE CREAM Bottles, with the NEW Cream Copper, Paulus Dairy milk sales are reaching a new "high" with this exclusive method of modern milk merchandising.
A COP THE CREAM franchise is available at minimum cost.

It's based on $5.00 per thousand population . . . just ½ cent per person . . . in your sales area. We buy back your old bottles to help you get the plan under way, too.
COP THE CREAM Bottles are adaptable to all makes of bottle washers and capping equipment, and can also be furnished with the Alseco finish.
Write for full details on this new, money-making plan today.

PAULUS SUPERIOR KIND DAIRY
PASTEURIZED MILK AND ICE CREAM
BUTZTOWN, PA.
October 25, 1939

Cop the Cream Bottle Company
Traders Bank Bldg.,
Hazleton, Penna.

Gentlemen: In Re: Letter of October 23rd.

Since the adoption of your bottles in March, this year, until we introduced the new Cream Coppers on the second of October we had increased our retail sales 50%. Since the new campaign, with the Cream Coppers, we have increased our sales another 28%. We reached a total increase of 1100 quarts in 8 months. Our campaign is really just getting started.

Speaking frankly, we believe your bottles and coppers are the finest means of getting business yet introduced to the milk industry. You may use our company as a reference at anytime. With best wishes, I am,

Cordially yours,
Norman L. Paulus
Paulus Dairy Company

We can guarantee you sales increases at maximum cost of $3.00 per quart customer. Write for full details today.

COP THE CREAM BOTTLE CO.
TRADERS BANK BLDG. • POST OFFICE BOX 356 • HAZLETON, PA.

USCC13
Semi-Rare
Royal farms
Baltimore,Md.
V-$150

USCC14
Rare
Furman Bros
Ithaca,N.Y.
V-$150+

Cows

USCW01
Uncommon
Parker's Dairy
Nichols.Ct.
V-$20

USCW02
Uncommon
Alta Crest Farms
Spencer,Ma.
V-$30

USCW03
common
Baker & Son

V-$20

USCW04
Uncommon
Jersey Milk

V-$50

USCW05
Uncommon

V-$20

USCW06
Semi-Rare
Maplehurst Dairy
Hinsdale,N.Y.
V-$50+

UCSCW07
reverse#06

V-$00

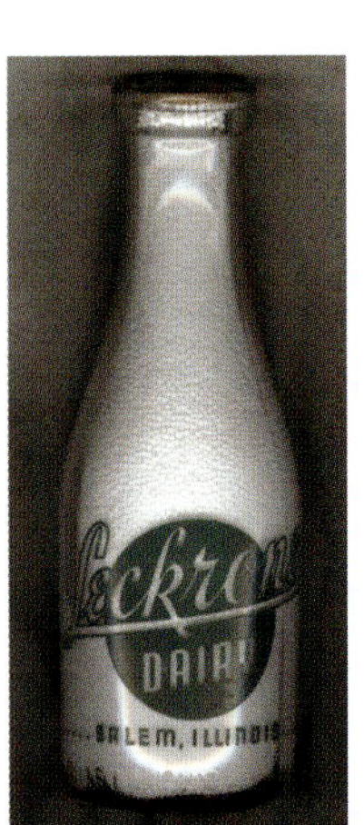

USCW08
Semi-Rare
Lackrone Dairy
Salem,Il.
V-$75+

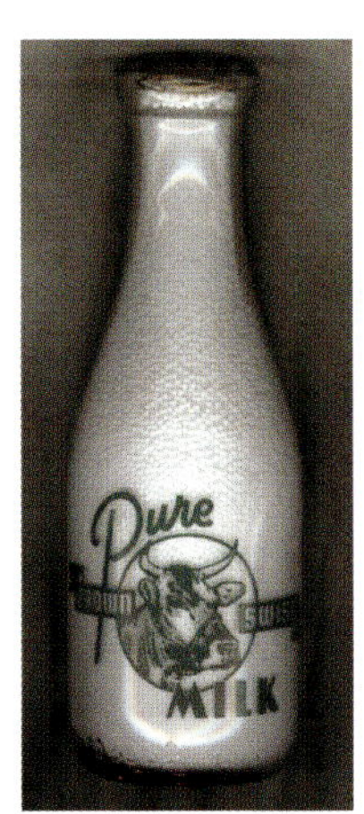

USCW09
reverse#08

V-$00

Thatcher Mfg.Co Saleman Catalog page 1944

USCW10
Uncommon
Chas,Nixon
Brocton,N.Y.
V-$30+

USCW11
Uncommon

V-$30

USCW12
Uncommon
Holstein Milk

V-$30

USCW13
Uncommon
Safe Milk

V-$30

USCW13a
Uncommon

V-$30

USCW14
Uncommon
Forest Hill Dairy
Menphis,Tn.
V-$50

USCW15
Uncommon
Holstein Holsom

V-$30

USCW16
Uncommon
Scott Farm
Portville,N.Y.
V-$50+

USCW17
Uncommon

V-$30

USCW18
Uncommon
Peter Hagner
Buffalo,N.Y.
V-$30

USCW19
Uncommon
Jersey Milk
Foster Mother
V-$30

USCW20
Uncommon
Sand Bank Farm
Contoocook,N.H.
V-$50+

USCW21
Uncommon
Loveridge Miller
Finley,Oh.
V-$50

USCW22
Uncommon
Jersey Creamline

V-$40

1USCW23
Uncommon
Spring Hurst

V-$30

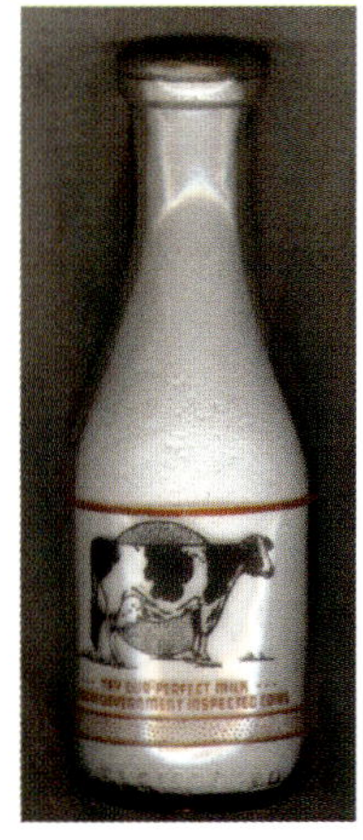

USCW24
Uncommon
Rosedale Farm
Greensburg,Pa.
-$50+

USCW25
Uncommon
Midacre Farm
Bethlehem,N.H.
V-$50+

USCW26
Uncommon
Jersey Milk

V-$30

USCW27
Uncommon
Holstein Milk

V-$30

USCW28
Uncommon
Bonnie Ayr Farm
Whitney,N.Y.
V-$50

USCW29
Uncommon
C.Graves & Sons
Clayton,N.Y.
V-$50

USCW30
reverse#29

V-$00

USCW31
Uncommon
Vista Grande Farm
Opseyville,N.Y.
V-$50+

USCW32
Rare
Carmel Dairy
Ca.
V-$250+

USCW33
reverse#32

V-$00

USCW34
Uncommon
Sheshequin Valley

V-$30

USCW35
reverse#34

V-$00

USCW36
Uncommon
H.Sanborn
Me.
V-$50+

USCW37
reverse#36

V-$00

USCW38
common
Earl Duncan
Troy,N.Y.
V-$25

USCW39
Uncommon

V-$50

USCW40
Uncommon
Rock Castle Dairy
Lynchburg,Va.
V-$30

USCW41
Uncommon
Robert's Dairy
Ma.
V-$50+

USCW42
Rare
Copper Gate Farm
Bernardsville,N.J.
V-$150+

USCW43
reverse#42

V-$00

USCW44
Uncommon
Rossignol's Dairy
Waterville,Me.
V-$20

USCW45
Semi-Rare
Claron Farm

V-$50+

USCW46
Uncommon
Clinch Haven
Norton,Va.
V-$70+

USCW47
Semi-Rare
Cresent Dairy
Paso Robles,Ca.
V-$70-

Disney

USDS01
Semi-Rare
KaVee
Belleville,Pa.
V-$450+

USDS02
Uncommon
Sanitary Dairy
Johnstown,Pa.
V-$250+

USDS03
Semi-Rare
Breezemont Dairy
Brookville,Pa.
V-$450+

USDS04
Semi-Rare
Breezemont Dairy
Brookville,Pa.
V-$350

USDS05
Rare
Snow White Dairy
Coos Bay,Or.
V-$?

USDS06
reverse#5

V-$00

USDS07
Semi-Rare
Sanitary Dairy
Johnstown,Pa.
V-$450

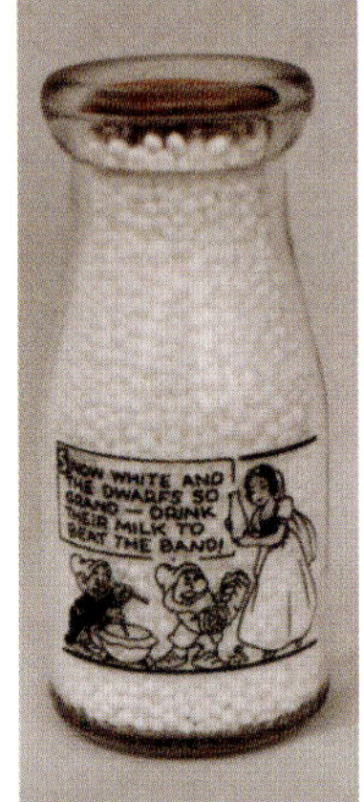

UDDS08
Semi-Rare
Somerset Dairy
Johnstown,Pa.
V-$250

Owens Illinois Glass Co. salemans samples

No. 9

WALT DISNEY'S
SNOW WHITE AND THE SEVEN DWARFS

No. 10

Here are characters from the most highly publicized motion picture of all time, inimitable little figures now endeared to every member of every household from coast to coast

No. 11

The designs and rhymes shown on this page were especially created for Owens-Illinois by Walt Disney's artists to help dairymen increase fluid milk consumption

TWO WISE MEN THE OWL AND DOC THEY DRINK THEIR MILK AROUND THE CLOCK

No. 12

All orders taken for Disney characters on dairy containers must be covered by a signed Advertising Agreement (three copies to Toledo). Orders are to carry an additional premium of 20c per gross on all sizes, and designs are to be one color applications only

No. 13

Snow White Dairy Recipes

USDS09
Uncommon
Wickenburg Dairy
Wickenburg,,Az.
V-$350

USDS10
Uncommon
Sanitary Dairy
Johnstown,Pa.
V-$250

USDS11
Uncommon
City Dairy
Mullan,Id.
V-$450

USDS12
Rare
Tip Top Dairy
Moscow,Id.
V-$350

USDS13
Semi-Rare
Sanitary Milk
Curwensville,Pa.
V-$350

USDS14
Uncommon
Sanitary Dairy
Johnstown,Pa.
V-$250+

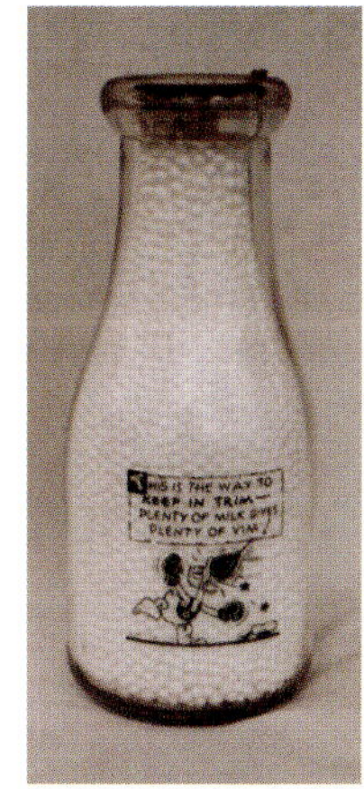

USDS15
Uncommon
Somerset Dairy
Johnstown,Pa.
V-$250

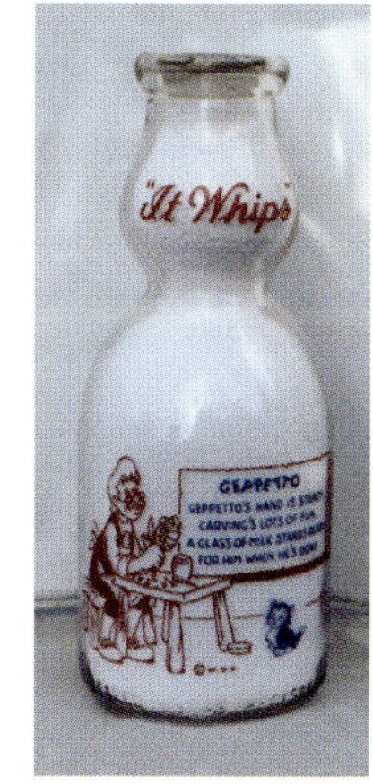

USDS16
Semi-Rare
Ka-Vee Milk
Belleville,Pa.
V-$450

Owens Illinois Glass Co Samples

MICKEY MOUSE ON MILK

All orders taken for Disney Characters on dairy containers must be covered by a signed Advertising Agreement (3 copies to Toledo). Orders are to carry an additional premium of 20¢ per gross on all sizes, and designs are to be one col. or application only.

USDS17
Semi-Rare
Marion Center Cry.
Indiana,Pa.
V-$350

USDS18
Semi-Rare
Johnstown Dairy
Johnstown,Pa.
V-$250+

USDS19
Semi-Rare
Marion Center
Indiana,Pa.
V-$250+

USDS20
Semi-Rare
Breezemont
Brookville,Pa.
V-$250+

USDS21
Semi-Rare
Sanitary Dairy
Johnstown,Pa.
V-$350

USDS22
Semi-Rare
Purity Milk
Oil City,Pa.
V-$350

USDS23
Rare
Dubois Dairy
Dubois,Pa.
V-$450+

USDS24
Semi-Rare
Titusville Dairy
Titusville,Pa.
V-$350

Disney

USDS25
Rare
Marion Center Cry.
Indiana,Pa.
V-$450+

USDS26
Rare
Sanitary Dairy
Johnstown,Pa.
V-$350+

Owens Illinois Glass Co. Samples

THE DESIGNS AND RHYMES SHOWN ON THIS PAGE WERE ESPECIALLY CREATED FOR OWENS-ILLINOIS BY WALT DISNEY'S ARTISTS TO HELP DAIRYMEN INCREASE FLUID MILK CONSUMPTION

WALT DISNEY'S

FERDINAND THE BULL

ALL ORDERS TAKEN FOR DISNEY CHARACTERS ON DAIRY CONTAINERS MUST BE COVERED BY A SIGNED ADVERTISING AGREEMENT (THREE COPIES TO TOLEDO). ORDERS ARE TO CARRY AN ADDITIONAL PREMIUM OF 20c PER GROSS ON ALL SIZES.

USDS27
Semi-Rare
Forest Grove Dairy
Forest Grove,Il.
V-$450+

USDS28
Uncommon
Sanitary Dairy
Johnstown,Pa.
V-$250

USDS29
Semi-Rare
Franz Dairy
Emlenton,Pa.
V-$350

USDS30
Semi-Rare
Dubois Dairy
Dubois,Pa.
V-$350

USDS31
Semi-Rare
Freeman's
Allentown,Pa.
V-$250+

USDS32
Semi-Rare
Dubois Dairy
Dubois,Pa.
V-$350+

USDS33
Rare
Dubois Dairy
Dubois,Pa.
V-$450

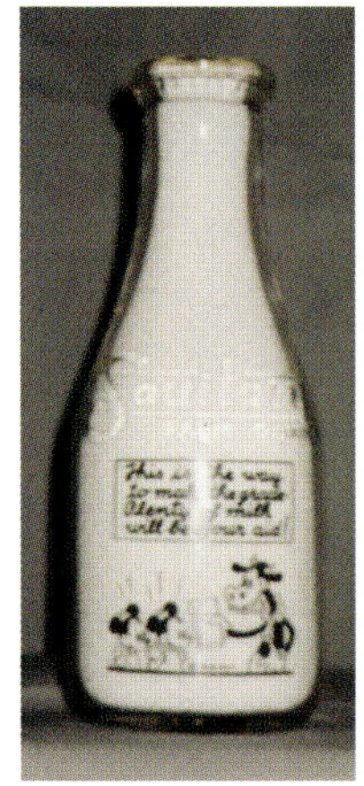

USDS34
Uncommon
Sanitary Farm
Mn.
V-$250

USDS35
Rare
Dubois Dairy
Dubois,Pa.
V-$450

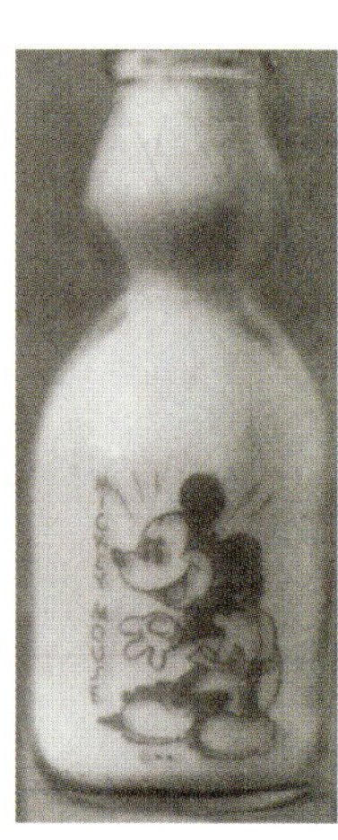

USDS36
Rare
Dubois Dairy
Dubois,Pa.
V-$450

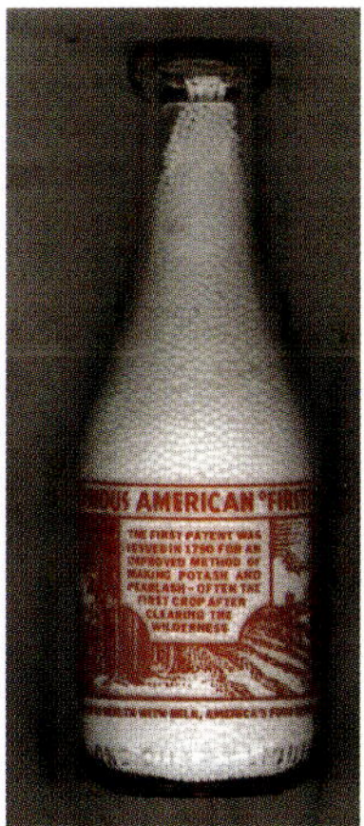

USAF01
Semi-Rare
Johnstown Dairy
Johnstown,Pa.
V-$120+

USAF02
Rare
Johnstown Dairy
Johnstown,Pa.
V-$120+

USAF03
Rare
Johnstown Dairy
Johnstown,Pa.
V-$120

USAF04
Semi-Rare
Ideal Farms
Fredrick,Md.
V-$150+

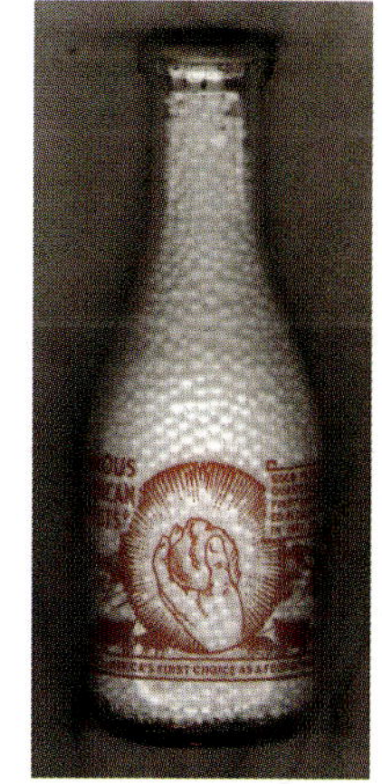

USAF05
Semi-Rare
Johnstown Dairy
Johnstown,Pa.
V-$120

USAF06
uncommon
Tuschlag Bros.
Greenville,Pa.
V-$150

USAF07
Semi-Rare
Johnstown Dairy
Johnstown,Pa.
V-$150

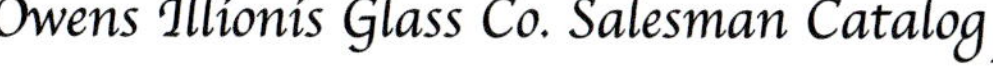

Owens Illionis Glass Co. Salesman Catalog page

Famous American "Firsts"
THE FIRST COAST-TO-COAST MAIL DELIVERY WAS MADE POSSIBLE IN 1860 BY THE "PONY EXPRESS" RIDERS, DEFYING THE DANGERS OF THE FAR WEST
FROM COAST TO COAST MILK RANKS FIRST AS A FOOD BEVERAGE
554

FAMOUS AMERICAN "FIRSTS"
BETSY ROSS
ACCORDING TO POPULAR BELIEF, MISS BETSY ROSS MADE OUR FIRST "STARS AND STRIPES"
MILK IS FIRST IN AMERICA AS A FOOD · BEVERAGE
555

FAMOUS AMERICAN "FIRSTS"
THE FIRST PATENT WAS ISSUED IN 1790 FOR AN IMPROVED METHOD OF MAKING POTASH AND PEARLASH - OFTEN THE FIRST CROP AFTER CLEARING THE WILDERNESS
BE FIRST IN HEALTH WITH MILK, AMERICA'S FOOD BEVERAGE
556

FAMOUS AMERICAN "FIRSTS"
GOLD IN PAYING QUANTITIES WAS FIRST DISCOVERED IN CALIFORNIA IN MAY, 1848...
MILK IS AMERICA'S FIRST CHOICE AS A FOOD-BEVERAGE
557

FAMOUS AMERICAN "FIRSTS"
DELAWARE, ACCEPTING THE CONSTITUTION ON DEC. 7, 1787 BY UNANIMOUS VOTE, WON THE HONOR OF BEING THE FIRST STATE TO ENTER THE AMERICAN UNION
MILK RANKS FIRST IN AMERICA AS FOOD AND BEVERAGE
558

FAMOUS AMERICAN "FIRSTS"
THE FIRST IRON ORE DEPOSIT IN AMERICA WAS DISCOVERED IN VIRGINIA IN THE YEAR 1715
MILK IS FIRST IN VALUE, HEALTH AND REFRESHMENT
559

E. L. DRAKE, IN POVERTY AFTER REPEATED FAILURES, SUNK THE FIRST SUCCESSFUL AMERICAN OILWELL AUG. 28, 1859 AT TITUSVILLE, PA.
FAMOUS AMERICAN "FIRSTS"
AMERICA'S FIRST CHOICE IS MILK, THE FOOD BEVERAGE
560

FAMOUS AMERICAN "FIRSTS"
The NEW YORK SKYLINE
THE FLATIRON BUILDING IS AMERICA'S FIRST STEEL-FRAME SKYSCRAPER-20 STORIES HIGH
MILK RANKS FIRST ON AMERICAN TABLES
561

FAMOUS AMERICAN "FIRSTS"
THE FIRST STEAM RAILWAY IN THE UNITED STATES WAS OPENED AT BALTIMORE, MD. AUG. 28, 1830, WITH 14 MILES OF TRACK
MILK IS FIRST AS AMERICA'S FOOD BEVERAGE
562

USAF08
Rare
Bay View Dairy
Plattsburg,N.Y.
V-$150

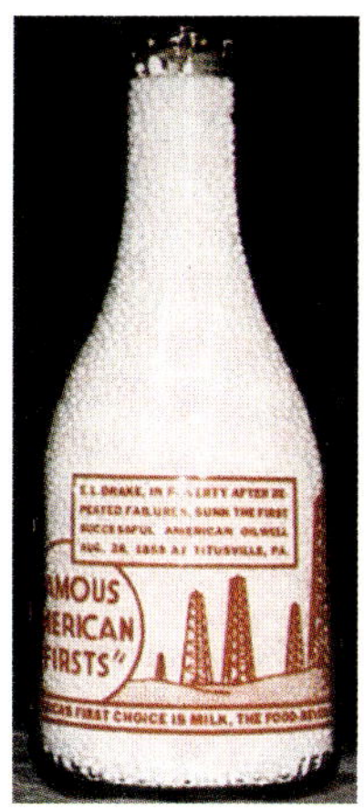

USAF09
Rare
Johnstown Dairy
Johnstown,Pa.
V-$150+

USFH01
Rare
Iowana Farms
Des Moines,Ia.
V-$250+

USFH02
Semi-Rare
Johnstown Dairy
Johnstown,Pa.
V-$120

USFH03
Semi-Rare
Johnstown Dairy
Johnstown,Pa.
V-$120

USFH04
Semi-Rare
Johnstown Dairy
Johnstown,Pa.
V-$120

USFH05
Semi-Rare
Johnstown Dairy
Johnstown,Pa.
V-$120

USFH06
Semi-Rare
Johnstown Dairy
Johnstown,Pa.
V-$120

USFH07
Semi-Rare
Johnstown Dairy
Johnstown,Pa.
V-$120

Owens Illinois Glass Co Salesman Sample Page

FAMOUS AMERICAN HEROES
1706 BENJAMIN FRANKLIN 1790
MILK—THE UNIVERSAL FOOD THRU THE CENTURIES
563

CONCERNING PYROGLAZE

PYROGLAZE is a copyrighted name of the Thatcher Manufacturing Company used for colored lettering and design fused into the glass surface of milk and other bottles. It is applied by means of the photographic silk screen method. Each color applied requires a separate application, as does every location. There are three locations on the bottle where lettering and designs may be applied. They are neck, shoulder and body. Pyroglaze dimensions used in these various locations are as follows:

SIZE	DIMENSIONS OF PYROGLAZE SPACE HEIGHT	WIDTH
All Sizes	5/8"	2-1/4"
B Quart	1-3/4"	
B Pint	1-1/2"	
Regular 1/3 Quart	1-1/8"	2-7/16'
Regular 1/2 Pint	1-1/8"	2-1/4"
D Quart	1-11/16"	
D Pint	1-1/4"	
D 1/2 Pint	1-1/8"	
B Quart	3"	5"
B Pint	2"	3-7/8"
B 10 oz. and 1/3 Qt.	1-5/8"	3-1/16'
B 1/2 Pint	1-5/8"	2-7/8"
Gill	1-1/8"	2-1/2"
D Quart	2-1/2"	5"
D Pint	2-1/4"	3-3/4"
D 10 oz.	1-5/8"	3-1/4"
D 1/2 Pint	1-1/2"	2-7/8"

USAE01
Rare
Johnstown Dairy
Johnstown,Pa.
V-$250

USAE02
Rare
Johnstown Dairy
Johnstown,Pa.
V-$250

USAE03
Semi-Rare
Tuschlag Bros.
Greenville,Pa.
V-$150

USAE04
Semi-Rare
Johnstown Dairy
Johnstown,Pa.
V-$150

USAE05
Rare
Tuschlag Bros.
Greenville,Pa.
V-$250

USAE06
Rare
Wiswell or Green
Mountain,Co.
V-$250

USAE07
Semi-Rare
Johnstown Dairy
Johnstown,Pa.
V-$150

USAE08
Semi-Rare
Johnstown Dairy
Johnstown,Pa.
V-$120

USAE09
Semi-Rare
Mullan Dairy
Mullan, Id.
V-$120

USAE10
Semi-Rare
Johnstown Dairy
Johnstown,Pa.
V-$120

Owens Illinios Glass Co. Salesmens Sample Pages

USGl01
uncommon
Sanitary Milk
Rantouli,Il.
V-$50

USGL02
Uncommon
Patten Dairy

V-$50

USGL03
Uncommon
Guernsey Milk
Champaign,Il.
V-$50

USGL04
Uncommon
Schaeffer Dairy

V-$50

UDGL05
reverse#4

V-$00

USGL06
Uncommon
Mutual Dairy

V-$50

USGL07
reverse#6

V-$00

USGL08
Uncommon
Capital Dairies
Il.
V-$50

USGL09
Uncommon
Furer's Milk
Pa.
V-$50

USGL10
Uncommon
Otto's Milk
Pittsburg,Pa.
V-$50

USGL11
Uncommon
Harmony Dairy
Pittsburg,Pa.
V-$50

USGL12
Uncommon
Marburger Dairy
Evans City,Pa.
V-$50

USGL13
Uncommon
P.S.McGee Dairy
Blair County,Pa.
V-$50

USGL14
Uncommon
Model Dairy
Corry,Pa.
V-$50

USGL15
Uncommon
Keystone Dairy
New Kensington,Pa.
V-$50

USGL16
Uncommon
Indiana Dairy
Indiana,Pa.
V-$50

USGL17
Uncommon
Wm.Colteryahn
Pa.
V-$50

USGL18
Uncommon
North Hills Dairy
Pittsburgh,Pa.
V-$50

USGL19
Uncommon
Page's Milk
Pittsburgh,Pa
V-$50

USGL20
Uncommon
R.W.Cramer
Pa.
V-$50

USGL21
Uncommon
Ka-Vee Milk
Belleville,Pa.
V-$50

USGL22
Uncommon
Bergman's Dairy
Derry,Pa.
V-$50

USGL23
Uncommon
Bolin Dairy
Bradford,Pa.
V-$50

USGL24
Uncommon
Lewis Dairies
Grove City,Pa.
V-$50

USGL25
Uncommon
Linger Light Dairy
New Castle,Pa.
V-$50

USGL26
Uncommon
Carron County Cry.
Rawlins,Wy.
V-$50

USGL27
Uncommon
Silvis Farms
Greensburg,Pa.
V-$50

USGL28
reverse#27
Sealtest

V-$00

USGL29
Uncommon
Purity Milk
Phillipsburg,Pa.
V-$50

USGL30
Uncommon
Dubois Dairy
Dubois,Pa.
V-$50

Historical

USHS01
Semi-Rare
Ligonier Dairy
Ligonier,Pa.
V-$100+

USHS02
Semi-Rare
Ligonier Dairy
Ligonier,Pa.
V-$100+

USHS03
Rare
Ferrers
Jeannette,Pa.
V-$150

USHS04
Semi-Rare
Co-operative Dairy
Ma.
V-$50+

USHS05
Rare
Steiner's
100th Annv.
V-$50+

USHS06
reverse#5

V-$00

USHS07
Rare
Harman Dairy
Bellefonte,Pa.
V-$150+

USHS08
Rare
reverse#7

V-$00

USHS09
Rare
reverse#7

V-$00

USHS10
Rare
revese#7

V-$00

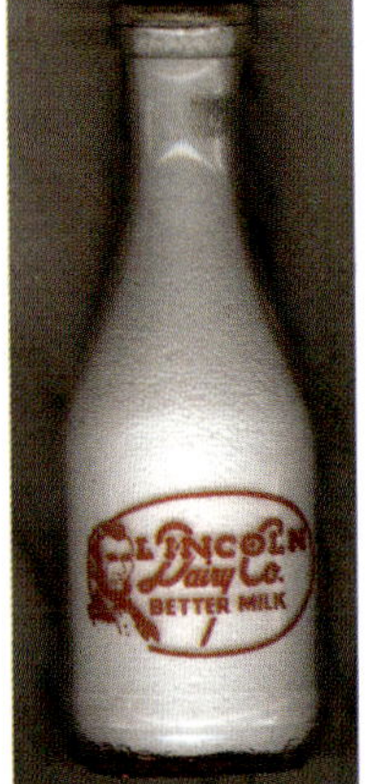

USHS11
Semi-Rare
Lincoln Dairy

V-$50+

USHS12
Uncommon

V-$50+

USHS12a
Semi-Rare
Franklin Dairy
Franklin,In.
V-$50+

USHS12b
Uncommon

V-$50+

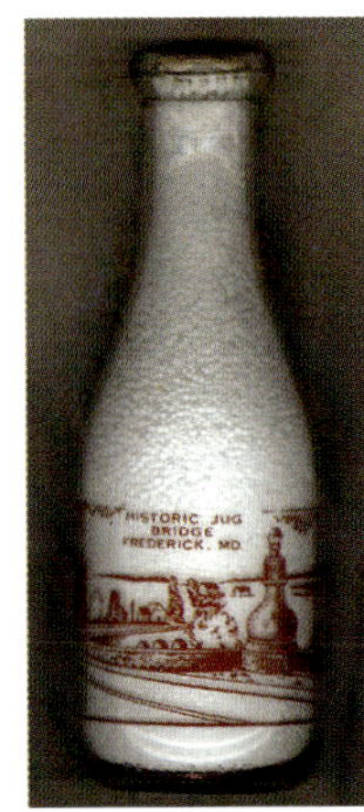

USHS13
Uncommon
Ideal Farms
Frederick,Md.
V-$70+

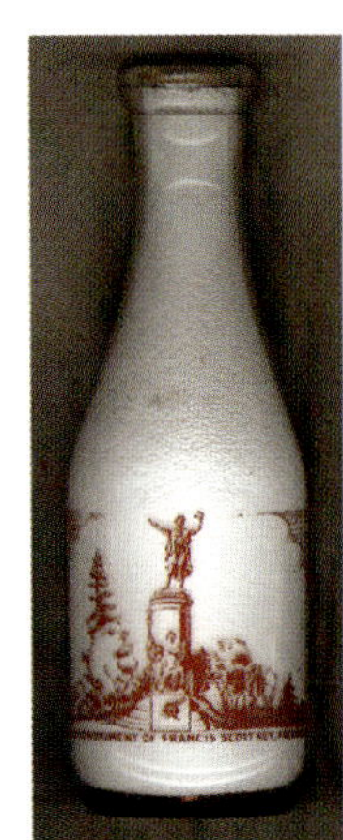

USHS14
Rare
Ideal Farms
Frederick,Md.
V-$150+

USHS16
Uncommon
Washington Dairy
Davenport.Ia.
V-$50+

USHS17
Rare

V-$?

USHS18
Semi-Rare
Fisher Dairy
Dedham,Ma.
V-$150

USHS19
Rare
Hilgenodrf Dairy
Meadville.Pa.
V-$150+

USHS20
Uncommon
Bier's Dairy

V-$50

USHS21
Uncommon
Rock Spring Coal
Rock Springs,Wy.
V-$150+

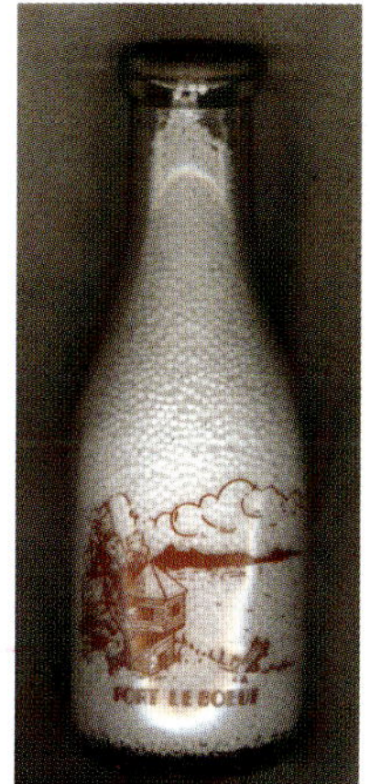

USHS22
Semi-Rare
LeBoeut Valley
Erie,Pa
V-$150+

USHS23
Rare
Markwell Milk
Sulpher,Ok.
V-$150+

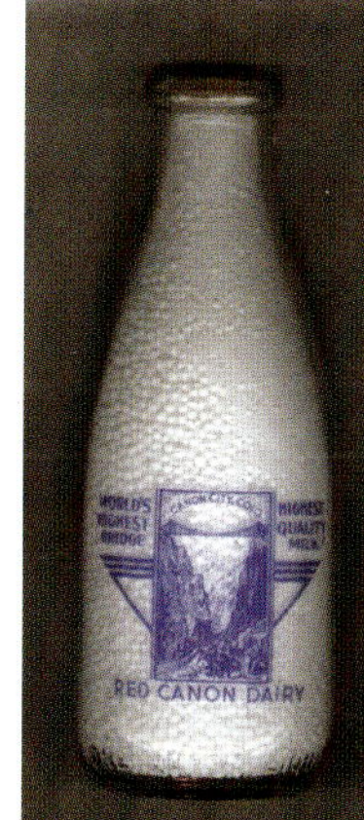

USHS24
Semi-Rare
Red Canon Dairy
Canon City,Co.
V-$150

USHS25
Rare
Biltmore Dairy
Ashville,N.C.
V-$150+

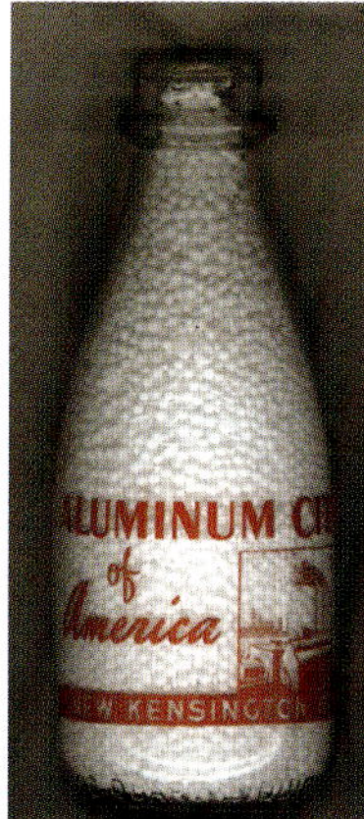

USHS26
Uncommon
Keystone Dairy
N. Kensington,Pa.
V-$70

USHS27
Uncommon
Robert's

V-$70

USHS28
Rare

Elmira,N.Y.
V-$?

USHS29
Uncommon
Purity Milk
Philipsburg,Pa.
V-$50+

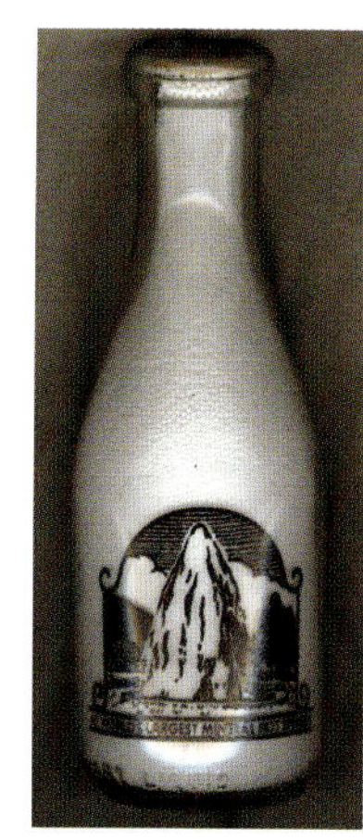

USHS30
Uncommon
Steward's Milk
Thermopolis,Wy.
V-$70+

Thatcher Mfg.Co. Salesman's Sample Page 1944

Owens Illinois Glass Co. Salesmans Sample Page 1941

SEE NIAGARA FALLS
BUFFALO DAIRY
290

OUR TOWN IS BEAUTIFUL
LET'S KEEP IT THAT WAY
285

JOIN
OUR CHILDREN'S WELFARE LEAGUE
284

THE NATION'S CAPITOL
VISIT THE HOME OF OUR GOVERNMENT
WASHINGTON DAIRY CO.
281

WE'RE PROUD TO BE SERVING GREATER
DETROIT
THE MODEL CITY OF MICHIGAN
650

OUR CENTENNIAL
1838 ★ 1938
280

VENANGO COUNTY
THE
Sportsman's
Playground
OF
NORTHWESTERN
PENNSYLVANIA
651

VACATION
IN
MICHIGAN
The Land of Lakes
287

Patronize the INDUSTRIES
that Support
YOUR COMMUNITY
652

Sec. III - Page 1 OWENS-ILLINOIS GLASS COMPANY, TOLEDO, OHIO COPYRIGHT 1941

USII01
Uncommon
Keokuk Ind
Dairy
V-$70+

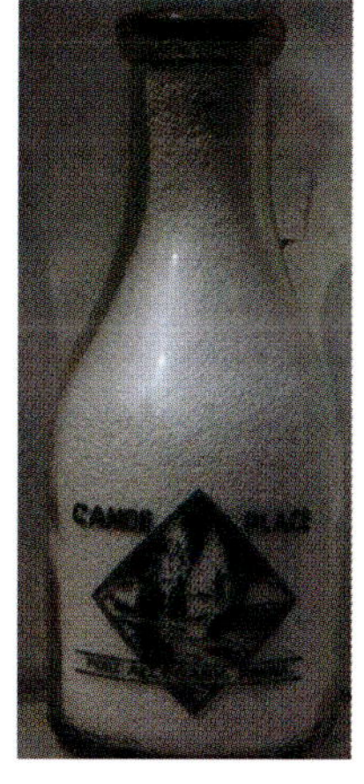

USII02
Semi-Rare
Canoe Place
Port Allegany,Pa.
V-$150+

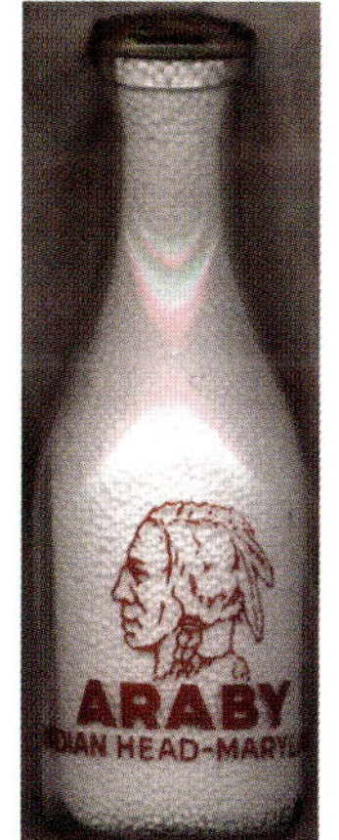

USII03
Rare
Araby
Indian Head,
Md.=V-$?

USII04
Semi-Rare
Long Sault
Canada
V-$150+

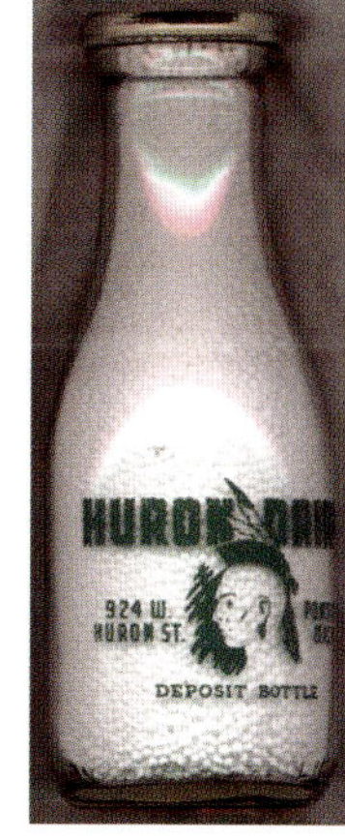

USII05
Semi-Rare
Huron Dairy
Potomac,Mi.
V-$70+

USII06
Semi-Rare
Decorah Farm
West Bend,Wi.
V-$50+

USII07
Uncommon
Caumsett Farm
Huntington,N.Y.
V-$80+

USII08
Uncommon
Frasure & Brown
Logan,Oh.
V-$80+

USII09
Uncommon
Shawsheen Dairy
Andover,Ma.
V-$80+

USII10
Uncommon
Winona
Winona Lake,In.
V-$100+

USII11
Rare
J.H.Gray
Pr.Frederick,Md.
V-$250+

USII12
Uncommon
The Dells
Wisconsin
V-$50+

USII13
Uncommon
reverse#12

V-$00

USII14
Semi-Rare
Redwood Dairy
Fortuna,Ca.
V-$150+

USII15
reverse#14

V-$00

Indian

USII16
Semi-Rare
Forest Hill Dairy
Memphis,Tn.
V-$150+

USII17
reverse#16
V-$00

USII18
Semi-Rare
Garvins Milk
V-$150

USII19
Semi-Rare
Hiawatha Milk
Brown County
V-$-80+

USII20
Uncommon
Mt.Dessert
Bar Harbor, Me.
V-$50

USII21
reverse#20
V-$00

USII22
Uncommon
Seneca Dairy
Syracuse,N.Y.
V-$50+

USII23
Semi-Rare
Apache Trail
Mesa,Az.
V-$150+

USII23a
Semi-Rare
Winona Dairy
Winona lk.,In.
V-$150

USII23b
Semi-Rare
Chillicothe Dairy
Chillicothe,Il.
V-$150+

USII24
Semi-Rare
Chickigami Dairy
Brutus,Mi.
V-$150

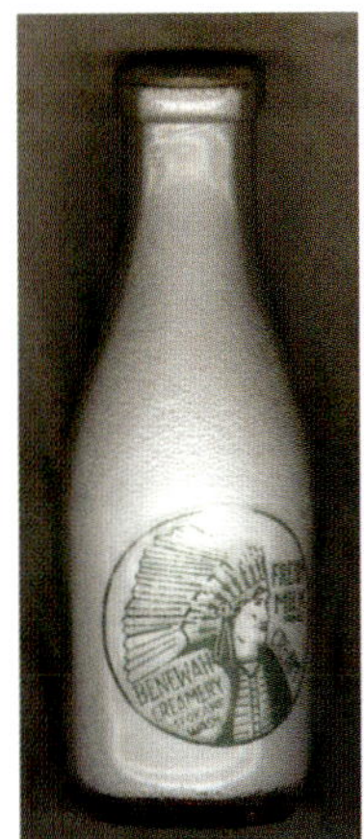

USII25
Uncommon
Benewah Cry.
Spokene,Wa.
V-$80

USII26
Uncommon
Kenotin Farm
Washington Mills
N.Y. V-$70

USII27
reverse#26
V-$00

USII28
Rare
Land O Lakes
Mankato,Mn.
V-$250+

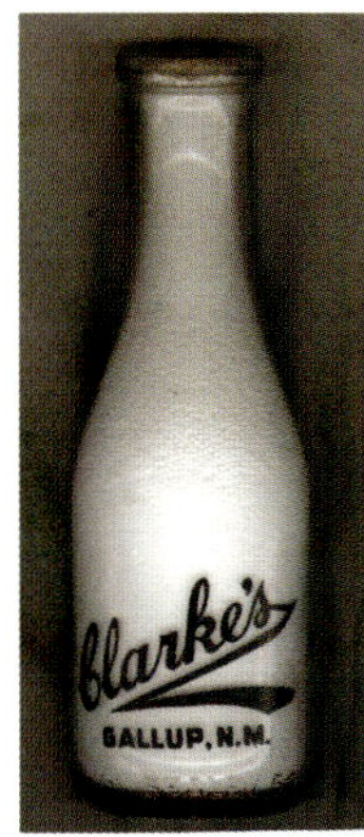

USII29
Uncommon
Clarke's
Gallup,N.M.
V-$70-

USII30
reverse#29

V-$00

USII31
Semi-Rare
Indian Valley Cry.
Taylorsville,Ca.
V-$150

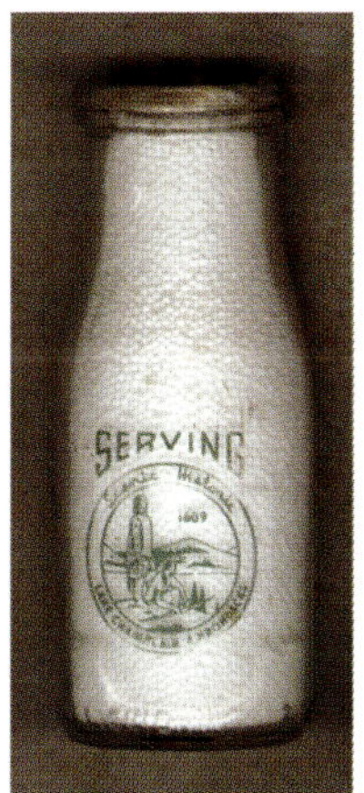

USII32
Uncommon
Northland Dairy
Lake Champlain
N.Y. V-$50+

USII33
Uncommon
Umpqua

V-$50

USII34
Rare
Redman Dairy

V-$?

USII35
Semi-Rare
Etowah Maid

V-$100+

USII36
Semi-Rare
Opekasit Farm

V-$50+

Thatcher manufacturing Co sales pamphlet undated

Design and Lettering

Creative designs pertaining to individual requirements may be obtained upon request. The Thatcher Art Department has created over five hundred stock designs which are available for Pyroglaze use. They may be seen in the Thatcher or Jobber salesmen's catalog. Because of certain limitations of the silk screen method, detailed designs and lettering should be avoided where the Pyroglaze space is small. Circle and oval designs on the shoulder generally appear distorted because of the contours of the bottle and are not recommended for this reason.

Color Separation

As a general rule when two colors are used, not superimposed, one-eighth of an inch must be allowed for color separation.

Superimpsed

Darker colors superimposed upon lighter colors are not only more legible but also more durable. The most successful superimposed combinations are those which show the greater contrast between the base color and the color superimposed.

Color

A color chart of the various colors available for Pyroglaze will gladly be shown you by your Thatcher or Jobber salesman.

Pyroglaze Lettered Ware

(a) In combination with any special blown lettering, including any special bottom plate lettering, minimum quantities shall be in accordance with paragraph (1) Blown Lettered Ware.

(b) Pyroglaze lettering will be available in 10 gross lots at the 10 gross pyroglaze differentials and in 5 gross at the 5 gross pyroglaze differentials. On such orders we will use plain bottles, without any special blown lettering—without special bottom plates — and in the standard No. 2 Common Sense finish. Such orders will be available in standard two-quart — standard 22 oz. quart—D 17¾ oz. quart, standard Sour Cream — Cottage Cheese and Fruit Juice Bottles.

Milk Trucks

USMK01
Uncommon
Hoopers Dairy
Jamestown,Pa.
V-$50

USMK02
Semi-Rare
Warners Dairy
Red Lion,Pa.
V-$50+

USMK03
Uncommon

V-$50

USMK04
Semi-Rare
Indiana Dairy
Indiana,Pa.
V-$50+

USMK05
Uncommon
Dairy Gold

V-$50+

USMKT01
restored
Elm Dairy,Oh.

USMKT02
Sterling Amherst Dairy
Amherst Buffalo,N.Y.
V-$50

USMKT03
Purity Dairy
Beaver,Pa

USMK06
Uncommon
Glenwood Farms
Massena,N.Y.
V-$50+

USMK07
Uncommon
Quality & Service

V-$30

USMK08
Semi-Rare
Ideal Farm
Frederick,Md.
V-$100

USMK09
Uncommon
Grants
Bangor,Me.
V-$50+

USMK20
DeKalb Truck Co.

USMKT04
Adohr Dairy
Los Angles,Ca.

USMKT05
Claude Wagner
McHenry,Md.

USMK10
Semi-Rare
Taylor's Dairy
Buffalo,N.Y.
V-$50+

Thatcher Mafg.Co Saleman Catalog Page 1944

USMKT06
Daisy Farms
New York City

USMKT07
Jersey Farm Dairy
Electric Truck

USMK11
Uncommon
Southend Farm
Millis,Ma.
V-$50

USMK12
Semi-Rare
Zimmerman Dairy
Peoria,Il.
V-$70+

USMKT08
Hesheldon Farms
Valencia,Pa.

USMKT09
Bordens's Milk Cream
New York City

USMKT10
H.Michaelsen
Long Island City,N.Y.

USMKT11
Dashiell Dairy
Midland,Md

USMKT12
Farmers Dairy
Cumberland,Md.

USMKT13
Maplehurst Dairy
Frostburg,Md.

USMKT14
Oak Grove Dairy
McHenry,Md

USMKT15
Queen City Dairy
Cumberland,Md.

USMKT16
Queen City Dairy
Cumberland,Md.

Milk Trucks

USMK13
Uncommon
Lansing Dairy
Lansing,Mi.
V-$50+

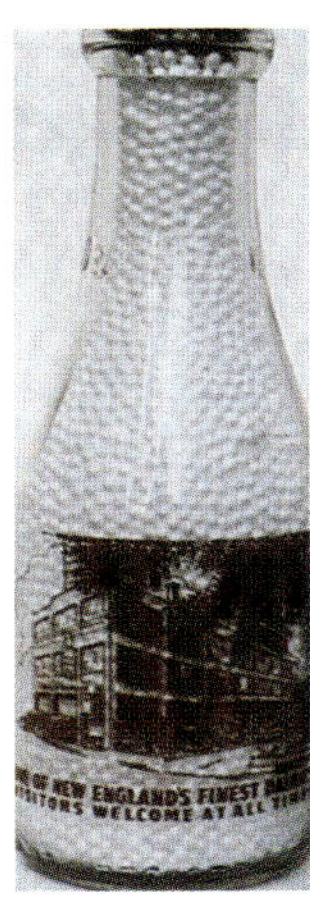

USMK14
Semi-Rare
Brookside Dairy
Waterbury,Ct.
V-$150+

USMK15
Semi-Rare
Cadillac Dairy
Cadillac,Mi.
V-$50+

USMKT17
Village Farm
Toledo,Oh.

A sketch of one of the Walker Electric Trucks which are to be delivered to the Bowman Dairy Company.

USMKT18
Bowmans Dairy
Chicago,Il.

USMKT19
Green Springs Dairy
Baltimore,Md.

USMKT20
Royal Palm Dairy
Miami,Fl.

klUSMKT21
Alba Dairy
Denver,Co.

LUSPM01
Semi-Rare
Cow over Moon

V-$100-

USPM02
Rare

V-$50

USPM03
Semi-Rare
I'm just a little girl

V-$100+

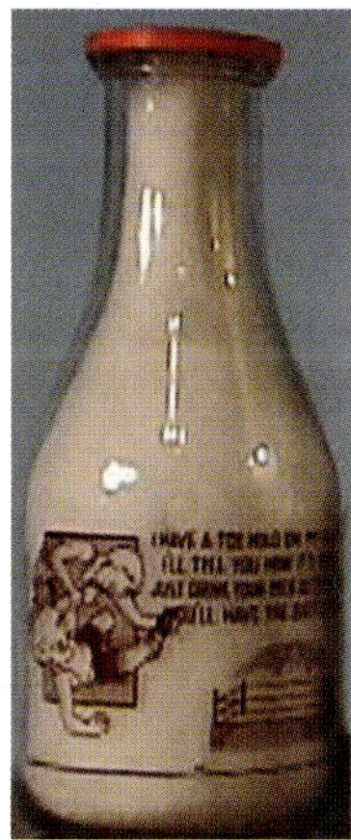

USPM04
Rare
I have a toe hold

V-$100+

USPM05
Semi-Rare
Jack is Nimble
reverse#6
V-$150-

USPM06
reverse#5

V-$50

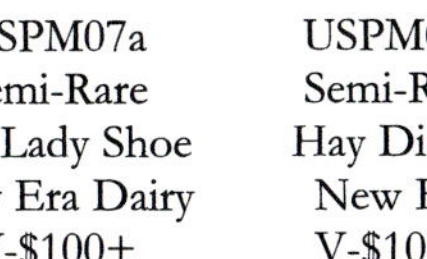

USPM07
Semi-Rare
Jack Sprat
New Era Dairy
V-$100+

USPM07a
Semi-Rare
Old Lady Shoe
New Era Dairy
V-$100+

USPM07b
Semi-Rare
Hay Diddle
New Era
V-$100+

KUSPM08
Semi-Rare
Mary Mary my
Crescent Cry.
V-$80+

USPM09
Uncommon
Once I met a girl
Model Dairy
V-$50+

USPM10
Rare
Winken & Blinken

V-$150-

USPM11
Semi-Rare
Tom,Tom the piper
Frear Dairy
V-$100+

USPM12
Semi-Rare
All the Little girls
and boys--music
V-$100+

USPM13
Uncommon
Peter Peter
Kinley's Dairy
V-$50

USPM14
Semi-Rare
All the Kids -shoe
Reiss Dairy
V-$150+

Poems

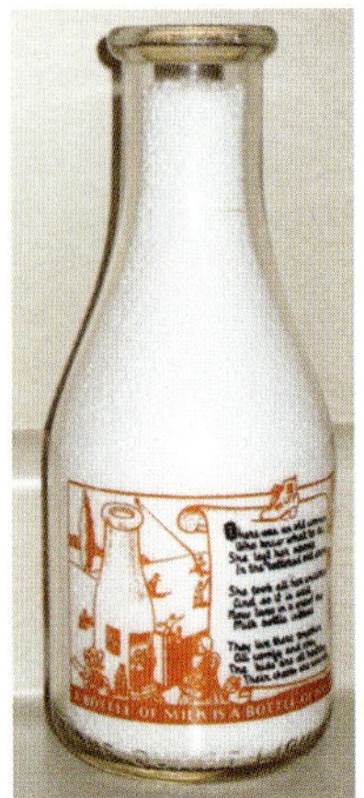

USPM15
Semi-Rare
Old Lady in shoe

V-$100+

USPM16
Semi-Rare
OldLady in shoe

V-$100+

USPM17
Semi-Rare
Old Mother
Hubbard
V-$80+

USPM18
Semi-Rare
Old King Cole

V-$100+

USPM19
Semi-Rare
Old King Cole

V-$100+

Lamb Glass Co. Mount Vernon, Ohio
Salesman Sample Page 1940

OR NOTHIN'

367

Jack Sprat was strong and fat
For he drank milk and cream.
When it came to REISS' DAIRY milk
He left his glass quite clean.

370

HEY DIDDLE DIDDLE
THE CAT AND THE FIDDLE

373

Little Bo-Peep, lost her sheep.
Which really did upset her.
But after a bottle of Eckert's Milk
She feels a great deal better.

374

Jack is nimble
And Jack is quick,
The milk he drinks
Explains the trick.

368

Jack is nimble.
Jack is quick.
Jack is never, never sick.
He drinks REISS' Milk each day.
To keep the aches & pains away.

371

Mary has a little lamb—
With fleece as fine as silk,
He follows Mary to the dairy,
When she goes for REISS' MILK.

375

Here are two kids chuck full of glee.
They like our milk it's plain to see.
If older folk more milk would drink,
We'd have less sickness, don't you think?

369

ONCE I met a little girl
Whose skin was fine as silk
For every day beside her plate
Was a glass of Purity Milk

372

Why are you so pretty my little Maid?
Your skin is white as silk—
Why you should know the answer, Sir,
I drink lots of REISS' MILK..

376

USPM20
Semi-Rare
Mary had a lamb
Illinois Valley
V-$100

USPM21
Semi-Rare
Mary had a lamb
Forest Hill Dairy
V-$100

USPM22
Uncommon
Mary had a lamb

V-$50+

USPM23
Semi-Rare
Mary had a lamb

V-$50+

USPM24
Semi-Rare
Mary had a lamb

V-$100+

Thatcher Mfg.Co Salesman Pg.

USPM25
Uncommon
Mary had a lamb
Kenbrook Milk
V-$80+

USPM26
Semi-Rare
Mary Mary Quite

V-$100+

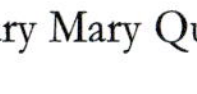

USPM27
Uncommon
Mary Mary Quite

V-$50+

USPM28
Semi-Rare
Little Miss Muffet

V-$100+

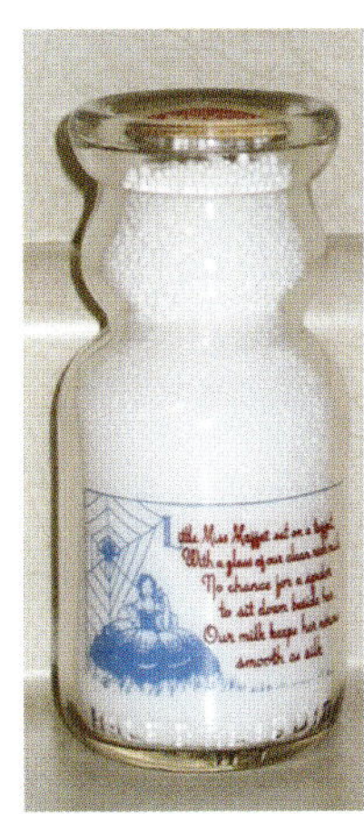

USPM29
Semi-Rare
Little Miss Muffet

V-$50+

USPM30
Semi-Rare
Little Miss Muffet

V-$100+

USPM31
Semi-Rare
Little Boy Blue

V-$70+

USPM32
Uncommon
Little Bo Peep

V-$100+

Poems

USPM33
Uncommon
Jack is Nimble

V-$70+

USPM34
Semi-Rare
Jack is Nimble
Hillview Milk
V-$100+

USPM35
Semi-Rare
Jack is Nimble

V-$100+

USPM36
Rare
Jack Bean Stalk
Hansen Dairy
V-$150+

USPM37
Semi-Rare
Jack & Jill

V-$150+

Thatcher Mfg.Co. Salesman Sample Page

USPM38
Rare
Jack is Nimble

V-$150+

USPM39
Semi-Rare
Humpty Dumpty

V-$150+

Owens Illinois Ad 1938

USPM40
Uncommon
Hatch Dairy
Salt Lake City,Ut.
V-$50+

USPM41
Rare
Goosey Gander

V-$150+

USPM42
Semi-Rare
Cow over Moon

V-$100+

USPM43
Semi-Rare
Fuzzy Wuzzy

V-$100+

USPM44
Rare
Curly Locks

V-$150+

UAPM45
Rare
Crocked Man
Roseville Milk
V-$150+

USPM46
Uncommon
Prince Charming
C.M.D.A.
V-$50+

USPM47
Uncommon
Supreme Dairy
Peru,Il.
V-$50+

Thatcher Mfg.Co. Salesman Sample Page 1944

Belview Dairy Phillipsburg,Pa.

Thatcher Mfg.Co. Saleman Sample Page 1944

Belview Dairy Phillipsburg,Pa.

Bottling and Capping Room at Belview Dairy

Please note article from Milk Dealer dated 1939.
Note next page with photos of bottles listed in this article.

Nursery Rhyme Treasure Hunt

Proved Effective Means of Advertising in Columbus, Ohio

WHEN the Columbus Milk Council, Columbus, Ohio, put into circulation about 800 gross of quart bottles with a variety of designs, slogans, etc., thereon in colors, the attention of the public was so favorably attracted to this idea of making attractive the homely container of man's most nearly perfect food that the idea of a nursery rhyme treasure hunt was instigated.

"This idea," comments Miss Marie Paulus, Industrial Health Service of the Columbus Milk Council, "was based on two fundamental facts—(1) the age-old interest of children in nursery rhymes, and (2) the unconquerable hankering of young and old to 'get something for nothing.'

"Six different nursery rhymes were prepared, paraphrased to include a message about milk. One, for example, read:

"Little Miss Muffet sat on a tuffet
Sipping her quart of milk,
This is why, she gaily cried,
My skin is soft as silk."

"Each of the six rhymes was applied in a different color, occupying about half the circumference of the bottle. The other half was occupied by an illustration appropriate to the verse. Five hundred gross of these nursery rhyme bottles were put into general circulation in Columbus.

"Here's where the treasure hunt came in. Two hundred similar nursery rhyme bottles were prepared, apportioned among the six different designs, but each had in the rhyme a misspelled word. To prevent faking normal bottles, the misspelling was by the addition of an unnecessary letter.

"These prize bottles were put into circulation and the announcement made by means of newspaper advertisements and a general circulation of bottle hangers that any one bringing one of these misspelled word bottles to the office of the Milk Council would receive one dollar. Only employees of milk companies were excluded from the treasure hunt.

"In the eight weeks the treasure hunt ran, 465 prize bottles were exchanged, each for a dollar bill. And during the final week of the treasure hunt more bottles were redeemed than for any similar period, proving the sustained interest of the public. Average number of prize bottles in circulation was about 200, because the redeemed bottles were put back in circulation. Of the number of prize bottles in circulation daily, about one-third (or 70) were in the homes on any given day. Out of this 70 daily average in homes, 10 (actually 9.7) of the prize bottles were found and redeemed. There are approximately 300,000 people in Columbus. Ten-seventieths of 300,000 equals 42,587. If among these 300,000 people, 10 found prize bottles out of the 70 bottles in homes each day, 42,587 people must have been watching for prize bottles—meaning that they, children and adults, were paying particular attention to every quart milk bottle delivered to the home or purchased at grocery. For, to find the misspelled word, a person had to read the verse carefully.

"At the beginning of the contest we found that the bottles were very apt to be kept in the home because of the novelty of applied color. However, as the contest ran on there was a much greater return on them. We felt that we were well compensated as far as interest was concerned for the loss of bottles."

DEALER CONTESTS CONSTITUTIONALITY OF UTAH MILK BOTTLE LAW

Constitutionality of Utah's "milk bottle law" which is designed to prevent one milk dealer from using the milk bottles of another, is being contested in the State Supreme Court in an action brought by E. L. Allen, dairy store owner in Salt Lake County.

The controversy arose after state authorities had seized 366 bottles bearing the names of other dealers but containing milk bottled by Mr. Allen. Allen contends he acquired the bottles by "purchase and exchange" and that the authorities acted beyond their power when they seized the bottles.

In his petition, Allen contended that the "milk bottle law" violates the "due process" clause of the constitution; that the statute is null and void because it does not require the judge issuing the warrant to find probable cause therefor; that it allows the issuance of a warrant based merely on information and belief; that it is special legislation in favor of a group or class, because it grants them the right to use criminal authorities and criminal procedure, instead of leaving them the usual civil remedy for the recovery of property.

USPM48
set of 6--Rare
C.M.D.A.
Columbus,O.
V-$?

USPM50
Uncommon
Peter Peter

V-$50+

USPM49
Reverse #48

V-$00

USPM51
Uncommon
Superior Milk

V-$50+

USPM52
Uncommon
Superior Milk

V-$50+

USPM53
uncommon
Haskell Dairy
Augusta,Ga.
V-$20+

USPM54
Uncommon
Tarrs Milk
N.Y.
V-$50+

USPM55
Uncommon

V-$5+0

USPM56
Rare
Let's look

V-$100+

USPM57
Semi-Rare
Jack & Jill

V-$150+

Reproductions--Milkbottles made to look like old milkbottles-made to fool collectors. these bottles are mostly round pyro or painted label milkbottles using milkbottles with out any emobssing or pyro labels-usually these bottles have case wear under the painted label. I know of no new round milk-bottles being made now but I expect someone will have a foreign company make them but will never look like the old bottles.

Modern milkbottle-- used to deliver milk--Only one company makes milkbottles to be used to deliver milk at this time--Stanpac Smithville,Ont. Canada These are usually square quarts no cap seat

Gift shop collectible--these bottles made for the gift trade,not made to fool but will fool the general public and then get into the antique collectible field.

Give-a-way--used a advertizing sales tool,promotion.

I am sure most milkbottle collectors have noticed a new type of milkbottle appearing at bottle shows, fleamarkets and on the internet.. A new technique has been developed by using the computer and heat to apply pyro or painted labels to milkbottles which look like the real pyro. This pyro is heat applied to bottle so it can not be scraped off as in the old fake way. This process can and is being used with very little expense and I expect will start the end of the collectible milkbottle. A person can now make a pyro milk-bottle that conmands a very high price at a very low price and fool the expert milkbottle collector. An example is the Mansfield Dairy Stowe,Vt with the skiing cow. This bottle was extremely rare and now it is seen regularly on internet sales. We now are seeing very rare war slogans and Disney milkbottles on all sizes of milkbottles with different dairy names. I would like to give one inportant clue in reproductions in the one half pint size-I believe Stan Pac, years ago, made a large quanity of this size bottle and embossed the base--Sun Brokers Inc.-I have seen all types of different pyro labels on these bottles and most are in the gift shop catagory. I expect the old embossed milkbottles will become more popular as these milkbot-tles will be extremely hard to reproduce. I will use the four terms in my discription of the reproductions pictured in this book.I would also like to say I have 90% of these reproductions in my collection and can verify their existence. Some of the milkbottles pictured are copies of real bottles and therefore put milk-bottle collectors on guard to look closely before they buy. One dairy that is being reproduced in great quanity is the Midwest Dairy. The originals has the initials MW embossed on the base.

USRP01
gift shop
Cape Farm Dairy
Rock Harbor
V-$10

USRP02
gift shop
Edgeman Milk
V-$10

USRP03
give-a way
Stan-Pac
V-$10

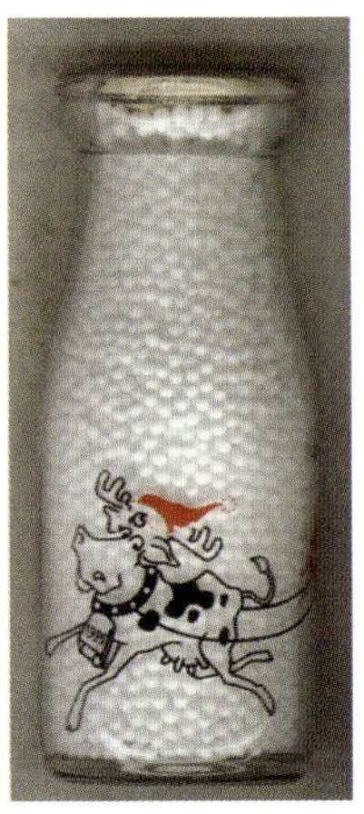

USRP04
reverse#3
V-$00

USPRP05
repro.
Shaker Farms
V-$10

USRP06
reverse#05

V-$00

USRP07
Repro.
Maple Farm

V-$05

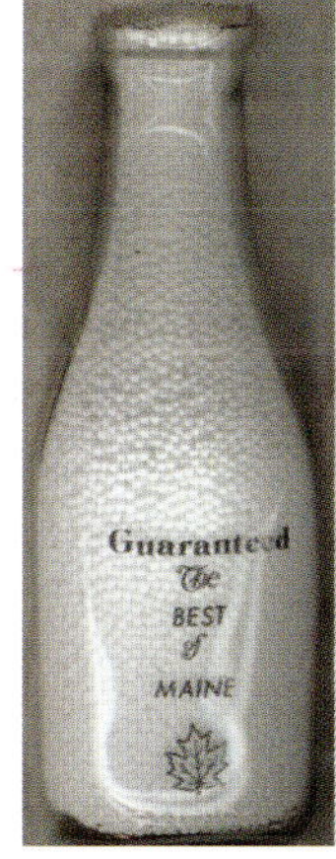

USRP08
reverse#07

V-$00

USRP09
Repro.
Rattlesnake

V-$50

USRP10
reverse#09

V-$00

USRP11
Modern
Farmer Dell
Pa.
V-$10

USRP12
reverse#11

V-$00

USRP13
Repro.
Fantasy

V-$00

USRP14
Repro.
babytop

V-$10

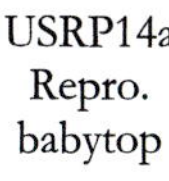

USRP14a
Repro.
babytop

V-$10

USRP15
Repro.
McDonald Farm

V-$05

USRP16
Repro.
babytop

V-$10

USRP16a
Repro.
babytop

V-$10

USRP17
Repro.
Akron Milk
creamtop
V-$10

USRP17a
reverse#17.

V-$00

Reproductions

USRP18
Repro.
Hilo Disney

V-$10

USRP18a
reverse#18

V-$00

USRP19
Repro.
Kuhl's Dairy

V-$10

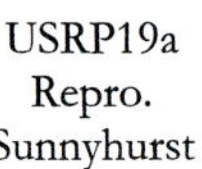

USRP19a
Repro.
Sunnyhurst

V-$10

USRP20
Repro.
Thatcher

V-$10

USRP21
Repro.
Santa Fe

V-$10

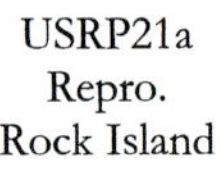

USRP21a
Repro.
Rock Island

V-$10

USRP22
Repro
Southern Pacific

V-$10

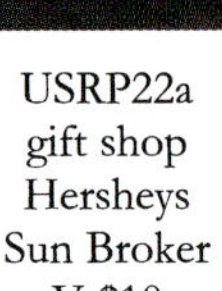

USRP22a
gift shop
Hersheys
Sun Broker
V-$10

USRP23
Modern
Promised Land

V-$10

USRP24
Repro.
Lawrence milk
1
V-$50

USRP25
reverse#24

V-$00

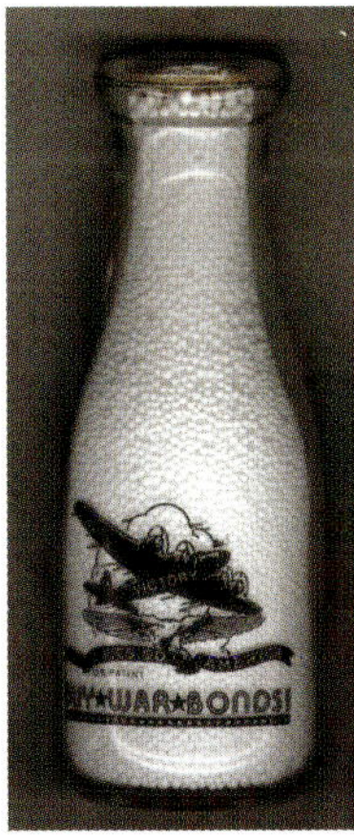

USRP26
Repro.
Sibbley Farm

V-$10

USRP27
Repro.
Liberty Milk
Buffalo,N.Y.
V-$10

USRP27a
Authentic
Liberty Milk
Buffalo,N.Y.
V-$20+

USRP27b
Repro
Liberty Milk
Buffalo,N.Y.
V-$10

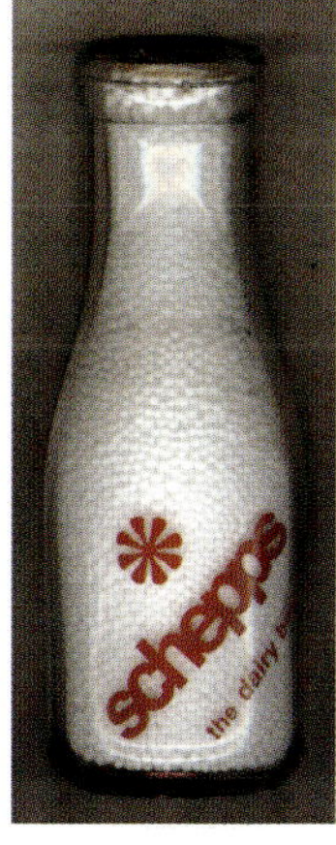

USRP28
Repro.
Liberty Milk
Buffalo,N.Y.
V-$10

USRP28a
Repro.
Liberty Milk
1
V-$10

USRP28b
Repro.
Liberty Milk
V-$10

USRP29
Modern
Homestead Cry.
Burnt Chimney,Va.
V-$10

USRP30
give-away
Schepps Dairy
Annv. 50th
V-$10

USRP31
Repro.
Sunrise Farms
Sun-Brokers
V-$10

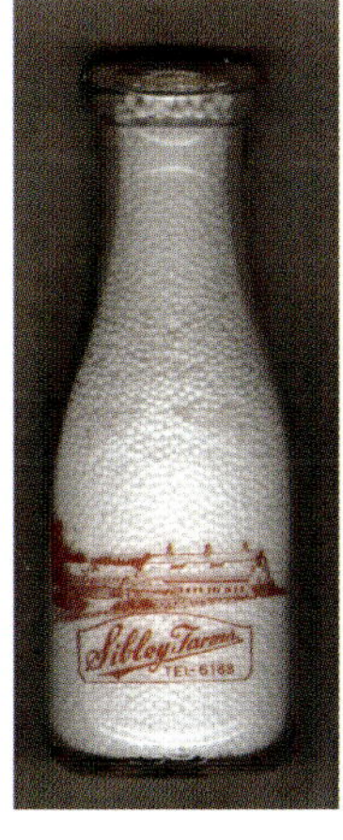

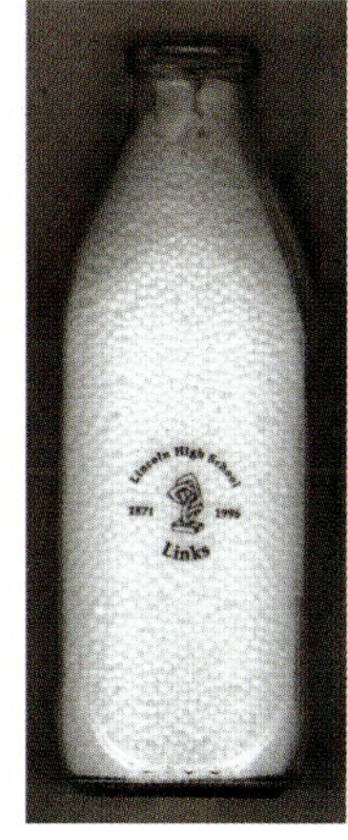

USRP32
reverse#31

V-$00

USRP33
reverse#31

V-$00

USRP34
reverse#26
Sibley Farm

V-$00

USRP35
give-away
Lincoln High
School
V-$10

USRP36
Repro.
Midwest Milk

V-$10

USRP37
reverse#36

V-$10

USRP38
gift shop
Milk Route
Collectors Club
V-$30

USRP39
side of #38

V-$00

USRP40
reverse#38

V-$00

USRP41
side of #38

V-$00

Reproductions

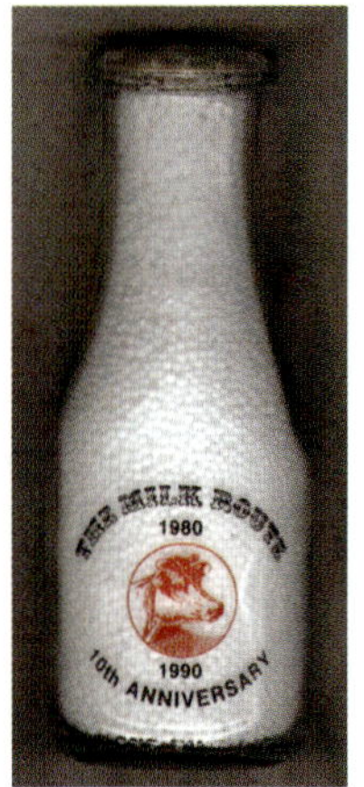

USRP42
gift shop
Milk Route
10th Anniv.
V-$20

USRP43
Modern
Broguiere's Dairy
Ca.
V-$20

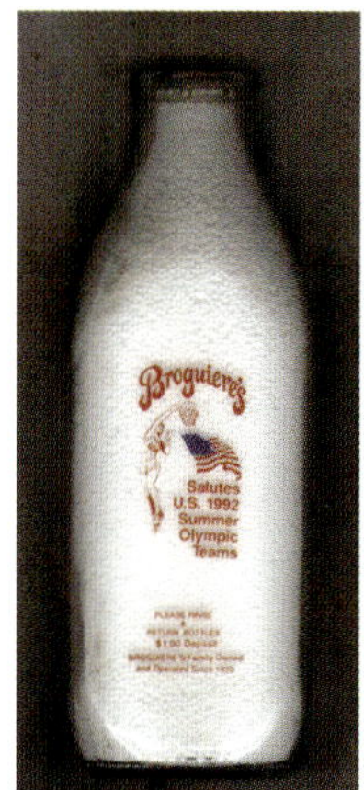

USERP44
reverse#43

V-$00

USRP45
reverse#43

V-$00

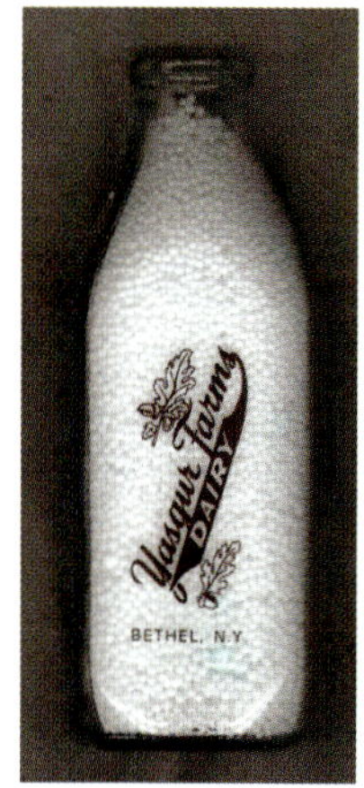

USRP46
Repro
Yasqur Farms
Bethel,N.Y.
V-$20

USRP47
reverse#46

V-$00

USRP48
Repro.
New Ulm Dairy
New Ulm,Mn.
V-$50

USRP49
reverse#48

V-$00

USRP50
Repro.
Maple Grove
Maple Grove,Il
V-$10

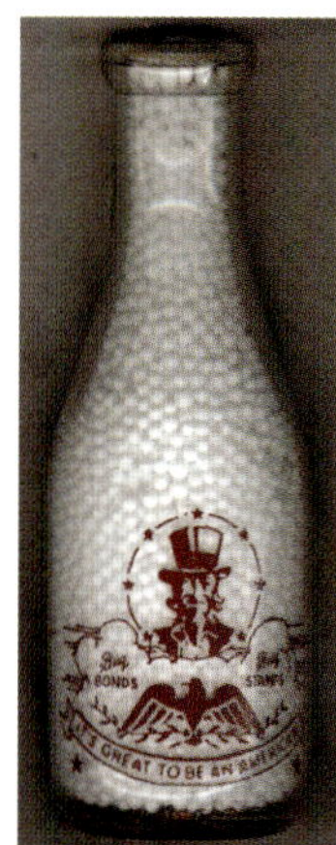

USRP51
reverse#50

V-$00

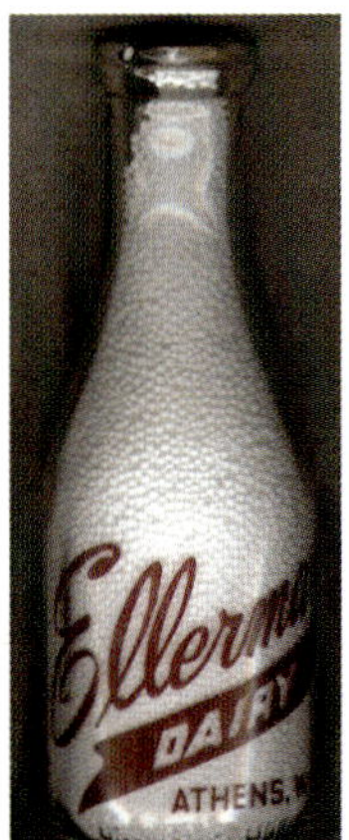

USRP52
Ellerman Dairye
Athens,Wi.

V-$10

USRP53
reverse#52

V-$00

USRP54
Modern
Shenville Cry.
Timberville,Va.
V-$20

USRP55
reverse#54

V-$00

USRP56
gift- shop
Maple Row Farm
Cherry Creek,N.Y.
V-$20

USRE01
Semi-Rare
Shy-Ann Milk
Cheyenne,Wy.
V-$50+

USRE02
common
always be careful

V-$10+

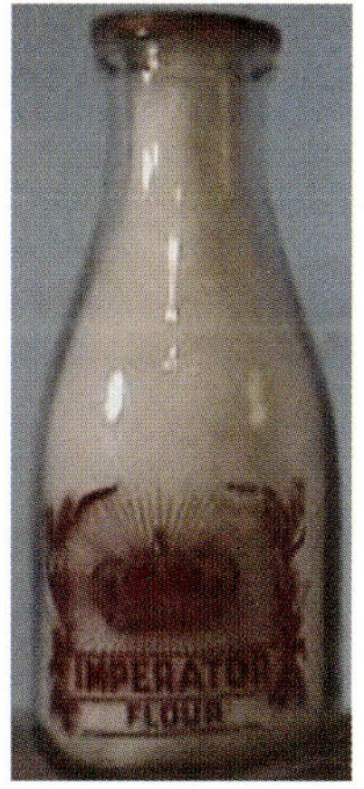

USRE03
Rare
Imperator Flour

V-$50+

USRE04
Rare
Conquest Coffee

V-$50+

USRE05
Semi-Rare
Willits Frontier

V-$50+

USRE06
Uncommon
Purity Milk

V-$50+

USRE07
Rare
Meadow Gold

V-$100+

USRE08
Semi-Rare
Doodland Dairy
Goat Milk
V-$100+

USRE09
Uncommon
Fit for a King

V-$50+

USRE10
Uncommon
Hansen Dairy
Grand Coulee
V-$50+

USRE11
Uncommon
Commercial

V-$20

USRE12
Uncommon
Drink more milk

V-$20

USRE13
Uncommon
Baby Brand Milk

V-$20

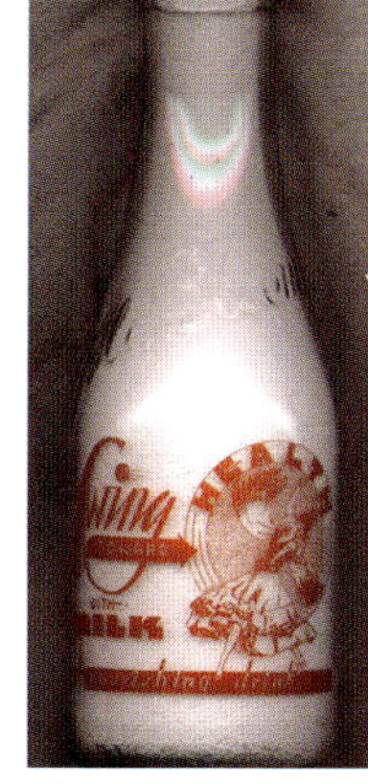

USRE14
Semi-Rare
Swing to Health

V-$50+

USRE15
Semi-Rare
Co-op Bread

V-$50+

Reverse side of Milkbottles

USRE16
Uncommon
Cresent Dairy

V-$30

USRE17
Uncommon
Health Hints

V-$20

USRE18
Uncommon
Hale's Dairy

V-$20

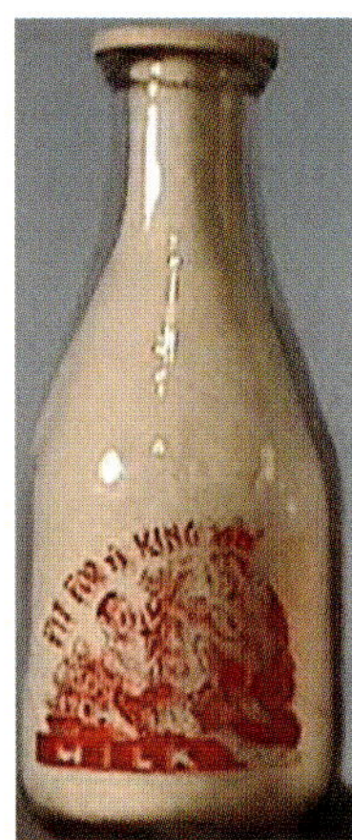

USRE19
Semi-Rare
Fit for a King

V-$30

USRE20
Uncommon
Wait's Dairy

V-$40

USRE21
Uncommon
Marion Pure Milk

V-$50

USRE22
Uncommon
Kristoferdons

V-$20

USRE23
Uncommon
Farm to You

V-$50+

USRE24
Uncommon
Priceless Protection

V-$30

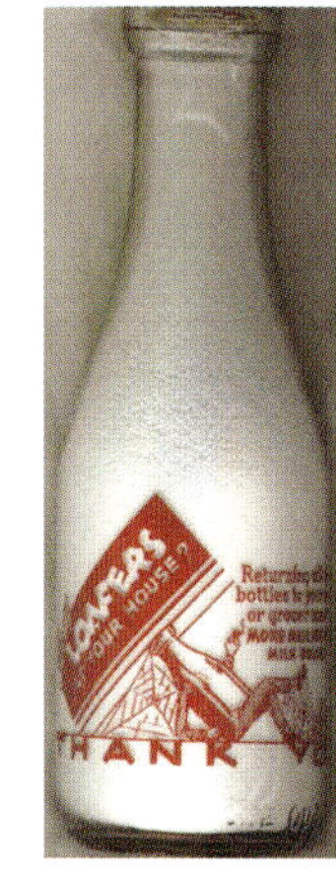

USRE25
Semi-Rare
Loafers

V-$50+

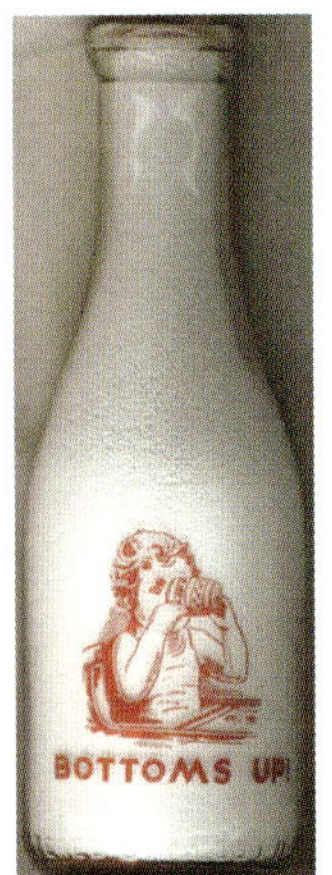

USRE26
Uncommon
Bottoms Up

V-$30

USRE27
Uncommon
Rose Dairy

V-$30

USRE28
Semi-Rare
Train

V-$50+

USRE29
Uncommon
Aldrich Dairy

V-$30

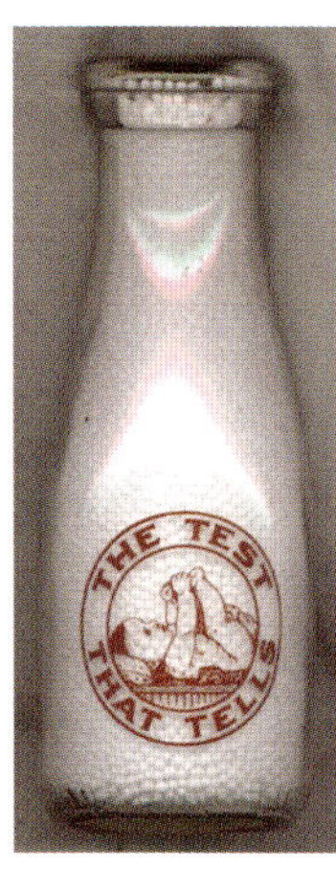

USRE30
Uncommon
Taste will tell

V-$20

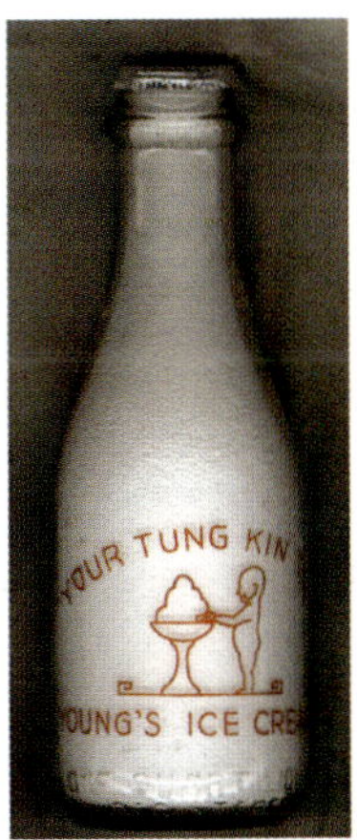

USRE31
Semi-Rare
Young's Ice Cream

V-S 30

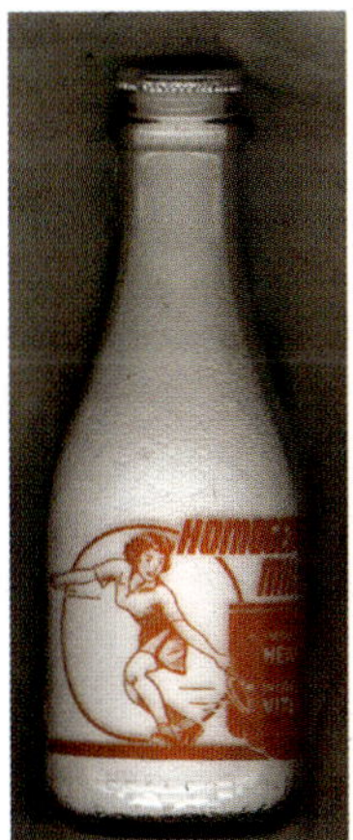

USRE32
Uncommon
Tennis Player

V-$30

USRE33
Semi-Rare
Morgan Bros.

V-$50

USRE34
Uncommon
Lakeside Dairy
Hoppy
V-$75+

USRE35
uncommon
Ohio State Fair

V-$50+

Thatcher Mfg.Co.Salesman Sample Page

USRE36
Rare
Iowa State Flower

V-$150+

USRE37
Rare
Kiddies Radio

V-$150+

USRE38
Uncommon
Do you know

V-$20

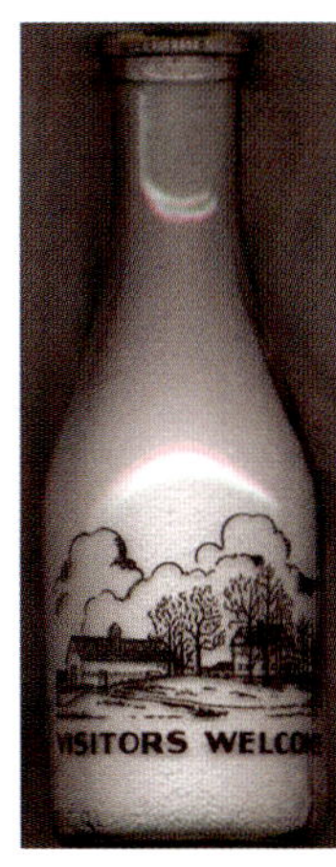

USRE39
Uncommon
Vistors Welcome

V-$30

Reverse side of Milkbottles

USRE40
Uncommon
Baseball Player

V-$30

USRE41
Uncommon
South Florida

V-$30

USRE42
Rare
Ruth's Green Vale

V-$150

USRE43
Semi-Rare
Dams & Steel

V-$50+

USRE44
Uncommon
Ayrshire

V-$50+

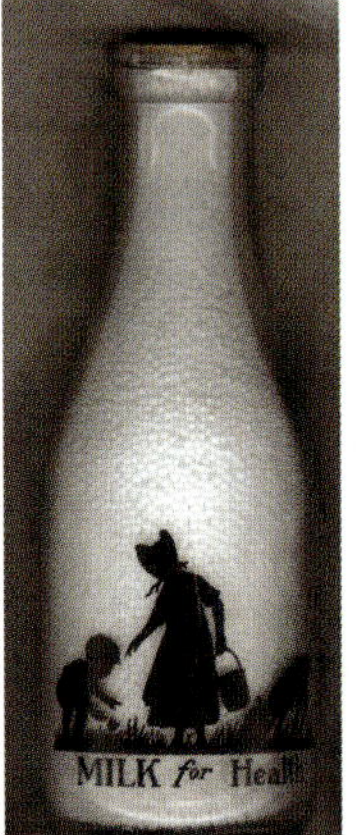

USRE45
Rare
Milk For Health

V-$50+

USRE46
Uncommon S
From Farm

V-$30

USRE47
Uncommon
From the Dairy

V-$30

USRE47a
Uncommon
Beauty

V-$30

Thatcher Mfg.Co Salesman Sample Page

USRE48
Uncommon
Bottle Washer

V-$30

USRE49
common
This is tested

V-$20

USRE50
Uncommon
Milk of Champions
V-$50

USRE50a
Uncommon
Coffee Crream

V-$20

USRE51
Rare
Blaids Milk

V-$100+

USRE52
Uncommon
Milk Sleep

V-$30

USRE53
Uncommon
Vonks Milk

V-$50

USRE54
Uncommon
Holstein Milk

V-$40

USRE55
Uncommon
We feed Baby

V-$30

USRE56
Semi-Rare
Look both Ways

V-$40

USRE57
Semi-Rare
Pendells Milk
Syracuse,N.Y.
V-$50

USRE58
Semi-Rare
Whoa Stop

V-$40

USRE59
Semi-Rare
Milk for a Pickup

V-$50+

USRE60
Uncommon
Wheatridge

V-$30

USRE61
Uncommon
Regard Character

V-$30

Reverse side of Milkbottles

USRE62
Uncommon
Keep your charm
2
V-$50

USRE63
Uncommon
Wesley Milk

V-$30

USRE63b
Uncommon
Drink Milk

V-$30

USRE66
Uncommon
Fountain of
Youth
V-$30

USRE66a
Semi-Rare
Messers Milk

V-$30

USRE64
Uncommon
Best for Baby

V-$50

USRE66
Rare
Sardis Cry.
Sardis,Ms.
V-$250+

c. XIII - Page 5 OWENS-ILLINOIS COMPANY, TOLEDO, OHIO COPYRIGHT 1941

Owens-Illinois Co. Toledo,Ohio Salesman Catalog Page 1941

USRE67
Rare
Yaples Dairy
Erie,Pa.
V-$150+

USQP01
Uncommon
Bay City
San Leamdro.Ca.
V-$30

USQP01a
Rare
Dairy Lab.
Buttermik
V-$50+

USQP01b
Uncommon
Elkhorn Farm
Watsonville,Ca.
V-$20+

USQP02
Uncommon
Prattr's Dairy
Visalia,Ca.
V-$30

USQP03
Uncommon
El Camino Cry.
San Bruno,Ca.
V-$30

USQP04
Uncommon
H.J.Whitmore
Clayton,N.Y.
V-$20

USQP04a
common
Hygionic Dairy
Watertown,N.Y.
V-$10

USQP04b
common
Gillette & Sons

V-$10

USQP05
Uncommon
Rivera Dairy
Santa Barbara,Ca.
V-$30

USQP06
Uncommon
Rock Castle
Lynchburg,Va.
V-$30

USQP06a
Semi-Rare
Virginia Dairy
Richmond,Va.
V-$50+

USQP07
Rare
Women's Missionary
Conference
V-$50+

USQP07a
reverse#7
Clarksburg,W.V.
V-$50

USQP08
Uncommon
Wildwood Dairy
Santa Rosa,Ca.
V-$30

USQP08a
Uncommon
Almida County
Oakland,Ca.
V-$30

USQP09
common
Bill Bros.
Cortland,N.Y.
V-$20

USQP09a
common
C.A.Dorr Dairy
Watertown,N.Y.
V-$20

One Quarter Pints

USQP10
Uncommon
J.RMc.Nulty
Watertown,N.Y.
V-$30

USQP10a
common
Zenda Farms
Clayton,N.Y.
V-$20

USQP10b
Uncommon
Bonnie Ayr Farms

V-$40

USQP11
Uncommon
Casey Dairy
Cortland,N.Y.
V-$20

USQP11a
Uncommon
Rutland Hills Farm
Watertown,N.Y.
V-$20

USQP12
Semi-Rare
Rice's Dairy
Lihue,Hi.
V-$50+

USQP13
Semi-Rare
Bently & Sons
Fairbanks.Ak.
V-$50+

USQP13a
Semi-Rare
Cramers Dairy
Fairbanks,Ak.
V-$50+

USQP14
Uncommon
Roof Garden Fish
Tuscon,Az.
V-$30+

USQP15
reverse#14

V-$00

USQP16
Semi-Rare
Cease Food Service
Dunkirk,N.Y.
V-$50+

USQP17
Semi-Rare
Bentley Renckens
Dunkirk,N.Y.
V-$50+

The Lamb Glass Company

Mount Vernon, Ohio

USSQ01
Uncommon
Woodlawn Dairy

V-$30

USSQ02
Uncommon
Ruthland Hills
Watertown,N.Y.
V-$20

USSQ03
reverse#2

V-$00

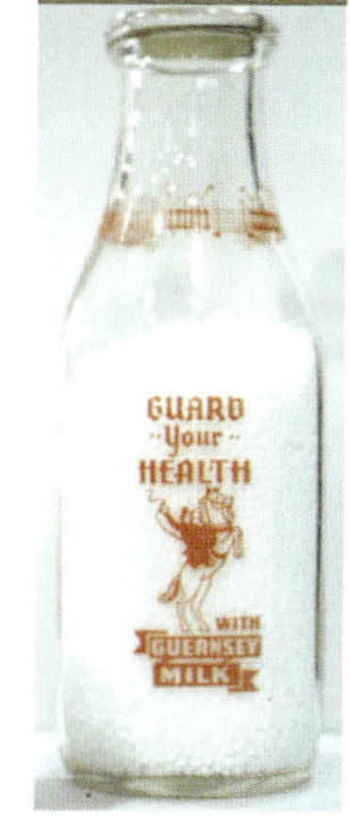

USSQ04
Uncommon
Guard your
health
V-$10

USSQ05
Semi-Rare
Parker
Cent.ennial
V-$50

USSQ06
reverse#05

V-$00

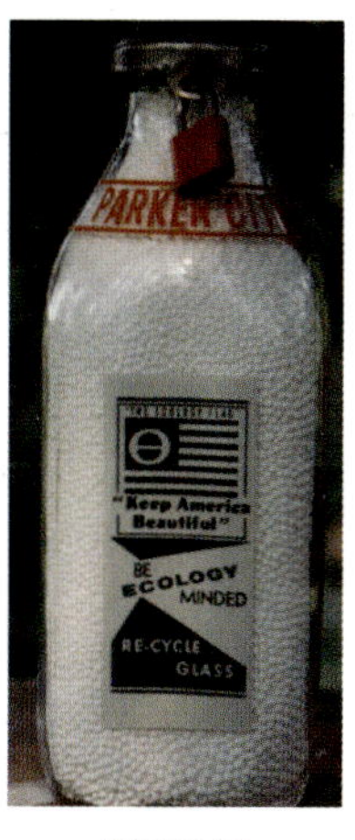

USSQ07
reverse#5

V-$00

USSQ08
reverse#5

V-$00

USSQ09
Semi-Rare
HyVita Milk
Ship Bottom,N.J.
V-$50+

USSQ10
Uncommon
Little Dairy
Namog,Id.
V-$30

USSQ11
Uncommon
J.D.Poole & Sons
Minford.Oh.
V-$20

USSQ12
Uncommon
Magic Milk

V-$10

USSQ12a
Uncommon
Monence
Monence,Il.
V-$10

USSQ12b
Uncommon
Crane Dairy

V-$10

USSQ12c
Uncommon
J&J Dairy
Alantic City
V$10

USSQ12d
Uncommon
Sunflower

V-$20

USSQ13
Uncommon
Brook Hill Farm
Acidophitus Milk
V-$20+

Square Quarts

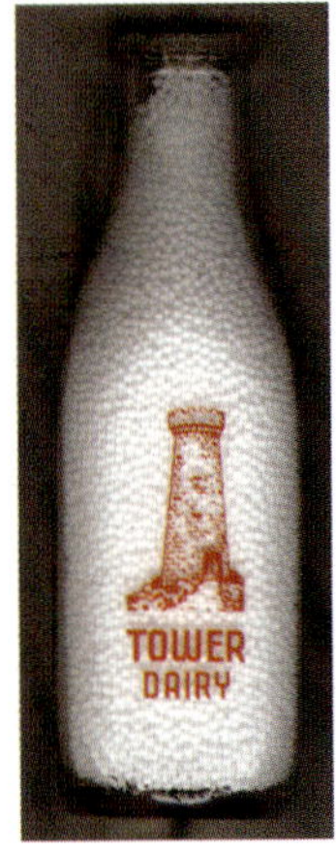

USSQ14
Rarew
Tower Dairy

V-$30

USSQ15
Semi-Rare
Wengert's

V-$50+

USSQ16
Uncommon
Burch Dairy
Jamestown.
V$50

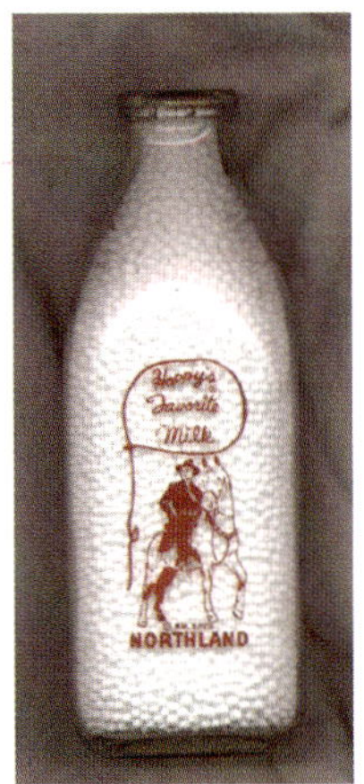

USSQ17
Uncommon
Northland

V-$50+

USSQ18
Rare
Gastafson Bros

V-$50+

USSQ19
reverse#18

V-$00

USSQ20
reverse#18

V-$00

USSQ21
reverse#18

V-$00

USSQ22
Rare
Sagtikos

V-$50+

USSQ23
reverse#22

V-$00

USSQ24
reverse#22

V-$00

USSQ25
reverse#22

V-$00

USSQ26
Semi-Rare
Armstrong
Locust Valley,N.J
V-$30

USSQ27
reverse#26
Boys Club

V-$00

USSQ28
uncommon
Meyer's Milk
57th Annv.
V-$30

USSQ29
Uncommon
Merry's Dairy
Ben Avon,Pa.
V-$30

USSQ30
Semi-Rare
Duncan's Dairy
Catskill,N.Y.
V-$30

USSQ31
reverse#30
Daniel Boone

V-$00

USSQ32
Uncommon
Blue Spruse Dairy
Freehold,M.J.
V-$20

USSQ33
Rare
Fitchett Bros.
Poughkeepsie,NY
V-$20

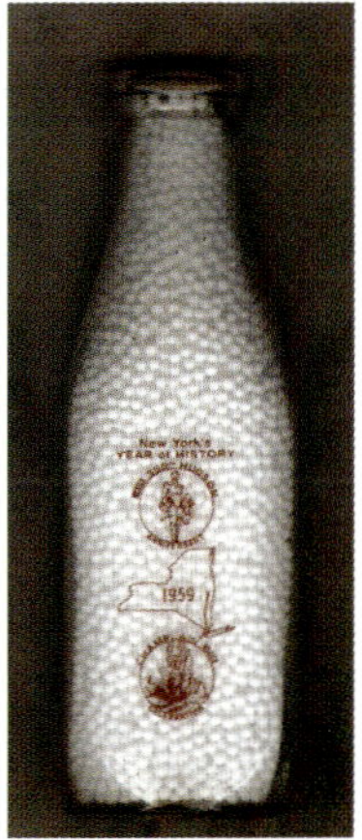

USSQ34
reverse#33

V-$30

USSQ35
Uncommon
Harrisburg Milk
Harrisburg,Pa.2V-
$50

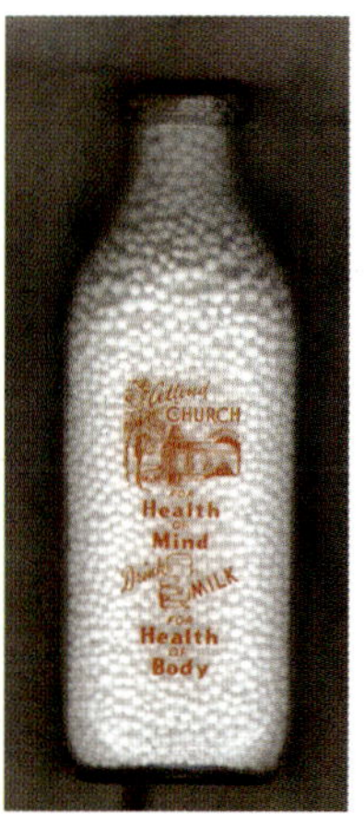

USSQ36
Uncommon
Maurer's Dairy
Pa.
V-$10

USSQ37
Uncommon
Seegert's Milk
Forestville,N.Y.
V-$20

USSQ38
Uncommon
Bechtel's Dairy
Pa.
V-$10

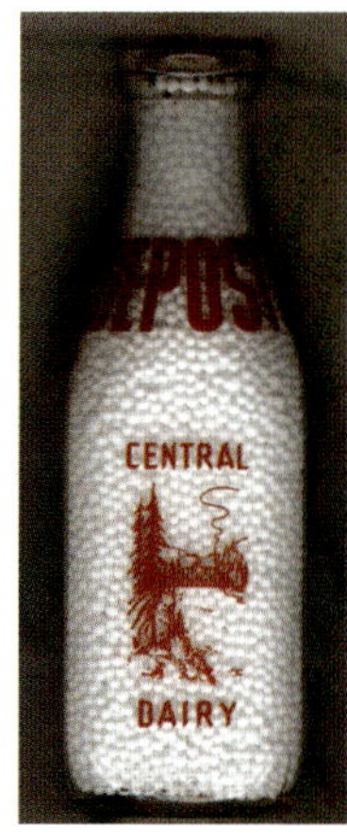

USSQ39
Semi-Rare
Central Dairy
Central Bridge
N.Y. V-$25

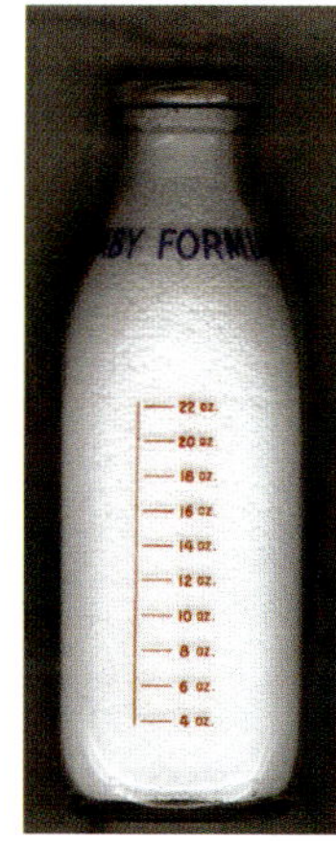

USSQ40
Uncommon
Baby Formula

V-$10

Square Quarts

USSQ41
Semi-Rare
Un.of N.Y.
Delhi,N.Y.
V-$30+

USSQ42
common
Bordens
V-$10

USSQ42a
common
golden Arrow
V-$10

USSQ42b
Uncommon
Park Ridge
Il.
V-$10

USSQ42c
common
Rutland Hills
V-$10

USSQ42d
common
Blue Boy Milk
Rochester,N.Y.
V-$10

USSQ43
Semi-Rare
Brook Road Dairy
V-$30

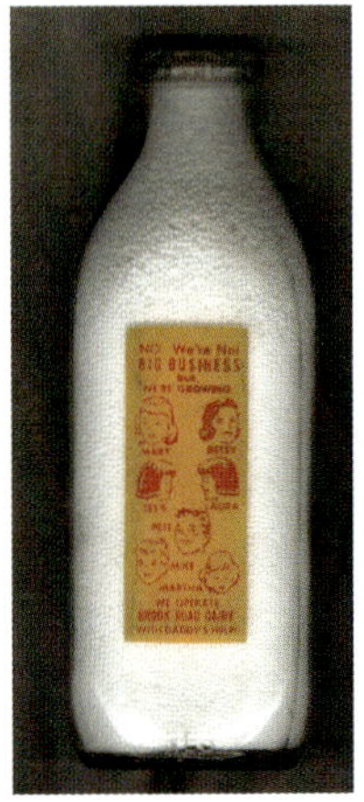

USSQ44
reverse#43
V-$00

USSQ45
Semi-Rare
Model Dairy
Huron,S.D.
V-$30

USSQ46
Uncommon
American Farm
School
V-$20

USSQ47
Uncommon
Broadway Dairy
New York City
V-$20

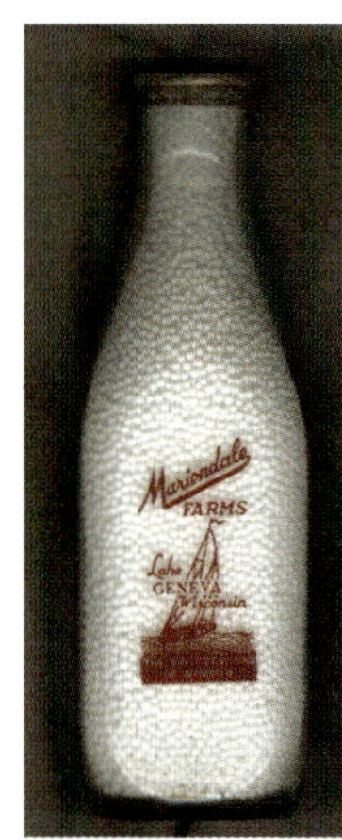

USSQ48
Uncommon
Mariondale Farm
Lake Geneva,Wi.
V-$30

USWS01
Semi-Rare
Gayoso Farms
Horn Lake,Ms.
V-$250+

USWS02
Rare
Walter Howe
York,Pa.
V-$350+

USWS03
Semi-Rare
Spring Grove Cry.
Willets,Ca.
V-$150+

USWS04
Semi-Rare
Troyer Dairy
Grants Pass,Or.
V-$250+

USWS05
Uncommon
America

V-$50

USWS06
Semi-Rare
For Safety
Buy War Bonds.
V-$150+

USWS07
Semi-Rare
Health Helps Him
Buy War Bonds
V-$150+

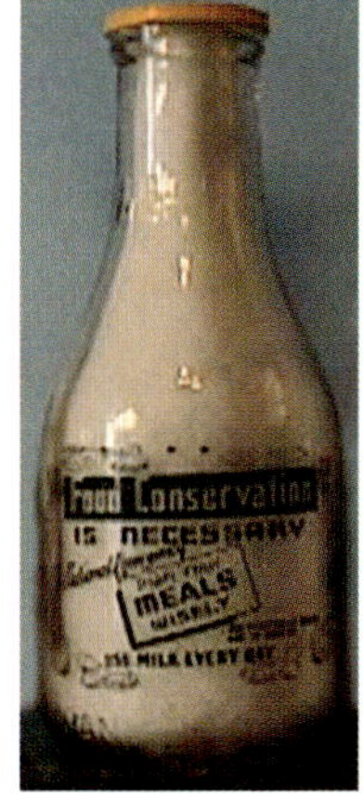

USWS08
Uncommon
Food
Conservation
V-$70+

USWS09
Semi-Rare
For Freedom
Buy War Bonds
V-$100

USWS10
Semi-Rare
V for Victory
Buy War Bonds
V-$50+

USWS11
Semi-Rare
Your Daily Dozen
For Victory
V-$150+

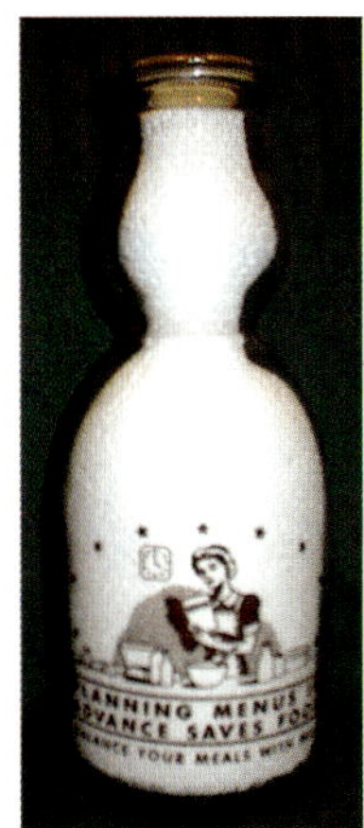
USWS12
Uncommon

V-$50+

USWS13
Rare
Unity-Freedom
Equality
V-$?

USWS14
Rare
HiGrade Dairy
Harrington,De.
V-$250+

USWS15
Rare
Highfield Dairy
Port Hope.Ont.
V-$250+

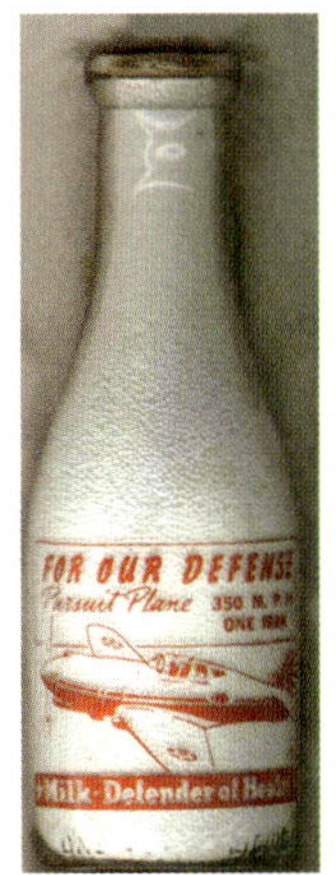

USWS16
Rare

V-$150+

kUSWS17
Uncommon
Food Fights

V-$50+

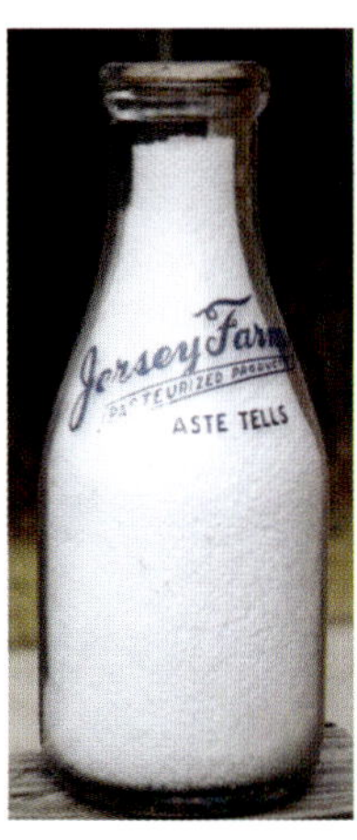
USWS18
Rare
Jersey farm

V-$150+

USWS19
reverse#18
NRA

V-$00

USWS20
Rare
M.G.Nevius

V-$250+

USWS20a
reverse#20

V-$00

USWS21
Semi-Rare
Cloverleaf Farm
Buy War Bonds
V-$150

USWS22
Uncommon
Food Fights Too

V-$50

USWS23
Uncommon
Food Fights Too

V-$50

USWS24
Uncommon
Denver Retail
Milk Dealers
V-$50

USWS24a
Uncommon
DRDA
V-$50

USWS24b
Semi-Rare
DRDA
V-$50+

USWS25
Uncommon
TitusvillDairy
Titusville,Pa.
V-$50+

USWS25a
Uncommon
Frear
Dover,De.
V-$70+

USWS26
Rare
V-$250+

985

Double PROTECTION
FOR THE HOME

986

Smart Kids save
DEFENSE
STAMPS!
ALBUMS FREE at POST OFFICE!

987

988

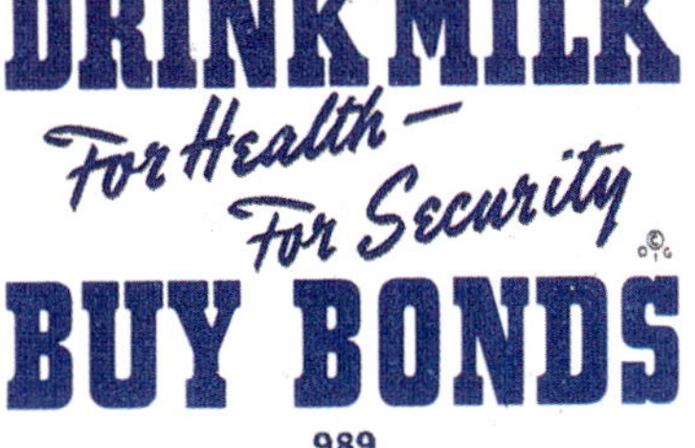

989

990

BUY DEFENSE STAMPS

991

992

993

OWENS-ILLINOIS GLASS COMPANY, TOLEDO, OHIO

War Slogans

USWS27
Rare

V-$150+

USWS28
Semi-Rare
Buy Bonds

V-$100+

USWS29
Semi-Rare
Dairy Coop Dairy
Vancover,Wa.
V-$150+

USWS30
Uncommon
Haskels
Augusta,Ga.
V-$50

USWS31
Uncommon
Buy War Bonds

V-$50

USWS32
Semi-Rare
Haskell's Dairy
Savanah,Ga.
V-$150+

USWS33
Semi-Rare
Disney
War Slogan
V-$150+

USWS33a
Rare
Columbia

V-$550+

USWS33b
Semi-Rare
Tuschlag Bros.
Greenville,Pa.
V-$150

USWS34
Rare
Haskell's Dairy
Augusta,Ga.
V-$450

USWS34a
Uncommon S
Conserve
Food
V-$50

USWS35
Uncommon
Buy War Bonds

V-$100

USWS35a
Uncommon
V.I.M.

V-$150

USWS35b
Uncommon
V.I.M.

V-$100

USWXS36
Semi-Rare
Haskell's Dairy
Augusta,Ga
V-$250+

USWS37
Rare
J.M.Adams& Brosl
Cheasea.Ma.
V-$250+

USWS38
Semi-Rare
For Victory

V-$150+

USWS39
Semi-Rare
Medo-Green Dairy

V-$150+

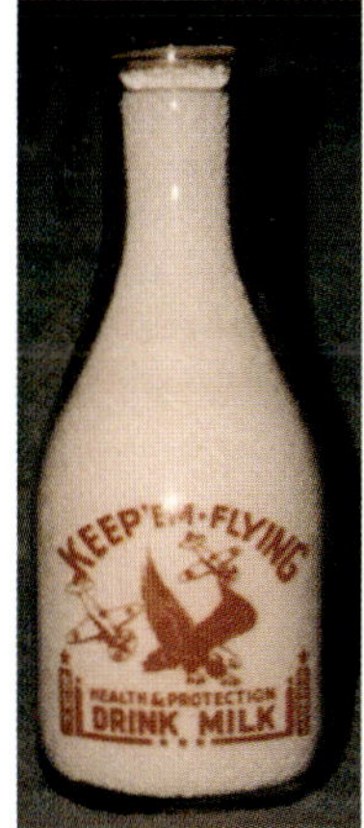

USWS40
Rare
Keep'em
Flying
V-$150+

USWS41
Semi-Rare

V-$150+

USWS42
Semi-Rare
Buy War Bonds

V-$150

USWS43
Semi-Rare
Everyday
Buy War Bonds
V-$150+

USWS44
Rare
Portland Milk
Portland,Or.
V-$350+

USWS45
Uncommon
Turner & Wescott

V-$70+

USWS46
reverse#45

V-$00

USWS47
Semi-Rare
Wilson Dairy
Ferndale,Wn
V-$150+

USWS48
Rare
V for Victory

V-$250+

USWS49
Rare
Grimm's Dairy
Mt.Carroll,Il.
V-$150+

USWS49a
reverse#49

V-$00

USWS50
Rare
Work for Victory

V-$150

USWS51
Uncommon
A Solid
foundation-Bonds
V-$100-

USWS52
Rare
Revenge
Manila
V-$250+

War Slogans

USWS53
Semi-Rare
Fortify your Health
V-$250+

USWS54
Semi-Rare
Bancroft Dairy
Madison,Wi.
V-$150+

USWS55
Rare
R.M.P.
Renovo.Pa.
V-$150+

USWS56
Semi-Rare
Gagnons
Huron,S.D.
V-$150+

USWS57
Uncommon
Rich's
Buffalo,N.Y.
V-$150+

USWS58
Super Rare
Reed's Dairy
Alexandria,Pa.
V-$unknown

USWS59
reverse#58

V-$00

USWS60
Semi-Rare
Rosedale Dairy
Laramie,Wy.
V-$250+

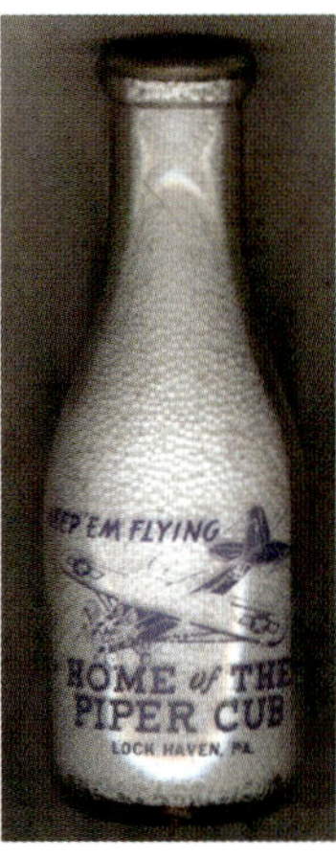

USWS61
Rare
Superior Dairy
Lock Haven,Pa.
V-$350+

USWS62
Semi-Rare
Bentley Renckens
Fredonia,N.Y.
V-$150

Owens Illinois Salesman Sample Page

Thatcher Manf.Co Sample Page

USAL01
Semi-Rare
Avondale Mills
Sylacauga.Al.
V-$70+

USAL02
Uncommon
Southern Dairy
Tuscaloosa,Al.
V-$50+

USAL03
Semi-Rare
Hollywood
Bessemer,.Al..
V-$70+

USAL04
Uncommon
Dixie Dairies
Prichard.Al.
V-$50+

USAL05
Semi-Rare
Mt.Meadow Dairy
Gadsden.Al.
V-$70+

USAL06
Uncommon
Talladega Cry.
Talladega.Al.
V-70+

USAL07
Uncommon
O.H. Dairy
Talladega.Al.
V-$70+

USAL08
Uncommon
Lone Oak Dairy
Leeds.Al.
V-$30

USAL09
Uncommon
Mo.La.Jac Farm
Bothan,Al.
V-$70+

USAL10
Semi-Rare
Joe Rosser Dairy
Bessemer.Al.
V-$70+

USAL11
Semi-Rare
Chandler Dairy
Moundsville,Al.
V-$70+

USAL12
Uncommon
Tro-Fe-Dairy
Gadsden.Al
V-$50+

USAL13
Rare
Bham City Dairy
Bessemer.Al.
V-$100+

USAL14
Rare
Christopher Dairy
Athens,Al.
V-$100+

USAL15
Uncommon
Jersey Dairy
Bessemer.Al.
V-$50+

Alaska

USAK01
Rare
Seward Dairy
Seward,Ak.
V-$150

USAK02
Rare
Anchorage Dairy
Anchorage,Ak.
V-$150

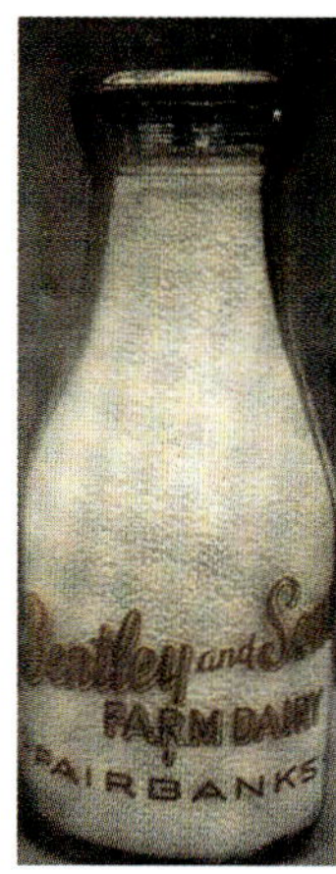

USAK03
Rare
Bentley & Son
Fairbanks.Ak.
V-$150

USAK04
Rare
Matanuska Maid
Anchorage,Ak.
V-$150

Thatcher Mafg.Co.Salesman Sample Page 1944

USAZ01
Uncommon
Mountain Meadow
Bisbee,Az
V-$150

USAZ02
Uncommon
Kruft Dairy
Phoenix,Az.
V-$70+

USAZ03
Semi-Rare
Sunland Dairy
Yuma.Az.
V-$100+

USAZ04
Uncommon
Pendergast Bros.
Tucson,Az.
V-$50+

USAZ05
Uncommon
The Modern Dairy
Globe.Az.
V-$50

USAZ06
Uncommon
Mission Dairy
Phoenix,Az.
V-$100+

USAZ07
Rare
Sunny South Dairy
Tucson,Az.
V-$100+

USAZ08
Rare
Fairview Dairy
Tucson,Az.
V-$150+

USAZ09
Uncommon
Central Ave.Dairy
Phoenix,Az.
V-$150+

USAZ10
Uncommon
Lindsey Dairy
Safford,Az.
V-$50

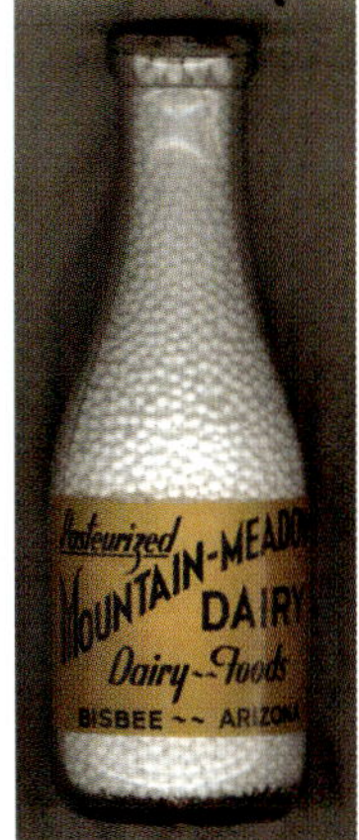

USAZ11
Rare
Mt. Meadow
Bisbee,Az.
V-$70+

Thatcher Mafg.Co. Salesman Sample Page 1944

USAZ12
Semi-Rare
Thumb Butte Dairy
Prescott,Az.
V-$50+

Arkansas

USAR01
Semi-Rare
American Dairy
Ft.Smith,Ar.
V-$70+

USAR02
Uncommon
Acee Milk
Ft.Smith,Ar.
V-$50

USAR03
Semi-Rare
R.M.Weir
Russellville,Ar.
V-$80+

USAR04
Uncommon
Pocahontas
Pocahontas,Ar.
V-$80+

USAR05
Uncommon
O.K. Ice Cream
Pine Bluff,Ar.
V-$50

USAR06
Semi-Rare
John Williams
Ft.Smith,Ar.
V-$100+

USAR07
Uncommon
Elsass Cry.
Rector.Ar.
V-$50+

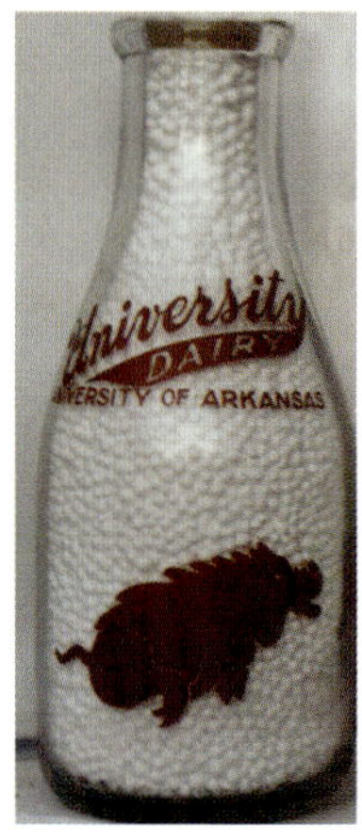

USAR08
Rare
University Dairy
Univ. of Arkansas
V-$450+

USAR09
Uncommon
Bennett's Dairy
Paris,Ar.
V-$50

USAR10
Uncommon
Walson Dairy
Wilson Ar.
V-$50

Thatcher Mfg.Co. Salesman Sample Page

USCA01
Uncommon
McCelland Dairy
Novato,Ca.
V-$70+

USCA02
Uncommon
Baywood Farm
Hollister,Ca.
V-$50+

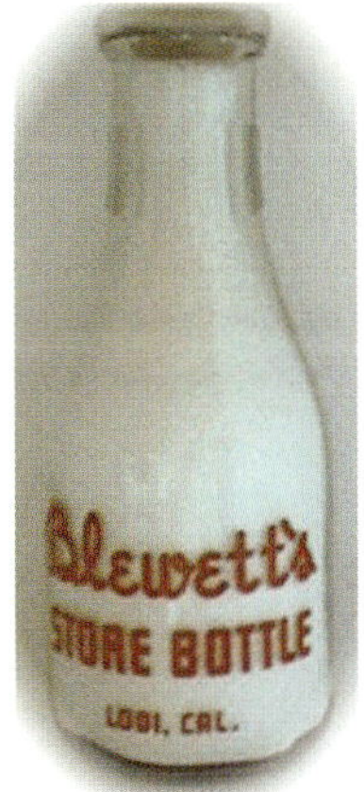

USCA03
Uncommon
Blewett's
Lodi,Va.
V-$50+

USCA04
Uncommon
Hale's Dairy
Escolon,Ca.
V-$50+

USCA05
Uncommon
Inderkums Dairy
Sacrmemto,Cal
V-$50

USCA06
Uncommon
Crystal Cry.
Sacramento,Ca.
V-$50+

USCA07
Uncommon
Souza's Dairy
Senicia,Ca.
V-$50+

USCA08
Uncommon
Gillespies Dairy
Ft.Bragg.Ca.
V-$50

USCA09
Semi-Rare
Carhams Dairy
Fresno.Ca.
V-$70+

USCA10
reverse#09

V-$00

USCA11
Uncommon
Serra Oaks Dairy
Sacarmento,Ca.
V-$70

USCA12
Uncommon
Purity Milk
Stockton,Ca.
V-$40

USCA13
Uncommon
Quality Dairy
Clovis,Ca.
V-$50

USCA14
Uncommon
Alameda Dairy
Alaneda.Ca.
V-$50+

USCA15
Uncommon
Warrendale Dairy
Loomis,Ca.
V-$50

California

USCA16-1
Semi-Rare
Adohr Milk
Los Angles,Ca..
V-$100+

USCA16-2
Rare
Adohr Milk
Los Angles,Ca..
V-$150+

USCA16-3
Semi-Rare
Adohr Milk
Los Angles,Ca..
V-$100+

USCA16a-1
Semi-Rare
Adohr Milk
Los Angles,Ca..
V-$100+-

USCA16a-2
reverse #
USCA16-2

V-$00+

USCA16a-3
reverse #16-3

.
V-$00+

USCA17
Uncommon
Thomas Dairy
Auburn,Ca..
V-$50

USCA18a
Semi-Rare
Happy Hollow
.
V-$100+

USCA18b
Semi-Rare
Burbiano Dairy.
Santa Barbara,Ca..
V-$70+

USCA18c
Rare
Challengle
San Luis Obispo
V-$250+

USCA16d
Rare
Christe Dairy
Pasadena,Ca.
V-$150+

USCA19
Semi-Rare
Loma Linda Sant.
Loma Linda,Ca..
V-$100

USCA20
Uncommon
Alves Dairy
Half Moon Bay,.
V-$50

USCA21
Uncommon
Lone Oak Dairy
Montecito,Ca.
V-$70+

USCA21a
Rare
Geyser Dairy
Geyserville,Ca.
V-$150+

USCA21b
Rare
Adohr Milk
Los Angles,Ca.
V-$150+

USCA22
Uncommon
Compsom Bros.
Corning,Ca.
V-$50+

USCA23
Uncommon
Ash Farm
St.Helena,Ca.
V-$50+

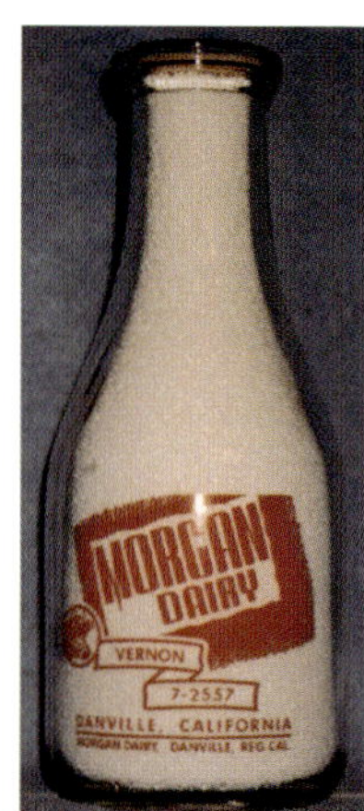

USCA24
Uncommon
Morgan Dairy
Danville,Ca.
V-$50+

USCA25
Uncommon
Cloverdale Cry.
Centerfville,Ca.
V-$50+

USCA26
Uncommon
Meadow View
Johnstonville,Ca.
V-$50+

USCA27
Semi-Rare
Driftwood Dairy
El Monte,Ca.
V-$80+

USCA28
Uncommon
Graham's Dairy
Eureka.Ca.
V-$50

USCA29
Semi-Rare
Greenwood Farm
Live Oak,Ca.
V-$70+

USCA30
Uncommon
Meadow Land
Yreka,Ca.
V-$70+

USCA31
Rare
Carmel Dairy
Carmel by the Sea
V-$250+

USCA32
reverse #31

V-$00

USCA33
Uncommon
Lone Pine Dairy
Lone Pine,Ca.
V-$70+

USCA34
Uncommon
Hales Milk
Escolon,Ca.
V-$50

USCA35
Uncommon
Scott Bros.
Pomona,Ca.
V-$50

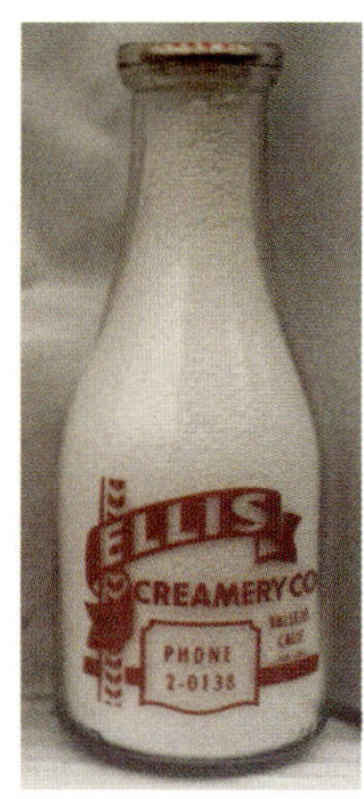

USCA35a
Uncommon
Ellis Cry.
Valleno,Ca.
V-$50

USCA36
Semi-Rare
Live Oak Dairy
Cloverdale,Ca.
V-$100+

USCA37
common
Cloverleaf Farm
Stockton,Ca.
V-$20

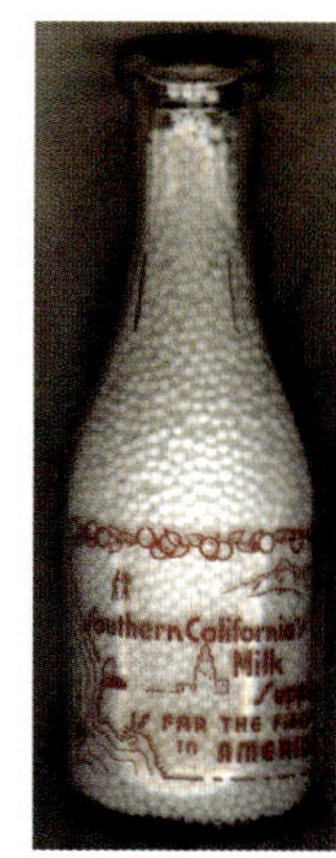

USCA38
Uncommon
Comolac Milk

V-$50+

USCO01
Rare
Hilltop Dairy
Victor,Co.
V-$450+

USCO02
Uncommon
Hy-Test Dairy
Pueblo,Co.
V-$7+

USCO03
Uncommon
Loving's Dairy
Pueblo,Co.
V-$30

USCO04
Uncommon
Gholson's Dairy
Las Animas,Co.
V-$50

USCO05
Uncommon
Comstock Dairy
Pueblo,Co.
V-$50+

USCO06
Uncommon
Wilson Dairy
Evergreen,Co.
V-$50+

USCO07
Semi-Rare
Clymer's Dairy
Grand Junction
V-$80+

USCO07a
Uncommon
Supreme
Butter
V-$50

USCO7b
Uncommon
Rye Creamery
Pueblo,Co.
V-$50

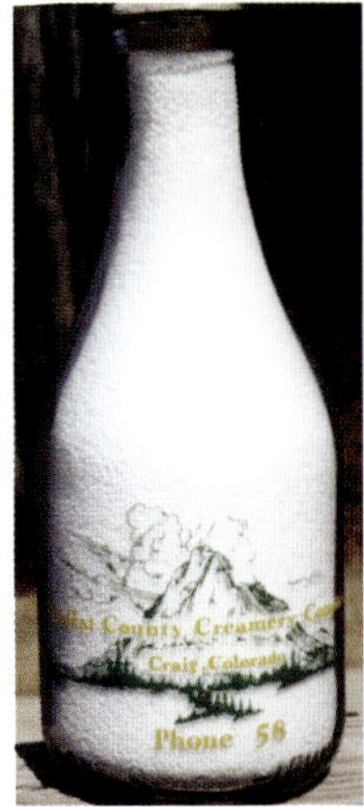

USCO08
Rare
Moffat County
Craig,Co.
V-$150+

USCO09
Uncommon
Diamond Farm
Pueblo.Co.
V-$50+

USCO10
Uncommon
City view Dairy
Colo.Springs,Co.
V-$30

USCO11
Uncommon
Alba's Dairy
Boulder,Co.
V-$50+

USCO12
Uncommon
Rye Dairy
Pueblo,Co.
V-$50+

USCO13
Uncommon
Thad Corey
Cannon City,Co.
V-$30

USCO14
Semi-Rare
Mt.Meadow Dairy
Hotchkiss,Co.
V-$70+

USCT01
Uncommon
Riverdaale Dairy
Avon,Ct.
V-$30+

USCT02
Uncommon
Clover Dairy
Torrington,Ct.
V-$30+

USCT03
common
Pleasant Hill
Preston,Ct.
V-$20+

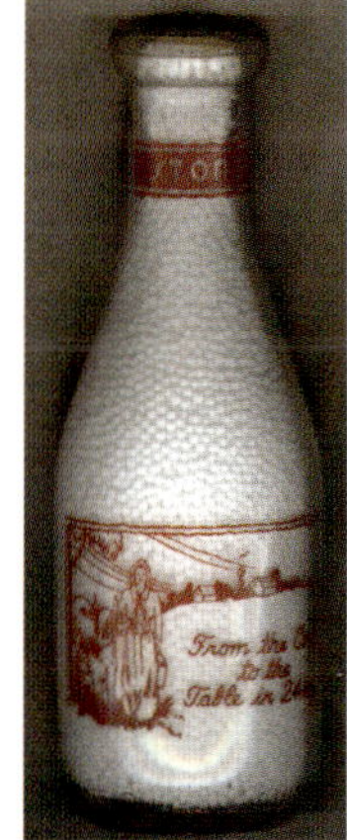

USCT04
reverse #USCT03

V-$00

USCT05
Uncommon
Burr Dairy
Clinton,Ct.
V-$30+

USCT06
Semi-Rare
Green Brier Dairy
Farmington,Ct.
V-$100+

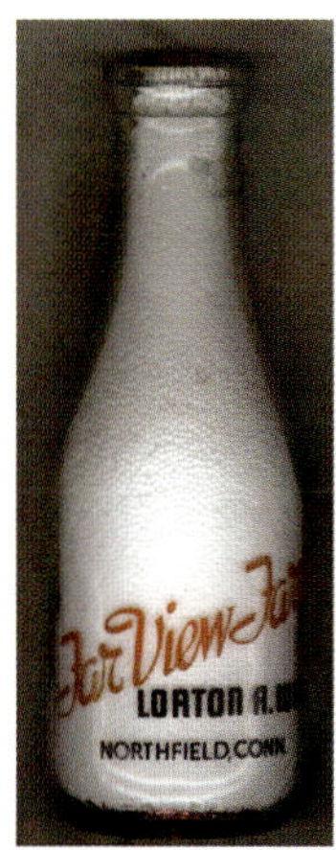

USCT07
Uncommon
Far View Dairy
Northfield,Ct.
V-$50+

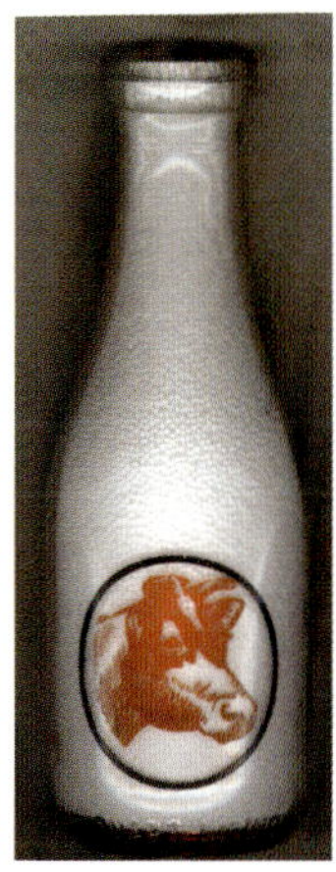

USCT08
reverse #USCT07

V-$o0

USCT09
Uncommon
Chris Nielsen
Bloomfield,Ct
V-$70+

USCT10
reverse #USCT09

V-$00

USCT11
Uncommon
Mortensen Dairy
Newington,Ct.
V-$50+

USCT12
Uncommon
Hilltop Farm
Newington,Ct.
V-$50

USCT13
Uncommon
Petersen Dairy

V-$50

USCT14
reverse#USCT13

V-$00

USCT15
Semi-Rare
Riverview Farm
Ct.
V-$70+

USCT16
Semi-Rare
Grandview Farms
Nedding,Ct..
V-$80+

USCT17
Uncommon
J.C.King
Windsor,Ct.
V-$50

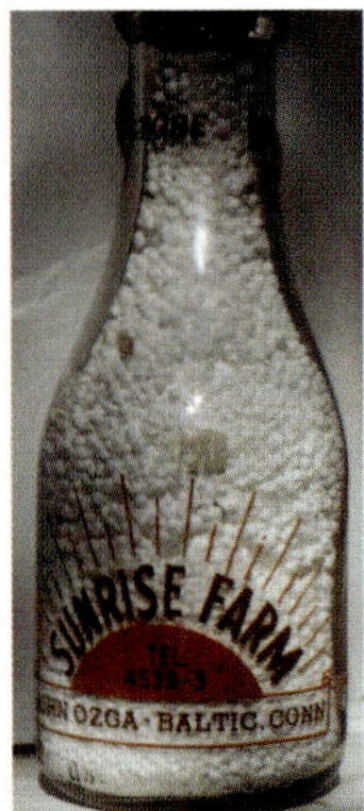

USCT18
Uncommon
Sunrise Farm
Baltic,Ct.
V-$70+

USCT19
Uncommon
Coltsfoot Farm
Cornwall,Ct.
V-$80+

USCT20
Uncommon
Sanford Overlook
Oakville,Ct.+
V-$70

USCT21
Rare
Cold Spring Farm
Milford,Ct.
V-$100+

USCT22
reverse #USCT21

V-$00

USCT23
Semi-Rare
Deepwell Farm
New Canaan,Ct.
V-$100+

USCT24
Semi-Rare
Fort Hill Dairy
Noank.Ct.
V-$80+

USCT25
Semi-Rare
Sunny Hill Farm
Terryville,Ct.
V-$150+

USCT26
reverse #USCT25

V-$00

USCT27
Uncommon
Frank King
Elmwood,Ct.
V-$70+

USCT28
Semi-Rare
Glendale Cry.
Newington,Ct.
V-$80+

USCT29
Uncommon
J.C.Gilbert
Newington,Ct.
V-$50

USCT30
Uncommon
rowley
Newington,Ct.
V-$50

USDE01
Uncommon
Longacres Farm
Seaford,De.
V-$150+

USDE02
Uncommon
Joseph Dairy
Cool Spring,De.
V-$50

USDE03
Uncommon
Frear
Dover,De.
V-$50+

USDE04
Uncommon
Richards Dairy
Newark,De.
V-$50+

USDE05
Uncommon
Clover Leaf Dairy
Frankford,De.l
V-$100+

USDE06
Rare
E.S.Knights
Wyoming,De.
V-$150+

USDE07
Semi-Rare
Mansion Farms
New Castle,De.
V-$100+

USDE08
Semi-Rare
Wilson & Parker
Ellendale,De.
V-$100+

USDE09
Semi-Rare
Given's Dairy
Laurel,De.
V-$100+

USDE10
Semi-Rare
Blue Hen Farms
Wilmington,De.
V-$50+

USDE11
Semi-Rare
Joseph Ennis
Smyrna,De.
V-$100+

USDE12
Semi-Rare
Silverside Dairy
Wilmington,De.
V-$100+

USDE13
Semi-Rare
Twaddell Bros.
Wilmington,De.
V-$100+

USDE14
Semi-Rare
Fry's Dairy
Milford,De.10V+-
$50

USDE15
Semi-Rare
Essex Cry.
Millsboro.De.
V-$150+

USFL01
Seim-Rare
Shore Acres Dairy
Leesburg,Fl.
V-$80+

USFL02
Semi-Rare
Pine Grove Dairy
Tampa.Fl.
V-$80

USFL03
Uncommon
Holly Hill Dairy
Jacksonville,Fl.
V-$50

USFL04
Semi-Rare
Davis Dairy
Lockhart,Fl.
V-$50+

USFL05
Uncommon
Spencer Harden
Sanford,Fl.
V-$80+

USFL06
Uncommon
Clay County Farm
Middleburg,Fl.
V-$50

USFL07
Uncommon
Sawyer Farm
Orlando,Fl
V-$50+

USFL08
Uncommon
Burnett's Dairy
Bradenton,Fl.
V-$50+

USFL09
Uncommon
Gilbert's Dairy
Tallahassee,Fl.
V-$50+

USFL10
Uncommon
Thomas Dairy
Miami,Fl.
V-$50+

USFL11
Uncommon
Magnolia Dairy
St.Augustine,Fl.
V-$50+

USFL12
Uncommon
Schach's Dairy
Greenwood,Fl.
V-$50+

USFL13
Rare
Adams Dairy
Key West,Fl.+
V-$150

USFL14
Semi-Rare
Meadowbrook
Miami,Fl.
V-$80+

USFL15
Uncommon
Schneider's Dairy
Eustis,Fl.
V-$50

USGA01
Uncommon
Breedlove Dairy
Monroe,Ga
V-$30

USGA02
Uncommon
Parker's Dairy
Dublin,Ga.
V-$50

USGA03
Uncommon
Pine Farm
Tifton,Ga.
V-$50

USGA04
Uncommon
Sunshine Milk
Macon,Ga.
V-$50

USGA05
Uncommon
Conn's Dairy
Thomasville,Ga.
V-$50

USGA06
common
Dublin Coop
Dublin,Ga.
V-$20

USGA06a
common
Harms Dairy
Savanneh.Ga.
V-$30

USGA06b
Uncommon
Augusta Dairy
Augusta,Ga.
V-$30

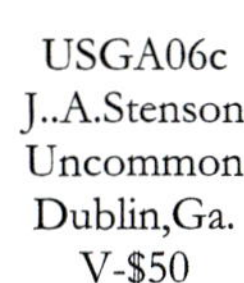

V-$00

USGA06c
J..A.Stenson
Uncommon
Dublin,Ga.
V-$50

USGA08
Uncommon
Long Meadow
Middleton,Ga.
V-$50

USGA09
Uncommon
Poplar Springs
Madison,Ga.
V-$50

USGA07
reverse
#USGA06

V-$00

USGA07a
reverse
#USGA06a

V-$00

USGA07b
reverse
#USGA07b

V-$00

USGA07a
reverse
#USGA06a

V-$00

USGA07c
reverse
#USGA06c

V-$00

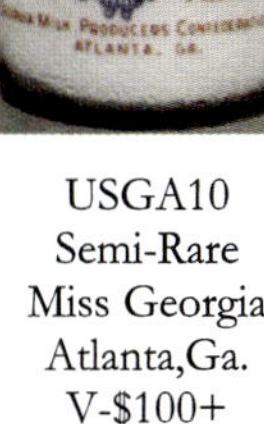

USGA10
Semi-Rare
Miss Georgia
Atlanta,Ga.
V-$100+

USGA11
Uncommon
Robert's Dairy
Savanneh,Ga.
V-$50

Hawaii

USHI01
Semi-Rare
Kalua Dairy
Hoolehua,T.H.
V-$100+

USHI02
Uncommon
Waihee Farm

V-$50+

USHI03
Semi-Rare
H.S.P.Co.
Naalehu Dairy
V-$100+

USHI04
Semi-Rare
W..H.Shipman
Hilo,Hi.
V-$100+

USHI05
Rare
Hind-Clarke Dairy

V-$150+

USHI06
Semi-Rare
Waimea Dairy

V-$100+

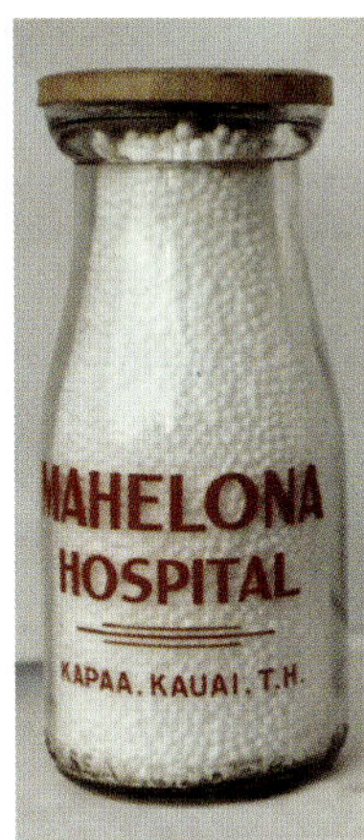

USHI07
Uncommon
Hahelona Hospital
Kapaa Kauai,T.H.
V-$50+

USHI08
Semi-Rare
National Dairy
Honolulu,Hi.
V-$100+

"AMERICA'S BEST MILK"

MOHAWK CONDENSED MILK CO.

FACTORIES:
ST. JOHNSVILLE, N.Y. DEANSBORO, N.Y. SHERMAN, N.Y.
CLYMER, N.Y. MAYVILLE, N.Y. WAVERLY, IOWA.
BEAR LAKE, PA. CORRY, PA. CAMBRIDGE SPRINGS, PA.
SANDY LAKE, PA. SAEGERTOWN, PA.

MAIN OFFICE
71 HUDSON STREET
TELEPHONE, LISPENARD 7510
NEW YORK

UNITED STATES FOOD ADMINISTRATION LICENSE NO. G-00644

CABLE ADDRESS, "MOHAWK, NEW YORK"
CODES: A.B.C. 5TH EDITION - WESTERN UNION.

PLEASE SEND REPLY TO CORRY, PA. May 22nd 1922.

Mohawk condensed Milk Co. Letter Head dated 1922

USID01
Uncommon
Korter's Milk
Moscow,Id
V-$50+

USID02
Semi-Rare
Haltom's Milk
Nampa.Id.
V-$70+

USID03
Uncommon
Hopper Dairy
Pacatello,Id.
V-$50

USID04
Uncommon
Creamtop Dairy
Idaho Falls,Id.
V-$50

USID04a
Uncommon
Creamtop Dairy
Boise.Id.
V-$50

USID05
Uncommon
Cammack Dairy
Blackfoot,Id.
V-$60+

USID06
Semi-Rare
Guernsey Dairy
Boise,Id.
V-$150+

KUSID07
Uncommon
Baker Dairy
Id.
V-$50

USID07a
Uncommon
Baker Dairy
Id.
V-$10

USID07b
Uncommon
Baker Dairy
Id.
V-$50

USID08
Semi-Rare
Sunnyside dairy
Weiser.Id.
V-$50+

USID09
Uncommon
Star Dairy
Namda.Id.
V-$30

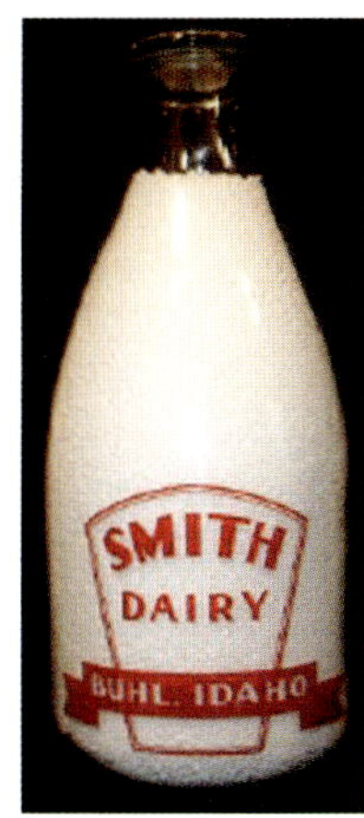

USID10
Uncommon
Smith Dairy
Buhl.Id.
V-$50+

USID11
Uncommon
Riverside Dairy
Gooding,Id.
V-$50+

USID12
Uncommon
Riderside Dairy
Gooding,Id.
V-$30

USID13
Uncommon
Modern Dairy
Idaho,Id.
V-$50+

USIL01
Uncommon
Rubins Dairy
Shelbyville,Il.
V-$50

USIL02
Uncommon
J.Johnsen & Son
Winthrop Harbor,Il
V-$50

USIL03
Semi-Rare
Nyman Dairy
Rockford,Il.
V-$70+

USIL04
Uncommon
Flint Dairy
Joliet,Il.
V-$50

USIL05
Uncommon
Flint Dairy
Joliet,Il.
V-$50

USIL06
Uncommon
Blue Ribbon Dairy
Chicago,Il.
V-$70+

USIL07
Semi-Rare
Batavia Dairy
Batavia,Il
V-$70+

USIL08
Uncommon
Tip Top Dairy
Polo,Il.
V-$50

USIL08a
Uncommon
Tip Top Dairy
Polo,Il.
V-$50

USIL09
Uncommon
Heath Dairy
Robinson,Il
V-$50

USIL10
Uncommon
Edgewater
Chicago,Il.
V-$50

USIL11
Uncommon
Stransdale Farm
Savanna,Il.
V-$50

USIL11a
Uncommon
Schuyler Dairy
Savanna,Il.
V-$30

USIL12
Uncommon
Marion Dairy
Marion,Il.
V-$40

USIL13
Uncommon
Nicolay's Dairy
Sandoval,Il
V-$50+

USIL14
Uncommon
Delmar Cox
Vandalia,Il.
V-$50+

USIL15
Uncommon
Durst Bros.
Quincy,Il.
V-$50+

USIL16
Uncommon
Ash Grove Dairy
Kankakee,Il.+
V-$50

USIL17
common
Quality Dairy
Geneseo,Il.3
V-$30

USIL18
Semi-Rare
Busy Bee Dairy
Hardin,Il.
V-$50+

USIL20
Uncommon
Four Star
Moline,Il.
V-$50

USIL21
Uncommon
Park's Dairy
Minonk.Il
V-$50

USIL22
Uncommon
Libertyville Dairy
Libertyville,Il.
V-$50

USIL23
Uncommon
Clearview Dairy
Tuscola.Il.
V-$50+

USIL24
Uncommon
Mooseheart Farm
Mooseheart,Il.
V-$50

USIL25
Uncommon
Oregon Dairy
Oregon,Il.
V-$50+

USIL25a
Uncommon
Hobb Dairy
Lena,Il.
V-$50+

USIL26
Uncommon
Hays Dairy
Waterman,Il.
V-$50+

USIL26a
Uncommon
Wolf & Sons
Kewanae,Il
V-$50+

USIL27
Uncommon
Strunk's Dairy
morton,Il.
V-$70+

USIL28
Uncommon
Ferry Hill Farm
Prairie View,Il.
V-$50+

USIL29
Uncommon
Peerless Dairy
Rock Island,Il.
V-$50+

USIL30
Semi-Rare
Montavon & Sons
Amboy,Il.
V-$70+

USIL31
Uncommon
Grimm's Dairy
Mount Carroll,Il.
V-$50

USIL32
Semi-Rare
Rubin Dairy
Shelbyville,Il.
V-$100+

USIL33
reverse #USIL32

V-$00

USIL34
Uncommon
Fitchome Farm
Aurora,Il
V-$50+

USIL35
Uncommon
Creamtop Dairy
LaSalle,Il.
V-$30

USIL36
Uncommon
Riverside Dairy
McHenry,Il.
V-$30

USIL37
Rare
Bob White Dairy
Decatur,Il.
V-$150+

USIL38
Semi-Rare
Round Lake Cry.
Round Lake,Il.
V-$100+

USIL39
Uncommon
Fred Rabe & Sons
Elmhurst,Il.
V-$50

USIL40
reverse #USIL39

V-$00

USIL41
Uncommon
Crabapple Creek
Matton,Il.
V-$50+

USIL42
Uncommon
Fitzpatrick's Dairy
Rock Island,Il.
V-$50+

USIN01
Semi-Rare
Winona Dairy
Winona Lake,In.
V-$150+

USIN02
Uncommon
Nottingham Dairy
Muncie,In.
V-$50

USIN03
Uncommon
Sunrise Dairy
Angola,In.
V-$50

USIL04
reverse #USIN03
V-$00

USIN05
Uncommon
Shively's Dairy
Greenfield,In.
V-$50

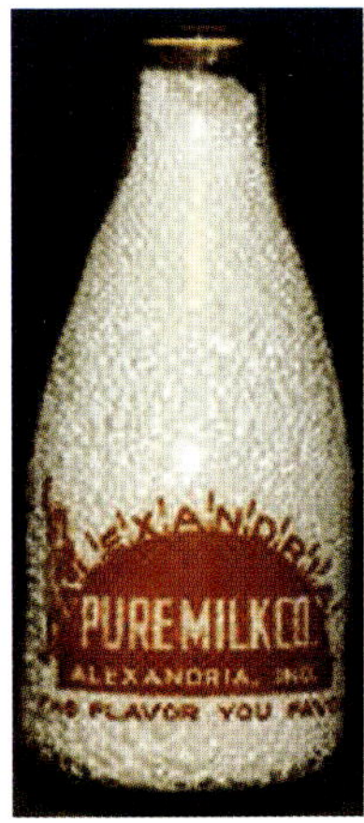

USIN06
Uncommon
Pure Milk Co.
Alexandria,IN.
V-$50

USIN07
reverse #USIn06
V-$00

USIN08
Uncommon
Pruitt Dairy
Edinburg,In.
V-$50

USIN09
Uncommon
Northside Dairy
Connersville,In.
V-$50+

USIN10
reverse #USIN09
V-$00

USIN11
Uncommon
babyBrand Milk
Fort Wayne,In.
V-$50

USIN12
Uncommon
Davis Dairy
Anderson,In.
V-$30

USIN13
common
Covalts Dairy
Muncie,In.
V-$30

USIN14
Uncommon
Northside Dairy
Aurora,In.
V-$50+

USIN15
Uncommon
Producers Dairy
Crawfordville,In.
V-$50

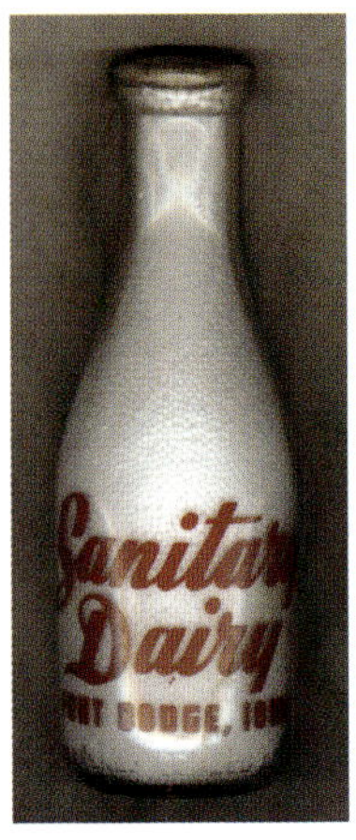

USIA01
Uncommon
Sanitary Dairy
Fort Dodge,Ia.
V-$30

USIA02
Uncommon
Quality Dairy
Des Moines,Ia.3V-
$50

USIA03
Semi-Rare
Kirchhoff
Maquoketa,Ia.
V-$50+

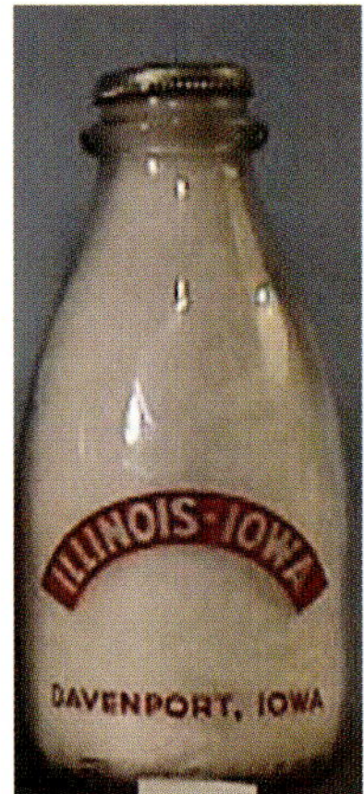

USIA04
Uncommon
Illinois-Iowa
Davenport.Ia.
V-$30

USIA05
Rare
Wild Rose
Ia.
V-$250+

USIA06
Uncommon
A.E.Whiting Dairy
Cedar Rapids,Ia.
V-$30

USIA07
Semi-Rare
Gustafson Bros.
Burlington,Ia.
V-$150

USIA08
Uncommon
H&L Dairy
Keokuk,Ia.
V-$30

USIA09
Uncommon
Walnut Dairy
Waterloo,Ia.
V-$30

USIA10
Uncommon
Independence
Independence.Ia.
V-$30

USIA11
Semi-Rare
Arlington Farm
Rock Rapids,Ia.
V-$70+

USIA12
Uncommon
Osceola County
Sibley,Ia.
V-$50

USIA13
Semi-Rare
Jersey Dairy
Spencer,Ia.
V-$80+

USIA14
Uncommon
Wapsie Vallley
Indenpendence,Ia.
V-$50

USIA15
Uncommon
Koerness Dairy
Klemme,Ia.
0V-$50

USKS01
Uncommon
Winfield Dairy
Winfield,Ks.
V-$30

USKS02
Uncommon
Producers Dairy
Hutchinson,Ks.
V-$30

USKS03
Uncommon
Richenburg Dairy
Wichita,Ks.
V-$50

USKS04
Uncommon
Whitworth Dairy
Chanute,Ks.
V-$50

USKS05
Uncommon
Silver Springs
Silver Springs,Ks.
V-$50

USKS06
Uncommon
City Dairy
Scott City,Ks.
V-$30

USKS07
Uncommon
Gardiners Dairy
Garden City,Ks.
V-$50

USKS08
Uncommon
Harter Creamery
Herington,Ks.3V-
$50

USKS09
Uncommon
Dicks Dairy
Garden City,Ks.
V-$50

USKS10
Uncommon
Nelson's Dairy
Humboldt,Ks.
V-$30

USKS11
Semi-Rare
Kirklawn Dairy
Topeka.Ks.
V-$70+

USKS12
Uncommon
United Dairies
Maysville,Ks.
V-$30

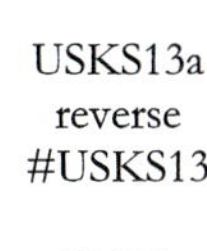

USKS13
Uncommon
Bennells Milk
Ottawa,Ks.
V-$50+

USKS13a
reverse
#USKS13

V-$00

USKS14
Uncommon
Duncan & Beery
Winfield,Ks.
V-$40

USKS15
Uncommon
Carlton Hall
Coffeyville,Ks.
V-$50

Kentucky

USKY01
Uncommon
Kentuvcky Acres
Crestwood,Ky.
V-$30

USKY02
Uncommon
Big Sandy Dairy
Paintsville,Ky.
V-$50

USKY03
Rare
Hmloland Dairy
Glascow,Ky.
V-$100+

USKY04
reverse#USKY03

V-$00

USKY05
Uncommon
Hy-Grade
Pineville,Ky.
V-$50

USKY06
reverse#USKY05

V-$00

USKY07
Uncommon
Jansing Dairy

V-$30

USKY08
Uncommon
L-N Dairy
Frankfort.Ky.
V-$30

USKY09
Uncommon
A.B.Snyder & Son
Middleboro,Ky.
V-$50

USKY10
Uncommon
Superior Ice Cream
Georgetown,Ky.
V-$30

USKY11
Uncommon
Crest Acre Dairy
Cave City,Ky.
V-$50

USKY12
Uncommon
Green Acres Dairy
Dry Ridge,Ky.
V-$50

USKY13
Rare
Locust Heights
Lexington,Ky.
V-$150+

USKY14
Uncommon
Winchester Dairy
Winchester,Ky.
V-$30

USKY15
common
Somerset Creamry
Somerset,Ky.
V-$30

USLA01
Semi-Rare
Fitz Dairy
Winnfield,La
V-$100+

USLA02
Rare
Alice C Dairy
Franklin,La.
V-$150+

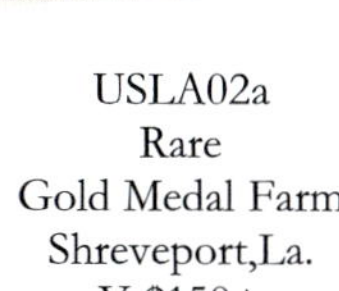

USLA02a
Rare
Gold Medal Farm
Shreveport,La.
V-$150+

USLA03
Semi-Rare
Lafayette Dairy
Lafayette,La.
V-$100+

USLA04
Rare
Evangeline Dairy
Lafayette,La.
V-$150+

USLA05
Rare
Monroe Milk
Monroe,La.
V-$150+

Sample butter Box 1928

USLA06
Rare
Robert Pessson
New Iberia,La.
V-$150+

Sample butter box 1928

USMD01
uncommon
Highs Dairy
Baltimore,Md
V-$30

USMD01a
Uncommon
Scott Key Dairy
Frederick,Md.
V-$30

USMD01b
Uncommon
Superior Dairy
Frederick,Md.
V-$30

USMD02
Rare
Brooke's Cross
Balwin,Md.
V-$?

USMD03
reverse#USMD02

V-$00

USMD04
Uncommon
Schauber's Dairy
Chestertown,Md.
V-$50+

USMD05
Uncommon
Bill Andale
Owings,Md.
V-$50+

USMD06
Uncommon
Frank Schauker
Chestertown,Md.
V-$50+

USMD07
Semi-Rare
Souder & Chick
Brunswick.Md.
V-$150+

USMD08
Uncommon
Ideal Farm Dairy
Fredick,Md.
V-$50+

USMD09
Reverse #USMD08
Carrilon At Barker
Park.
V-$150+

USMD10
reverse#USMD08
Hood College

V-$150+

USMD11
reserve#USMD08
Barbara Fitchie

V-$150+

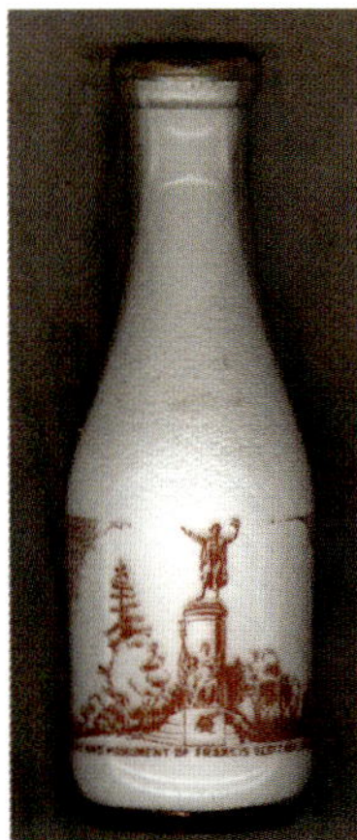

USMD12
reverse#USMD08
Francis Scott
Key
V-$150+

USMD13
Semi-Rare
Eden Plans Dairy
Hagerstown,Md.
V-$150+

USMD14
Uncommon
Cedar Farm
Calvert., Md
V-$50+

USME01
Uncommon
W.Bowley & Son
Bangor,Me.
V-$50+

USME02
Semi-Rare
Katahdin Cry.
Fort Fairfield,Me.
V-$100+

USME03
Uncommon
Norway Cry.
Norway,Me.
V-$50+

USME04
Uncommon
Maine Dairy
Portland,Me.
V-$50+

USME05
Semi-Rare
Pine Cone Dairy
Fairffield,Me
V-$100+

USME06
Semi-Rare
Springmont Farm
Frysburg,Me.
V-$50+

MUSME07
Semi-Rare
Webber's Dairy
Winslow,Me
V-$100+

USME08
Uncommon
Shaw's Ridge
Sanford,Me
V-$50

USME09
Uncommon
Grant Dairy
Bangor,Me.
V-$50

USME10
Semi-Rare
Bachvale Farm
Farmington,Me.
V-$150+

USME11
Uncommon
Webbers Dairy
Waterville,Me.
V-$50+

USME12
Semi-Rare
Richvale Farm
Farmington,Me.
V-$100+

USME13
Uncommon
Round Top Farm
Darariscotta.Me
V-$50

USME14
Semi-Rare
Wendell Wathen
Fort Fairfield,Me.
V-$100+

USME15
Uncommon
Elm'Aple Dairy
Lisbon Falls,Me.
V-$50+

Massachusetts

USMA01
common
Hank's Bros.
E.Longmeadow,Ma.
V-$20

USMA02
Uncommon
Southend Farm
Millis,Ma.
V-$50

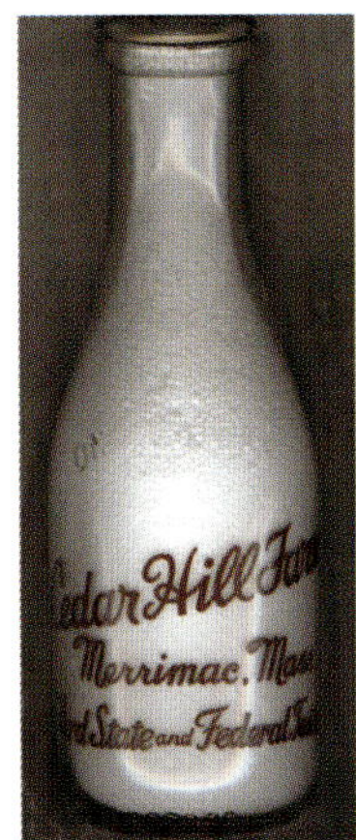

USMA03
Uncommon
Cedar Hill Farm
Merrimac,Ma.
V-$50

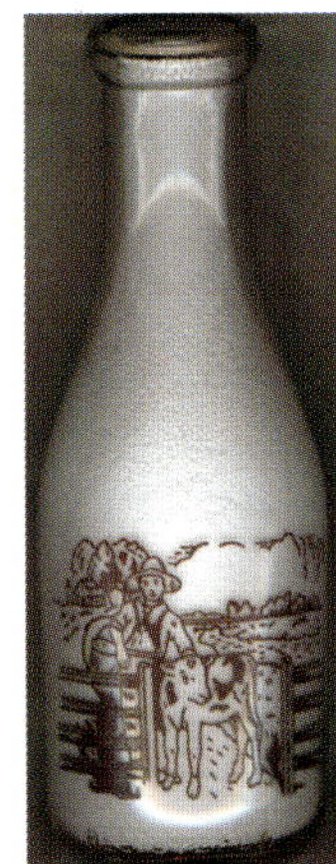

USMA04
reverse#USMA03

V-$00

USMA05
Uncommon
Timberlost Dairy
Ashburnham,Ma
V-$50

USMA06
Uncommon
Greenwood Dairy
Worcester,Ma.
V-$50+

USMA07
reverse#USMA05

V-$00

USMA08
Uncommon
Bonnie View Dairy
Dudley,Ma.
V-$30

USMA09
Uncommon
Pleasanview Dairy
Newton,Ma.
V-$30

kUSMA10
Uncommon
Producers Dairy
Brookton,Ma
V-$30

USMA11
Uncommon
Pleasant View
Taunton,Ma.
V-$50+

USMA12
Uncommon
Clover Valley
So.Easton,Ma.
V-$50+

USMA12a
Semi-Rare
Greenleaf Dairy
Brocton,Ma.
V-$80+

USMA13
Semi-Rare
Ferndale Dairy
Weston,Ma.
V-$80+

USMA14
Uncommon
Wollow Tree Dairy
S.Dartmouth,Ma.
V-$50

USMA15
Rare
Sibley Farm
Spencer,Ma.
V-$250+

USMI01
Uncommon
West Side Dairy
Owosso,Mi.
V-$50

USMI02
Uncommon
A.G.Nelson
Owosso,Mi.
V-$50+

USMI03
Uncommon
Producers's Cry.
Benton Harbor,Mi.
V-$30

USMI04
Uncommon
Emery Kinney
Ludington,Mi.
V-$50

USMI05
Uncommon
Highland Dairy
Hasting,Mi.
V-$50

USMI06
common
Rond Dairy
Battle Creek,Mi
V-$30

USMI07
Semi-Rare
Mill's Creamery
Grand Rapids,Mi.
V-$100+

USMI08
reverse#USMI07

V-$00

USMI09
Uncommon
South Haven Dairy
South Haven,Mi.
V-$30

USMI10
Uncommon
Bohrers Dairy
Traverse City,Mi.
V-$50

USMI11
Uncommon
Lowes Dairy
Flint,Mich.
V-$50

USMI12
Semi-Rare
Maple Lawn Dairy
Pymouth,Mi.
V-$150+

USMI13
common
Sherman Dairy
South Haven,Mi.
V-$30

USMI14
Semi-Rare
Nelson's Dairy
Manistique,Mi.
V-$150+

USMI15
reverse#USMI14

V-$00

USMN01
Rare
Spencer Dairy
Minn.
V-$150+

USMN02
Semi-Rare
Ohleens Milk
Minn,Mn.
V-$100+

USMN03
Uncommon
Allen Dairy
Caledonia,Mn.
V-$30

USMN04
Uncommon
Tetonka Dairy
Waterville,Mn.+
V-$50

USMN05
Uncommon
Gilbertson Dairy
Battle Lake,Mn.
V-$30

USMN06
Rare
Land O'Lake
Mankato,Mn.+
V-$250

USMN07
reverse#USMN06

V-$00

USMN08
Rare
The City Dairy
St. .Paul,Mn.
V-$150+

USMN09
Uncommon
Forest's Dairy
Luverne,Mn.
V-$50+

USMN10
Semi-Rare
St.Paul Milk Co.
St..Paul,Mn.
V-$80+

USMN11
Uncommon
Johnson bros
Virginia,Mn.
V-$50

USMN12
Uncommon
Glidden Dairy
Hallock,Mn.
V-$50+

USMN13
common
Farmers Coop Cry
Fairmont,Mn.
V-$30

USMN14
Uncommon
Duluth Milk Co.
Duluth,Mn.
V-$50

USMN15
Semi-Rare
Holstein Holsom
Virginia,Mn.
V-$100+

USMS01
Semi-Rare
Sunset Dairy
Farrell,Ms.
V-$100+

USMS02
Rare
Leflore Dairy
Greenwood,Ms.
V-$150+

USMS03
Semi-Rare
Avent Dairy
Oxford,Ms
V-$100+

USMS04
Rare
Meredith's Dairy
Batesville.Ms.
V-$150+

USMS05
Uncommon
Gayoso Farms
Horn Lake,Ms.
V-$50+

USMS06
Semi-Rare
Kirkpatrick Dairy
Amory,Ms.
V-$100+

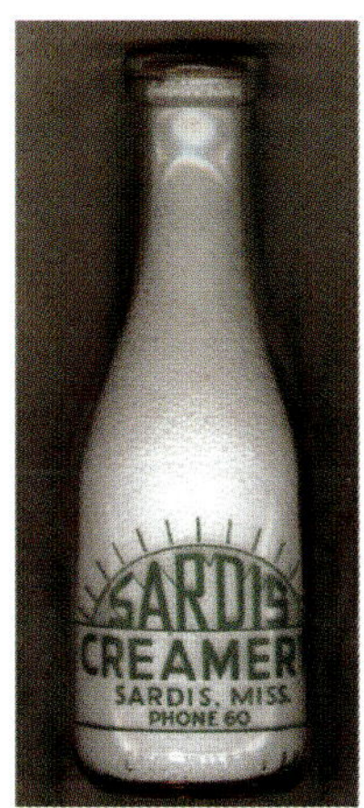

USMS07
Rare
Sardis Creamery
Sardis,Ms.
V-$250+

USMS08
reverse#USMS07

V-$00

Butter Carton Sample -Shelley Equip.Co. Lincoln,Nebr. 1928

Missouri

USMO01
Uncommon
Reiss Dairy
Sikeston,Mo.
V-$50+

USMO02
Semi-Rare
Melody Farm
Chesterfield,Mo.
V-$150+

USMO03
Uncommon
Woods Dairy
Sikeston,Mo.
V-$50

USMO04
Uncommon
Harris Dairy
St.Joseph,Mo.
V-$50

USMO05
Uncommon
Blakeney Dairy
Poplar Bluff,Mo.
V-$50

USMO06
Semi-Rare
Vaughn Dairy
Festus,Mo.
V-$70+

USMO07
reverse#USMO06

V-$00

USMO08
common
Willis-Case Dairy
Poplar Bluff,Mo.
V-$30

USMO09
reverse#USMO08

V-$00

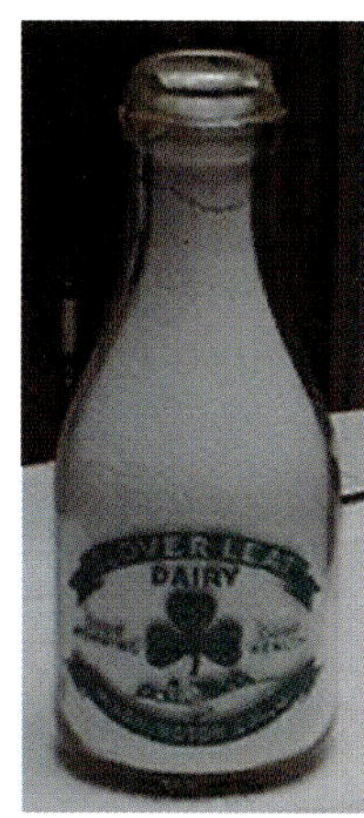

USMO10
Uncommon
Cloverleaf Dairy
Mo.
V-$50+

USMO11
Uncommon
Martins Milk
Union,Mo.
V-$50+

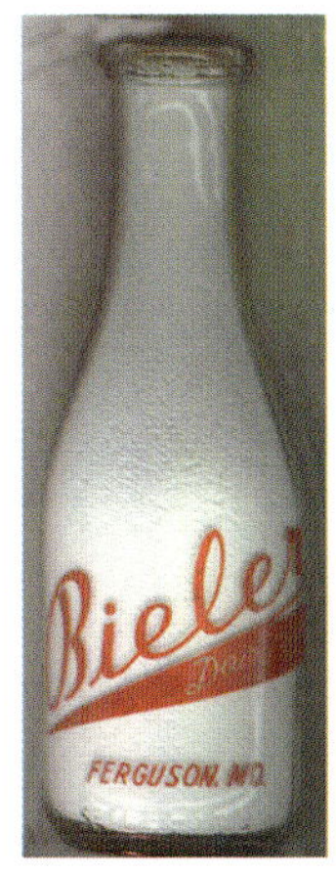

USMO12
common
Bieler dairy
Ferguson,Mo.
V-$30

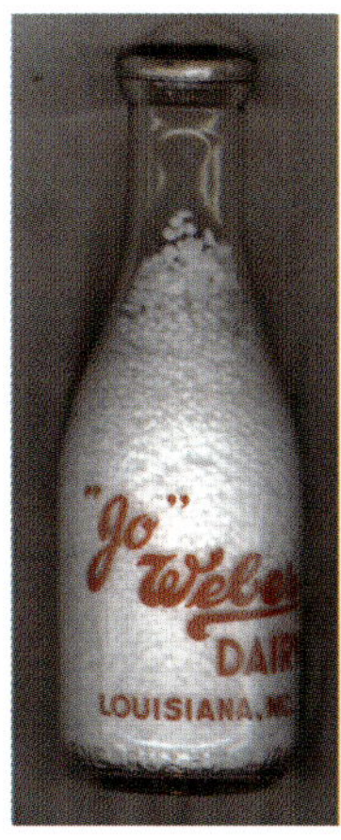

USMO13
common
Jo Weber Dairy
Louisana,Mo
V-$30

USMO14
Uncommon
Wahlig Dairy
Kirkwood,Mo.
V-$50

USMO15
Semi-Rare
Schonhoff Dairy
Cape Giraideau,Mo.
V-$80+

USMT01
Uncommon
South Side Dairy
Butte,Mt.
V-$50

USMT02
Uncommon
Western Milk Co
Butte,Mt.
V-$50+

USMT03
Rare
Jack Hoffman
Miles City,Mt.
V-$150+

USMT04
reverse#USMT03

V-$00

USMT05
Uncommon
Green's Market
Townsend,Mt.
V-$70+

USMT06
Uncommon
Kessler Dairy
Bozeman,Mt.
V-$70+

USMT07
Uncommon
Crystal Dairy
Butte,Mt.
V-$50

USMT08
Uncommon
Ayrshire Dairy
Great Falls,Mt.
V-$70+

USMT09
Uncommon
Dickert Dairy
Helena,Mt.
V-$70+

Ice Cream Sample Carton Shelley Equip.Co. 1928

Nebraska

USNE01
Uncommon
Village Dairy
Southerland,Ne.
V-$50+

USNE02
Uncommon
Hand's Dairy
Sidney,Ne.
V-$50

USNE03
Uncommon
Ravenswood Milk
McCook,Ne.
V-$50

USNE04
Uncommon
Ernst Dairy
McCook.Ne.
V-$50

USNE05
Semi-Rare
Terry's
Scottsbluff,Ne.
V-$50+

USNE06
reverse#USNE05

V-$00

USNE07
common
Skyline Dairy
Lincoln.Ne.
V-$30

USBNE08
Uncommon
Wiebe's Dairy
Beatrice,Ne.
V-$50

Butter sample box 1928

USNV01
Uncommon
Pershing Cry.
Lovelock.Nv.
V-$50+

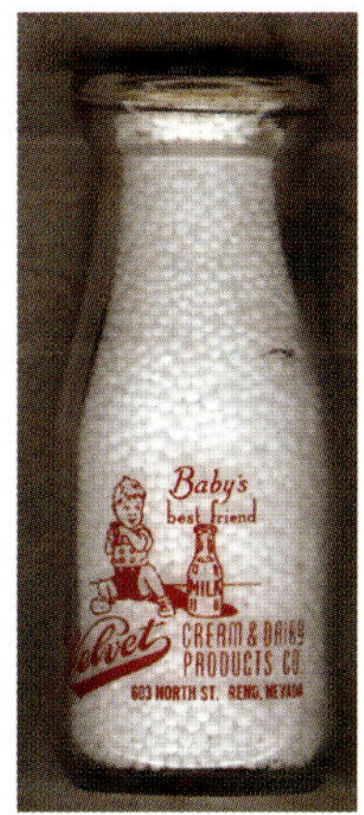

USNV02
Uncommon
Velvet Dairy
Reno,Nv
V-$30

USNV03
Uncommon
Sanitary Dairy
Tonopah.Nv.
V-$50+

USNV04
Uncommon
G.J.Seidel & Son
Poland,Nv.
V-$50+

USNV05
Semi-Rare
Model Dairy
Reno,Nv.
V-$100+

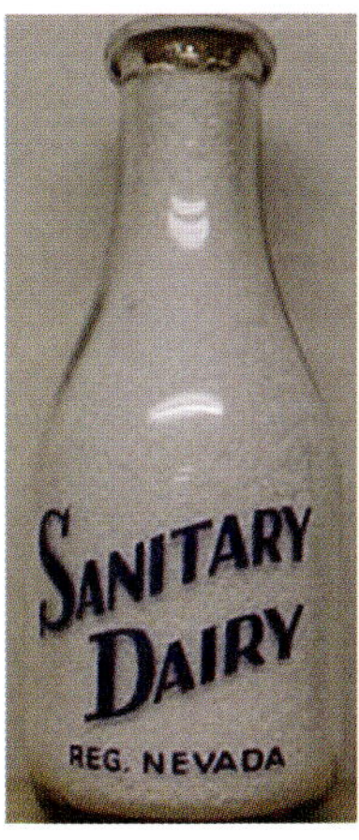

USNV06
Uncommon
Sanitary Dairy
Nv.
V-$50+

USNV06
Uncommon
Yorks Dairy
Fallon's Nv.
V-$50+

USNV07
Semi-Rare
Oppedyk Dairy
Las Vegas,Nv.
V-$70+

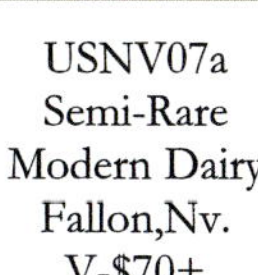

USNV07a
Semi-Rare
Modern Dairy
Fallon,Nv.
V-$70+

USNV07b
Semi-Rare
Model Dairy
Reno,Nv.
V-$100+

USNV07c
Semi-Rare
Knadstedt Dairy
Nv.
V-$50+

USNV09
Semi-Rare
Eagle Valley Dairy
Carson City.Nv.
V-$100+

USNV10
Uncommon
Nevada Dairy

V-$50+

USNV11
Uncommon
Valley Dairy
Yerington,Nv.
V-$30

USNV12
Uncommon
Pomeroy Dairy
Fallon,Nv.
V-$50+

USNV13
Uncommon
Yates Dairy
Reno,Nv.
V-$80+

New Hampshire

USNH01
Uncommon
Purity Dairy
Manchester,N.H.
V-$50

USNH02
Uncommon
Littleton Dairy
Littleton,N.H.
V-$50+

USNH03
Uncommon
E.E. Beland
Bedford,N.H.
V-$50+

USNH04
Uncommon
D.B.Lawrence
Claremont,N.H.+
V-$50

USNH05
Uncommon
Churchill's Dairy
Bethlehem,N.H.
V-$30

USNH06
Uncommon
H.F.Morrill
Concord,N.H.
V-$50

USNH07
Uncommon
Mosher Farm
Keene,N.H.
V-$50

USNH07a
uncommon
Worcester Farm
Keene,N.H.
V-$50

USNH08
Uncommon
McCready's Dairy
Berlin,N.H.
V-$50

USNH09
Uncommon
Farm House Dairy
Bingham Falls,N.H.
V-$50

USNH10
Uncommon
Rosewald Farm
Hillboro,N.H.
V-$50

USNH10a
Uncommon
Schofield's Daiyr
Bristol.N.H.
V-$50

USNH11
common
Messers Dairy
New London,N.H.
V-$30

USNH12
Rare
Northland Dairy
Littleton,N.H.
V-$150+

USNH13
reverse#USNH12

V-$00

USNJ01
Uncommon
Hamilton Farm
Somerville,N.J.
V-$50

USNJ01a
Uncommon
Coombs
Millville,N.J.
V-$50

USNJ01b
uncommon
Phillips Dairy
Cold Spring,N.J.
V-$50

USNJ02
Uncommon
Doherty's Dairy
Florence,N.J.
V-$50

USNJ02a
Uncommon
Mahwin Farms
Mahwah,N.J.
V-$50

USNJ02b
Uncommon
Sickler's Dairy
Williamtown,N.J.
V-$50

USNJ03
Uncommon
Elliott Dairy
Freehold,N.J.
V-$30

USNJ04
Uncommon
Coddington Dairy
Martinsville,N.J.
V-$30

USNJ05
Uncommon
Eugsters Dairy
Rochelle Park,N.J.
V-$50

USNJ05a
Uncommon
J.C.Allen
Manasquan,N.J.
V-$50

USNJ05b
Uncommon
Wardells Dairy
Nephune,N.Y.
V-$50

USNJ06
Uncommon
Hillcrest Dairy
Egg Harbor,N.J.
V-$50

USNJ06a
Uncommon
Garden State
Midland Park,N.J.
V-$50

USNJ06b
Uncommon
Sever's Dairy
Beverly,N.J.
V-$50

USNJ07
Uncommon
Berry's Milk
Port Norris,N.J.
V-$50

USNJ07a
Uncommon
Krauszen Dairy
New Brunswick,N.J.
V-$50

USNJ08
Uncommon
Kenwood Dairy
Pennington,N.J.
V-$50

New Jersery

USNJ09
Uncommon
Hidden Acres
Washington,N.J.
V-$50

USNJ09a
Uncommon
Mapledale Dairy
Philipsburg,N.J.
V-$50

USNJ09b
Uncommon
River Edge Dairy
Somerville,N.J.
V-$50

USNJ10
Uncommon
White Dotte Farm
Vincentown,N.J.
V-$50

USNJ11
Uncommon
J.Maurice Huff
Clarksboro,N.J.
V-$50

USNJ12
Uncommon
Hope Dairy
Madison,N.J.
V-$50

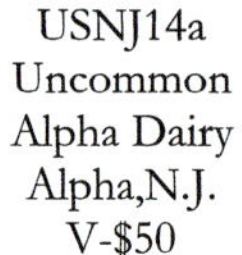

USNJ13
common
Cream Valley
Woodstown,N.J.
V-$30

USNJ13a
Uncommon
Golden Glow
Paterson,N.J.
V-$50

USNJ14
Uncommon
Somerset Dairy
Middlebush,N.J
.V-$30

USNJ14a
Uncommon
Alpha Dairy
Alpha,N.J.
V-$50

USNJ14b
Uncommon
Preakness Dairy
Preakness,N.J.
V-$50

USNJ15
Rare
Crestall Dairy
Carlstadt,N.J.
V-$150+

USNJ16
Uncommon
Shrewsburg
Shrewsburg,N.J.
V-$50+

USNJ16a
Uncommon
Sisco Dairy
Clifton,N.J.
V-$50+

USNJ16b
Semi-Rare
Robertson's
Camden,N.J.
V-$100+

USNJ17
Rare
Hills & Dales Farm
Oldwick,N.J.
V-$150+

USNJ18
Semi-Rare
Bordens
Burlington,N.J.
V-$100+

USNJ19
Uncommon
Spring Lake Dairy
Spring Lake,N.J.
V-$50+

USNM01
Uncommon
Polmood Farm
Santa Fe,N.M.
V-$70+

USNM02
Rare
Red Fern Dairy
Albuqerque,N.M.
V-$150+

USNM03
reverse#USNM02

V-$00

USNM04
Uncommon
Ferguson Bros.
Santa Fe.N.M.
V-$50+

USNM05
Uncommon
Emmett's Dairy
Central,N.M.
V-$70+

USNM06
Semi-Rare
LaPuerta de Sol
Gerson Gusdorf
V-$50+

USNM07
reverse#USNM06

Taos,N.M.
V-$00

USNM08
Uncommon
Sumset Cry.
Roswell,N.M.
V-$50+

USNM09
Uncommon
Shades Dairy
Santa Fe,N.M.
V-$50+

USNM10
Uncommon
Campbell's Dairy
Clovis,N.M.
V-$50+

USNM11
Rare
Del Rico Dairy
Santa Fe,N.M.
V-$100+

USNM012
Uncommon
T&M Dairy
Hanover,N.M.
V-$50

USNM13
uncommon
Ferguson Bros Dairy
Santa Fe,N.M.
V-$50

USNY01
Uncommon
Fairfield Dairy
Batavia,N.Y.
V-$50

USNY02
Uncommon
Liberty Dairy
Utica,N.Y.
V-$30

USNY03
Uncommon
Card-Sock Dairy
Dunkirk,N.Y.
V-$30

USNY04
Uncommon
Brush's Dairy
Huntington,N.Y.
V-$30

USNY04a
reserve#USNY04

V-$00

USNY05
Uncommon
Seiberg Cream
Jamestown,N.Y.
V-$50

USNY06
Uncommon
Mather Dairy
Whallonsburg,N.Y.
V-$30

USNY07
Uncommon
Meadowland

V-$30

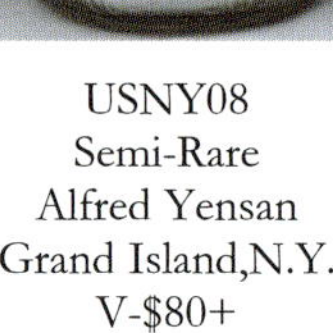

USNY08
Semi-Rare
Alfred Yensan
Grand Island,N.Y.
V-$80+

USNY08a
Uncommon
McCarty Dairy
Filmore,N.Y.
V-$50

USNY09
Uncommon
Flushing Dairy
Maspeth,N.Y.
V-$30

USNY09a
Uncommon
Hamilton Milk
Brooklyn,N.Y.
V-$50

USNY10
Semi-Rare
M.B.Thurston
Sherrill,N.Y.
V-$100+

USNY11
reserve#USNY10

V-$00

USNY12
Semi-Rare
C.Graves & Sons
Clayton,N.Y.
V-$80+

USNY13
Uncommon
H.B.Archer
Randolph,N.Y.
V-$50

USNY14
Uncommon
C.A. Miller Dairy
Fredonia,N.Y.
V-$50

USNY15
Rare
Fishkill Milk Bar
Fishkill,N.Y.
V-$150+

USNY16
Uncommon
Ryan's Dairy
Newport,N.Y.
V-$50

USNY17
Uncommon
Hillcrest Dairy
Wading River,N.Y.
V-$50

USNY18
Uncommon
Fisher Dairy
Ravena,N.Y.
V-$50

USNY19
Uncommon
Oak Tree Dairy
Elwood,N.Y.
V-$50+

USNY20
Uncommon
J.D.Mager
Little Valley,N.Y.
V-$50+

USNY21
Uncommon
Supreme Dairy
Mohawk,N.Y.
V-$50

USNY22
Uncommon
Orchard Hill Dairy
Orchard Park,N.Y.
V-$50

USNY23
Uncommon
Pryibil Farm
Glen Cove,N.Y.
V-$50

USNY24
Uncommon
Douglaston Manor
Plaski,N.Y.
V-$80+

USNY25
Uncommon
Ramelio's Dairy
Frankfort,N.Y.
V-$50+

USNY26
Uncommon
Cornell Dairy
Jamesville,N.Y.
V-$50

USNY27
Semi-Rare
Andrews Dairy
Canandaigua,N.Y.
V-$70+

USNY28
Rare
Blue Eagle Dairy
Rome,N.Y.
V-$250+

USNC01
Uncommon
Odom's Dairy
Ahoskie,N.C.
V-$50+

USNC02
Uncommon
Charlotte Dairy
Charlotte,N.C.
V-$50+

USNC03
Uncommon
Lakeside Dairy
Hendersonville,N.C.
V-$50+

USNC04
Uncommon
R.S.Edmiston
Mooresville,N.C.
V-$50+

USNC05
common
Surry Dairies
Mt.Airy,N.C.
V-$30

USNC06
Rare
Fanning Field Farm
Fletcher,N.C.
V-$150+

USNC07
Uncommon
Mada Milk
New Bern,N.C.
V-$50+

USNC08
Uncommon
Archdale Farms
King's Mountain,N.C.
V-$7+

USNC09
Uncommon
Springside Dairy
Charlotte,N.C.
V-$50+

USNC10
Uncommon
Warrenton Dairy
Warrenton,N.C.
V-$50+

USNC11
Uncommon
Butlers Dairy
Tryon,N.C.
V-$50+

USNC12
Uncommon
Sutton's Dairy
Kinston,N.C.
V-$50+

USNC13
Uncommon
Lomax Dairy
Spencer,N.C.
V-$50+

USNC14
Uncommon
G.L.Hamrick
Lattimore,N.C.
V-$50+

USNC15
Uncommon
Towery's Dairy
Lattimore,N.C.
V-$50+

USNC16
Uncommon
Evergreen Dairy
Kannapolis,N.C.
V-$50+

USNC17
Uncommon
Edwards Dairy
Kinston,N.C.
V-$50+

USNC18
Uncommon
Zimmerman's
Lexington,N.C.
V-$50+

USNC19
Uncommon
Golden Valley
tryon,N.C.
V-$50+

USNC20
Uncommon
Lee's Dairy
Lawndale,N.C.
V-$50+

USNC21
Uncommon
Nantahala Cry.
Bervard,N.C.
V-$50+

USNC22
Uncommon
Hall's Dairy
Mt.Ulla,N.C.
V-$50+

USNC23
Uncommon
Rockwell Park
Rockwell,N.C.
V-$50+

USNC24
common
Stanly Dairies
Albermale,N.C.
V-$30

USNC25
common
Slected Dairies
Winston Salem,N.C.
V-$50

USNC26
reverse#USNC25

V-$00

USNC27
Rare
Swan Ponds Dairy
Morganton,N.C.
V-$150+

USNC28
Uncommon
Hickory Grove
Mt.Ulla,N.C.
V-$50+

USNC29
Uncommon
White's Dairy
Kinston,N.C.
V-$50+

North Dakota

USND01
Rare
Bismark Dairy
Bismark,N.D.
V-$150

USND02
Rare
Cloverdale
Bismark,N.D.
V-$350+

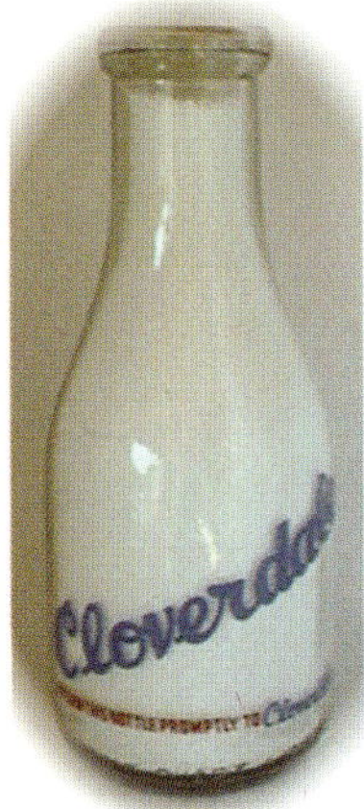

USND03
reverse#USND02

V-$00

USND04
Semi-Rare
Cloverdale
Bismark,N.D.
V-$50+

USNC05
Rare
Whites
Minot,N.D.
V-$150

USNC06
Rare
Acme Dairy
Fargo,N.C.
V-$150+

USNC07
Semi-Rare
Bridgeman Milk
N.D.
V-$100

USOH01
Uncommon
Lone Pine Dairy
Bucyrus,Oh.
V-$50

USOH02
Uncommon
Miami Belle
Germantown,Oh.
V-$50

USOH03
Uncommon
Tattersell Dairy
Elyria,Oh.
V-$50

USOH04
Uncommon
Kinley's Dairy
Upper Sandusky.O.
V-$50

USOH05
Uncommon
Townsend West
Cincinnati,Oh.
V-$50

USOH06
Uncommon
Linton & Linton
Wilmingtoon,Oh.
V-$50

USOH07
Uncommon
Borden's
Akron,Oh.
V-$50+

USOH08
Uncommon
Turkey Bend Dairy
Warsaw,Oh.
V-$50

USOH09
Uncommon
Slagle's Jersey
Poland,Oh.
V-$50

USOH10
Semi-Rare
Cappeldale Farm
Dover,Oh.
V-$80+

USOH11
Uncommon
El Dora Farms
Lima,Oh.
V-$50

USOH12
Uncommon
Maple Park
Middletown,Oh.
V-$50

USOH13
Uncommon
Spring Brook Dairy
Greenville,Oh.
V-$50

USOH14
Uncommon
Olenick Dairy
Youngstown,Oh.
V-$50

USOH15
Uncommon
Valley Run Dairy
Fredericktown,Oh
V-$50

USOH15a
Uncommon
Pine Tree Dairy
Delta,Oh.
V-$50

Oklahoma

USOK01
Uncommon
Jerry Oven
Enid,Ok.
V-$50

USOK02
Rare
Markwell Milk
Sulphur,Ok.
V-$150+

USOK03
reverse#USKOK02

V-$00

USOK04
Uncommon
McNabb Dairy
Mounds.Ok.
V-$30

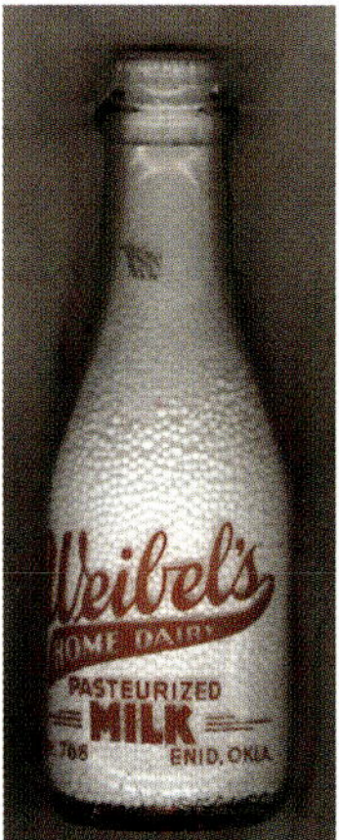

USOK05
Uncommon
Weibel's Milk
Enid,Ok.
V-$50

USOK06
Uncommon
Bill's Hometown
Pawhuska,Ok.
V-$50

USOK07
Uncommon
Wrights Dairy
Hobart,Ok.
V-$50

USOK08
Uncommon
Essary Dairy
Clinton,Ok.
V-$50

USOR01
Semi-Rare
Golden Top Milk
Salem,Or.
V-$100+

USOR02
Rare
Garner Dairy
Grants Pass.Or.
V-$150+

USOR03
Uncommon
Orchard View
Dallas,Or.
V-$50

USOR04
Semi-Rare
Chula Vista Dairy
Eugene,Or.
V-$100+

USOR05
Uncommon
Mountain Dairy
Klamath Falls,Or.
V-$70+

USOR06
Semi-Rare
Myrtles Dairy
Coss Bay,Or.
V-$100+

USOR07
Semi-Rare
Springfield Cry.
Springfield,Or.
V-$100+

USOR08
Rare
Brown's milk
Baker,Or.
V-$150+

USOR09
Rare
Kola Tepee
Salem,Or.
V-$150+

USOR10
Semi-Rare
Holly Dairy
Or.
V-$100

USOR11
Uncommon
Alpenrose Dairy
Portland,Or.
V-$50

USOR12
common
Valley Dairy
LaGrande.Or.
V-$30

USOR13
Semi-Rare
Ginger Roger's
Medford,Or.
V-$150+

USOR14
Uncommon
Sunflower Dairy
Austoria,Or.
V-$50+

USOR15
Semi-Rare
Curly's
Salem,Or.
V-$100+

USPA01
Uncommon
Valley Dairy
Cochranton,Pa
V-$30

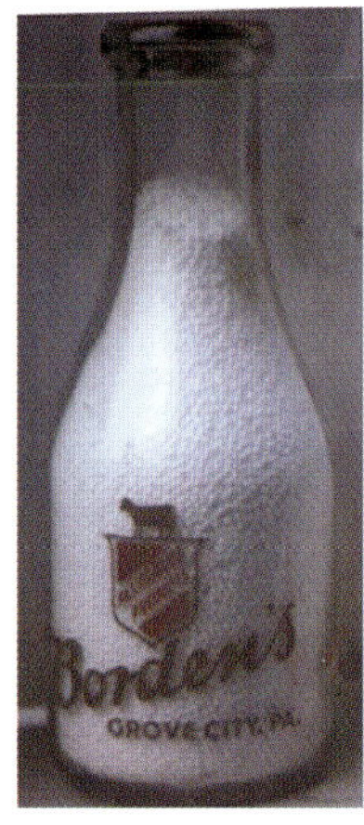

USPA02
Uncommon
Borden's
Grove City,Pa
V-$50

USPA03
Semi-Rare
C.V. Danielson
Mt.Jewell,Pa
V-$100

USPA04
Semi-Rare
Hershey Chocolate
Lebanon,Pa.
V-$150+

USPA05
Semi-Rare
Ayrshire Dairy
Sharon,Pa
V-$100+

USPA06
Semi-Rare
Woodside Farm
Landisville,Pa.
V-$100+

USPA07
Semi-Rare
Willowdale Farm
Lancaster,Pa.
V-$100+

USPAO08
reverse#USPA07

V-$00

USPA09
Rare
Spruce Villa Dairy
Lititz,Pa
V-$150+

USPA010
uncommon
Drinkmor Dairy
Aliquippa,Pa
V-$-30

USPA10a
Uncommon
Rust's Milk
Sharon,Pa.
V-$50

uSPA11
Semi-Rare
Anderson Dairy
Ebensburg,Pa
V-$100+

USPA12
reverse#USPA11

V-$00

USPA13
Uncommon
Otto's Milk
Pittsburg,Pa.
V-$30

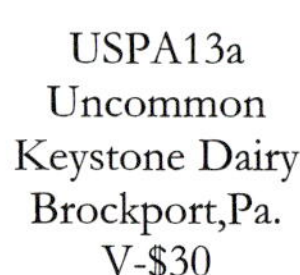

USPA13a
Uncommon
Keystone Dairy
Brockport,Pa.
V-$30

USPA14
Rare
Lenkerbrook
Harrisburg,Pa.
V-$150+

USPA15
Semi-Rare
Lencoski's Dairy
Latrobe,Pa.
V-$150+

USPA16
reverse#USPA15

V-$00

USPA17
Semi-Rare
Lauver's Dairy
Mifflintown,Pa.
V-$100+

USPA18
Rare
Cole's Dairy
Monongehela,Pa.
V-$150+

USPA19
Uncommon
Green Meadow
Kent,Pa.
V-$50+

USPA20
Semi-Rare
Meadow View
Red Lion,Pa.
V-$100+

USPA21
reverse#USPA20

V-$00

USPA22
Uncommon
Martin Farm
Scenery Hill,Pa.
V-$70+

USPA23
Uncommon
Cedar Spring Dairy
Mill Hall,Pa.
V-$70

USPA24
Uncommon
Hendrick Dairy
Perkasie,Pa.
V-$50+

USPA25
Semi-Rare
Campbell's Dairy
Grove City,Pa
V-$100+

USPA26
Semi-Rare
Walthour's Dairy
Greensburg,Pa
V-$100+

USPA27
Uncommon
Homecroft Dairy
Bessemer,Pa.
V-$70+

USPA28
Uncommon
Spring Valley Farm
McKeansburg,Pa.
V-$70+

USPA29
reverse#USPA28

V-$00

USPA30
Rare
Mumper's Dairy
Elizabethtown,Pa.
V-$150+

USPA31
Rare
Hertzler's Dairy
Elizabethtown,Pa.
V-$150+

USPA32
Uncommon
Sylvan View
Lancaster,Pa.
V-$70+

USPA32a
Rare
Magrisn Dairy
New Danville,Pa
V-$150+

USPA33
Uncommon
Kulikowski Dairy
Coal Center,Pa.
V-$50+

USPA34
Uncommon
Pine Hill farms
Effort,Pa.
V-$70+

USPA35
Uncommon
Michelitsch's Dairy
Port Allegany,Pa
V-$50+

USPA36
Semi-Rare
Bradford's Dairy
Lewistown,Pa.
V-$80+

USPA37
Semi-Rare
Pine Tree Dairy
Backmanville,,Pa.
V-$100+

USPA38
Uncommon
Roseraver Dairy
Monessen,Pa
V-$50+

USPA39
Uncommon
Antietam Farm
Waynesboro,Pa.
V-$70+

USPA40
Uncommon
Check's Dairy
Latrobe,Pa.
V-$50+

USPA41
Rare
Sunset Dairy
Laebanon,Pa
V-$150+

USPA42
Uncommon
Lone Pine Dairy
Grove City,Pa
V-$50

USPA43
Uncommon
Tromknecht &
Erie,Pa.
V-$50+

USPA44
Uncommon
L.Dibble Dairy
Wesleyville,Pa.
V-$50+

USPA45
Uncommon
Ideal Farm
New Stanton,Pa.
V-$50+

USRI01
Uncommon
Lincoln Woods
Sayesville,R.I.
V-$50

USRI02
Uncommon
Shawdow Lawn
E.Providence,R.I.
V-$50

USRI03
Uncommon
Romey's Dairy
Woonsocket,R.I.
V-$50

USRI04
common
Consomers Dairy
Westerly,R.I.
V-$30

USRI05
Uncommon
DeWolf Farm
Bristol,R.I.
V-$50+

USRI06
Uncommon
Horse Shoe Falls
Shannock,R.I.
V-$50+

USRI07
Uncommon
I.H.Sweet
Oakland,R.I.
V-$50+

USPRI08
Uncommon
Hennessey's Dairy
No.Providence,R.I.
V-$50

USRI09
Uncommon
B .N .Smith
Cranston,R.I.
V-$50

USRI10
Uncommon
Mann's Sunny Acre
Chepachet.R.I.
V-$50

USRI11
Rare
Hill View Dairy
No.Providence,R.I.
V-$150+

USRI12
Semi-Rare
Lee's Brook
No.Providence,R.I.
V-$70+

South Carolina

USSC01
Uncommon
Reyaola Dairy
W. .Columbia,S.C.
V-$50+

USSC01a
Uncommon
Allison's Milk
W. Columbia
V-$50+

USSC01b
Uncommon
Four Columns
Landum,S.C.
V-$50+

USSC01c
Uncommon
Reyaola Dairy
W. Columbia
V-$50+

USSC02
Uncommon
St. .Stephen Dairy
St. Stephen,S.C.
V-$50

USSC03
Uncommon
Edgewood Dairy
Greenville,S.C.
V-$50

USSC04
common
Columbia Dairy
Columbia,s.C.
V-$30

USCSC05
common
Chinguapa Dairy
Inman,S.C.
V-$30

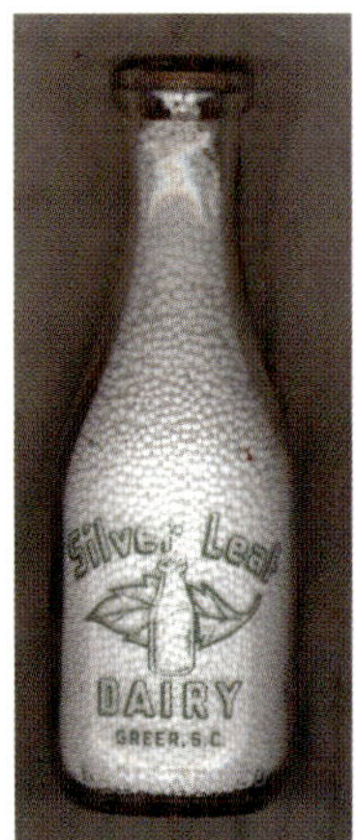

USSC06
Uncommon
Silver Leaf Dairy
Greer,S.C.
V-$50

USSC07
Uncommon
T.H. Thomas
Columbia,S.C.
V-$50

USSC08
Uncommon
Blue Ribbon Dairy
Sumter, S.C.
V-$50

USSC09
Semi-Rare
Laurens Past. Plant
Laurens, S.C.
V-$50+

USSC10
Uncommon
Gippy Plantation
Moncks Corner-
$50

USSC11
Rare
Rock Spring Dairy
Belton, S.C.
V-$100+

USSC12
Uncommon
Service Creamery
Sumter, S.C.
V-$50

USSC13
Uncommon
Winter Park Dairy
Columbia, S.C.
V-$50

USSD01
Rare
Yankton State
Yankton,S.D.
V-$150+

USSD02
Rare
Sunnyside Dairy
Comaon, S.D.
V-$150+

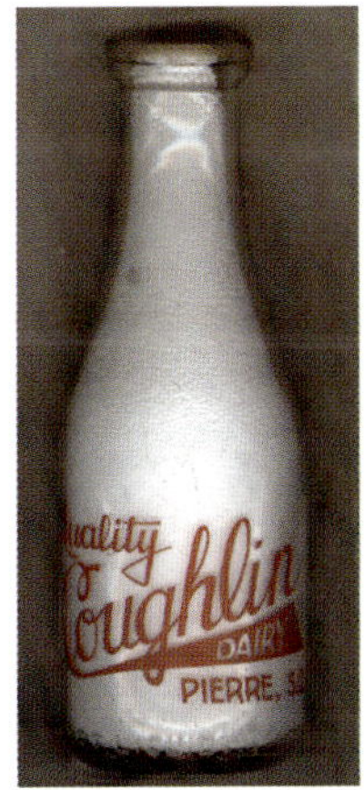

USSD03
Uncommon
Coughlin Dairy
Pierre, S.D.
V-$80=

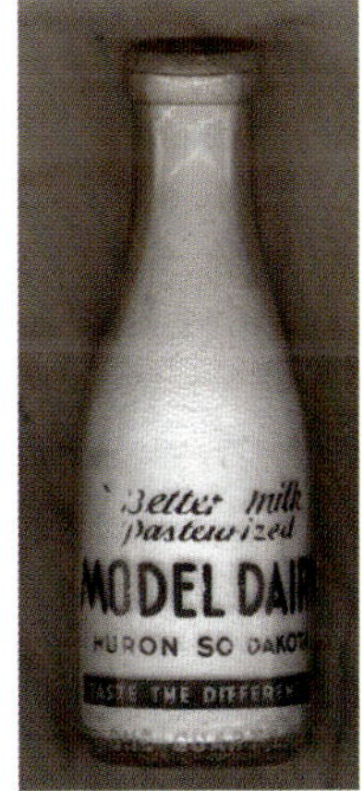

USSD04
Uncommon
Model Dairy
Huron. S.D.
V-$80+

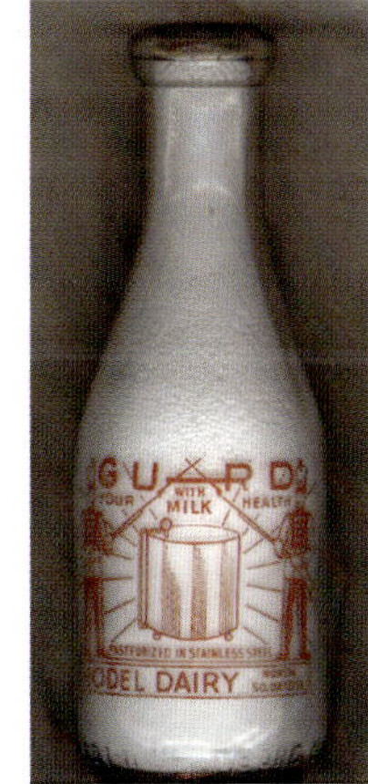

USSD05
Semi-Rare
Model Dairy
Huron, S.D.
V-$80+

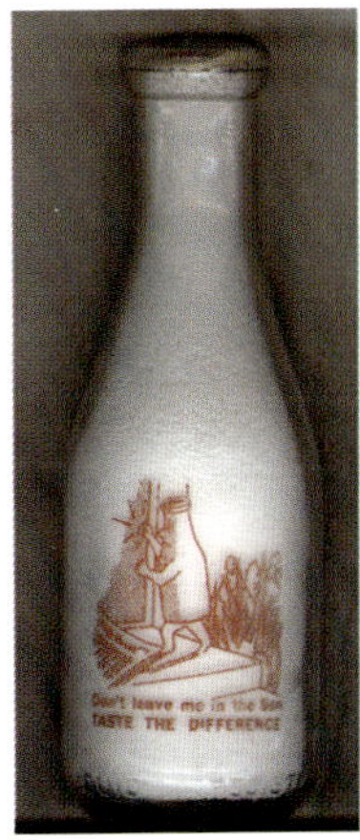

USSD06
reverse#USSD05

V-$00

USSD07
Semi-Rare
J.March & Son
Hot Springs, S.D.
V-$80+

USSD08
Uncommon
Gold Medal Milk
Huron, S.D.
V-$80+

USSD09
Uncommon
Gagnon's Milk
Huron, S.D.
V-$80+

USDSD10
Semi-Rare
Peerless Dairy
Madison, S.D.
V-$80+

USSD11
Rare
Goldhammer Dairy
Mitchell, S.D.
V-$100+

USSD12
Rare
Dollenback Dairy
Cavour, S.D.
V-$250+

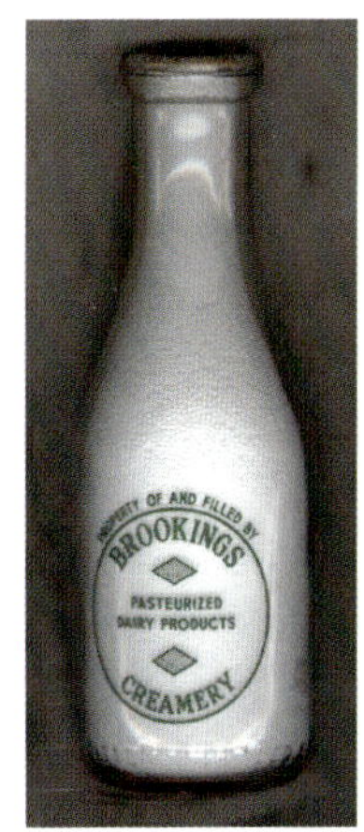

USSD13
Uncommon
Brookings Cry.
Brookings, S.D.
V-$100+

USTN01
Semi-Rare
Red Rose Dairy
Murfresboro.TN.-
V-$80+

USTN02
Uncommon
Guy Pollard
Maryville, Tn.
V-$50

USTN03
Semi-Rare
Pilot Knob Dairy
Cookeville, Tn.
V-$50+

USTN04
reverse#USTN03
V-$00

USTN05
Uncommon
US 51 South
Memphis, Tn.
V-$50

USTN06
common
Jersey Pride Cry.
Columbia, Tn.
V-$30

USTN07
Uncommon
Stedland Jersey
Memphis, TN.
V-$50

USTN08
Uncommon
T.H. Brown
Maryvill,. Tn.
V-$50

USTN09
Uncommon
Bassett Dairy
Bristol. TN.
V-$30

USTN10
Uncommon
Simmons Dairy
Paris. Tn.
V-$30

USTN11
Uncommon
Forest Hill Dairy
Memphis, TN.
V-$30

USTN12
Rare
Jersey Farm
Nashville, Tn.
V-$150+

USTN13
reverse#USTN12
National Recovery
Act
V-$00

USSTN14
Uncommon
Tuell Dairy
Columbia, Tn.
V-$50+

USTN14a
Uncommon
Pegus & Hollow
Jackson, Tn.
V-$50+

USTN15
Uncommon
Lusk & Bryan
Mt.Pleasant, Tn.
V-$50

USTX01
Uncommon
Model Dairy
Galveston, Tx.
V-$50

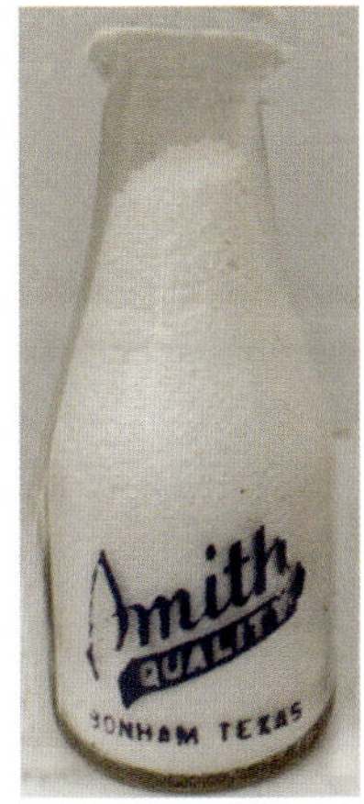

USTX02
Uncommon
Smith Dairy
Sonham, Tx.
V-$50

USTX03
Uncommon
Producers Milk
Greenville, Tx.
V+-$50

USTX04
Semi-Rare
Snow Flake Milk
Glenburne, Tx.
V-$150+

USTX05
Uncommon
Hemphill Produce
Canadian, Tx.
V-$100+

USTX06
Uncommon
Star Dairy
Galveston,Tx,
V-$100+

USTX07
Uncommon
Lee's Dairy
Electra,Tx
V-$100+

USTX08
Semi-Rare
T & M Dairy
Huston,Tx.
V-$150=

USTX09
Semi-Rare
Golden Jersey
Dinborg,Tx.
V-$80+

USTX10
Uncommon
Longhorn Cry.
Abilene,Tx.
V-$100+

USTX11
Semi-Rare
Malsby Cry.
Mineral Wells.Tx
V-$100+

USTX12
Uncommon
Kleen Kap Milk
Waco,Tx.
V-$150+

USTX13
Uncommon
R.C.Ivey Dairy
Childress,Tx.
V-$100+

USTX14
Semi-Rare
Greenbelt's
Quanah,Tx.
V-$150+

USTX15
Uncommon
Thomas Dairy
Weathorford.Tx,
V-$100+

Washington,D.C.

USDC01
Uncommon
Chestnut Farms
Washington,D.C.
V-$50+

USDC02
Uncommon
Highland Farm
Washington,D.C.
V-$50+

USDC03
Uncommon
Highland Dairy
Washington,D.C.
V-$50+

USDC04
Uncommon
Embassy Fairfax
Washington,D.C.
V-$50+

USDC05
Rare
Embassy Dairy
Washington,D.C.
V-$250+

USDC06
Uncommon
Chestnut Farm
Washington,D.C.
V-$50+

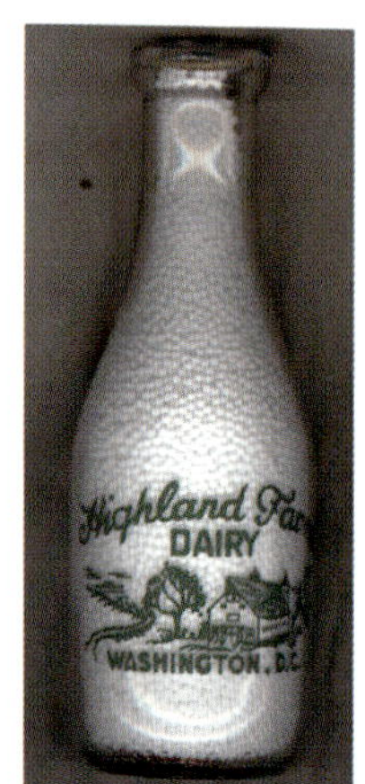

USDC07
Uncommon
Highland Dairy
Washington,D.C.
V-$80+

USUT01
Semi-Rare
Clark Dale Dairy
Panguitch,Ut.
V-$80+

USUT02
Uncommon
Home Owed Dairy
Salt Lake City,Ut.
V-$50+

USUT03
Uncommon
Rosehill Farm
Salt Lake City,Ut.
V-$70+

USUT04
Uncommon
Riverside Dairy
Moab,Ut.
V-$50+

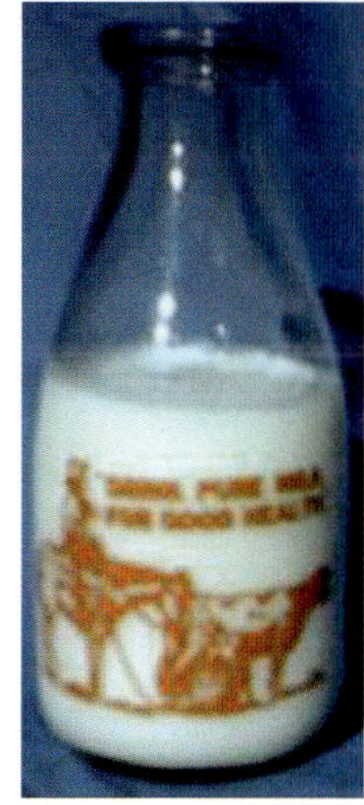

USUT05
reverse#USUT04

V-$00

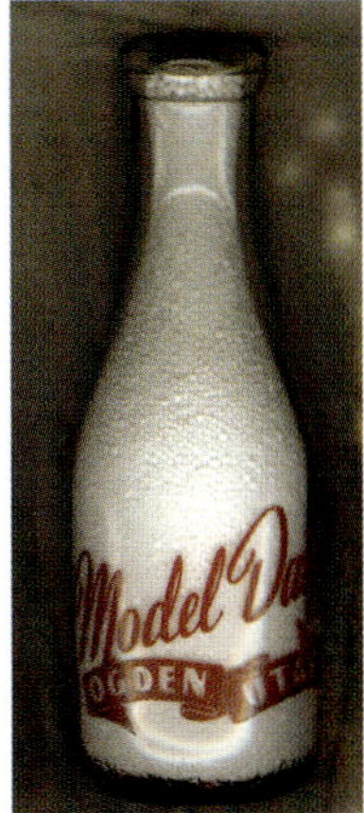

USUT06
Uncommon
Model Dairy
Ogden,Ut.
V-$50+

USUT07
Uncommon
Royal Dairy
Salt Lake City,Ut.
V-$80+

USUT08
Uncommon
Hatch Dairy
Salt Lake City,Ut.
V-$50+

USUT09
Uncommon
Store Bottle
Provo,Ut.
V-$50+

USUT10
Uncommon
Cache Meadow
Logan,Ut.
V-$50

Vermont

USVT01
Uncommon
Guernsey Milk
Lyndonville,Vt.
V-$50+

USVT02
Uncommon
Winnisquam Farm
waterbury,Vt.
V-$50+

USVT03
Semi-Rare
Pride of Vermont

V-$70+

USVT04
Uncommon
M.J.Mercure Dairy
Winooski,Vt.
V-$50

USVT05
Uncommon
Kenolie Dairy
Newfane,Vt.
V-$30

USVT06
Uncommon
Riverside Dairies
St.Johnsbury,Vt.
V-$50

USVT07
Uncommon
Orin Thomas
Rutland,Vt.
V-$70

USVT08
Rare
George Godin
Richfield,Vt.
V-$150+

USVT09
Rare
College View Dairy
Northfield,Vt.
V-$150+

USVT10
Uncommon
Palmer's Dairy
Middlebury,Vt.
V-$50

USVT11
Uncommon
Kilfasset Farm
St. Johnsburg,Vt.
V-$50

USVT12
Semi-Rare
Trinity Farm Dairy
Fair Haven Vt.
V-$150

USVT14
Semi-Rare
Mansfield Dairy
Stowe,Vt.
V-$150+

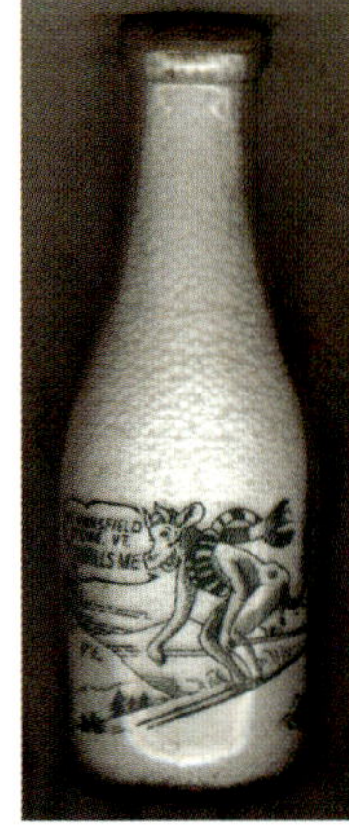

USVT14
reverse#USVT13

V-$00

USVT15
Uncommon
M.Dumas Dairy
Burlington,Vt.
V-$50

USVA01
Uncommon
Rock Castle Dairy
Lynchburg,Va.
V-$50

USVA02
Uncommon
Garst Dairy
Roanoke,Va.
V-$50

USVA03
Rare
Loudoun Farms
Purcellville,Va.
V-$100+

USVA04
Semi-Rare
Mapleton Farm
Va.
V-$50+

USVA05
Sem i-Rare
J. .Paul Warren
Townsend.Va.+
V-$70

USVA06
Uncommon
Richmond Dairy
Richmond,Va.
V-$50+

USVA07
Uncommon
Wood's Dairy
Petersburg,Va.
V-$50+

USVA08
Semi-Rare
J.L.Whitehead
Nassawadox.Va.
V-$100+

USVA09
Semi-Rare
C.S.McKay
Front Royal,Va.
V-$100+

USVA10
Uncommon
Patrick Jersey Milk
Rustburg,Va.
V-$70+

USVA11
Semi-Rare
Walkers Folly Farm
Melfa,Va.
V-$100+

USVA12
Semi-Rare
Gladston Dairy
Cape Charles,Va.
V-$100+

USVA13
common
Ashton Dairy
Petersburg,Va.
V-$20

USVA14
Uncommon
Salem Cry.
Salem,Va.
V-$50

USVA15
Uncommon
W.E.Flory.
Dayton,Va.
V-$50+

USVA15a
Rare
Warrenton Store
Warrenton,Va.
V-$100+

USVA16
Rare
Dozier Guernsey
Lee Hall,Va.
V-$150

USVA17
Uncommon
Sanitary dairy
Front Royal,Va.
V-$80+

USVA18
Uncommon
Peerless Cry
Covington,Va.
V-$30

USVA18x
Semi-Rare
Winchester Cry.
Winchester,Va.
V-$70+

USVA18a
Uncommon
Cooperedge Dairy
Lilian,Va.
V-$50+

USVA18b
Uncommon
Meadow Brook
Culpeper,Va,
V-$50+

USVA19
Semi-Rare
Poole's Dairy
Petersburg,Va.
V-$100+

USVA20
Semi-Rare
Hampton Hieghts
Hampton,Va.
V-$100+

USVA21
Semi-Rare
Shockey
Stuart,Va.
V-$100+

USVA22
Semi-Rare
Sawyer's Dairy
Smithfield,Va.
V-$100+

USVA23
Semi-Rare
Salem Dairy
Schackleford,Va.
V-$100+

USWA01
Uncommon
Benewah Cry.
Spokane,Wa.
V-$50

USWA02
Uncommon
Enfield Dairy
Ellensburg,Wa.
V-$50+

USWA03
Semi-Rare
Yakima City Cry.
Yakima,Wa.
V-$80+

USWA04
Uncommon
Stratton Dairy
Pullman,Wa.
V-$50+

USWA05
Uncommon
Kitsap Dairy
Breamerton,Wa.+
V-$50

USWA06
Uncommon
Statton's
Ellensburg,Wa.
V-$50+

USWA06a
Uncommon
Graham's
Seattle,Wa.
V-$50+

USWA07
Uncommon
Nemah Dairy
Raymond,Wa.
V-$50+

USWA08
Uncommon
Standard Dairy
Longview,Wa.
V-$50+

USWA09
Uncommon
Standard Dairy
Longview,Wa.
V-$50+

USWA10
Uncommon
Scudder Ranch
Yakima,Wa.
V-$50+

USWA11
Uncommon
Oak Grove Dairy
Clinton,Wa.
V-$50

USWA12
Uncommon
Tip Top Dairy

V-$50+

USWA13
Uncommon
Deppings Dairy
Wa.
V-$50+

USWA13a
Uncommon
Highland Pacific
Mt.Vernon,Wa.
V-$50

USWA14
Uncommon
Cloverleaf Dairy
Everett,Wa.
V-$50

USWA15
Uncommon
Standard Dairy
Longview,Wa.
V-$50

West Virginia

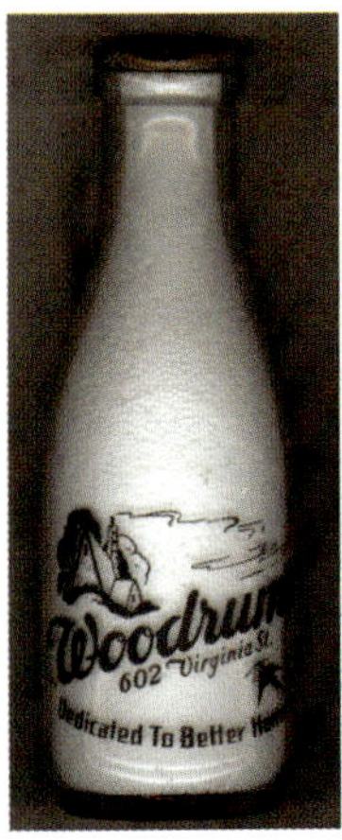

USWV01
Uncommon
Woodrum
Charlestown,WV
V-$50

USWV02
Uncommon
West-Mar
Elkins,W.V.
V-$50

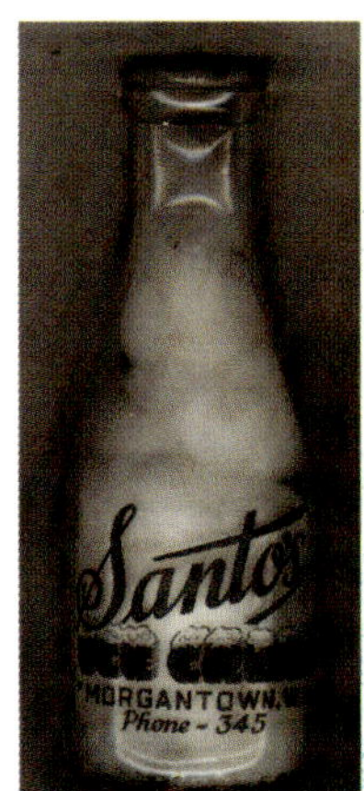

USWV03
Uncommon
Santos Ice Cream
Morgontown,W.V.
V-$50

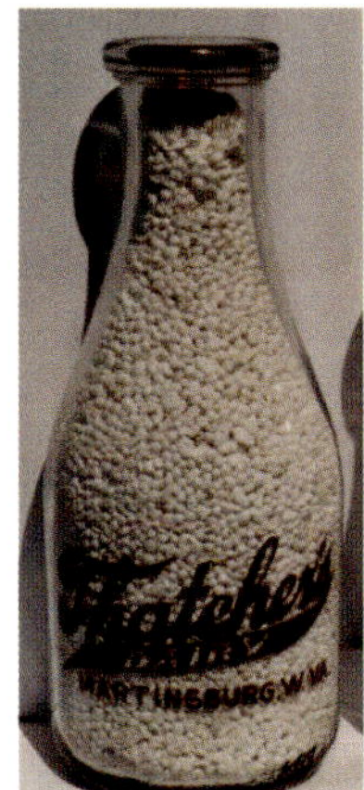

USWV04
Uncommon
Thatcher Dairy
Martinsburg,.WV
V-$70+

USWV05
Uncommon
Webster Springs
Wesbster Spr.W.V.
V-$50

USWV06
Uncommon
Woodworth Farm
Hurricane,W.V.
V-$50

USWV07
Uncommon
Dailey's Dairy
Charles Town,WV
V-$100+

USWV08
Uncommon
Hough's Dairy
Harpers Ferry,WV
V-$150+

USWV09
Uncommon
Oak Branch
White Sulphur Sp.
V-$50+

USWV10
Uncommon
Home Dairy
Fairmont,W.V.
V-$50

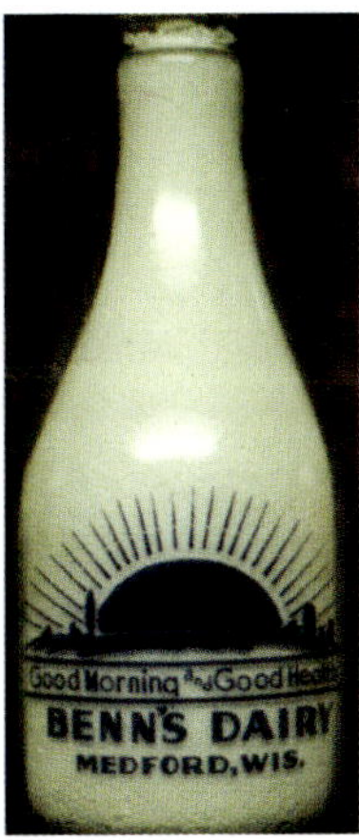

USWI01
Uncommon
Benn's Dairy
Medford,Wi.
V-$50

USWI02
common
Midwest
Plymouth,Wi
V-$20

USWI03
Uncommon
Schuchardt's
Sheboygan,Wi.
V-$50+

USWI04
Rare
Piper's
Sharon,Wi.
V-$150+

USWI05
Uncommon
Morning Star
Portage,Wi.
V-$50

USWI06
Uncommon
Fern Grove Dairy
Cornell,Wi.
V-$50+

USWI07
Rare
Butte des Morts
Neehah,WI.
V-$150+

USWI08
Uncommon
Boulevard Dairy
Marinette,Wi.
V-$50

USWI09
Uncommon
Better Farms
Fond Dulac,Wi.
V-$50+

USWI10
Uncommon
Bonnie Bro.Dairy
Eau Claire,Wi.
V-$50

USWI11
Semi-Rare
Manor Dairy
Madison,Wi.
V-$150+

USWI12
common
Brancroft
Madison.Wi.
V-$20

USWI13
Semi-Rare
Schlichting's Dairy
Sheboygan
Falls,Wi.
V-$100+

USWI14
Uncommon
Noll's Dairy
Marshfield,Wi.
V-$50

USWI15
Uncommon
New Glarus Dairy
New Glarus,Wi.
V-$50

Wyoming

USWY01
Uncommon
McNiff Dairy
Rawlings,Wy.
V-$50

USWY02
Rare
Shy Ann Dairy
Cheyenne,Wy.
V-$250+

USWY03
Uncommon
Judevines
Douglas,Wy.
V-$50+

USWY04
Rare
Center of Trans.
Cheyenne,Wy.
V-$250+

USWY05
Rare
Collegian Dairy
Laramie,Wy.
V-$150+

USWY06
reverse#USWY05

V-$00

USWY07
Rare
Rosedale
Laramie,Wy.
V-$350+

USWY08
Uncommon
Carson County Cry.
Rawlins,Wy.
V-$70+

USWY09
Rare
Challenge
Wy.
V-$150+

USWY10
Semi-Rare
Eden Valley Dairy
Rock Springs,Wy.
V-$100+

USWY11
Semi-Rare
Sunshine Farm
Cheyenne,Wy.
V-$150+

USWY12
Semi-Rare
Judvine Creamery
Douglas,Wy.
V-$150+

USWO13
Semi-Rare
Creek Valley Dairy
Aroola.Wy.
V-$150+

USWY14
Uncommon
Adams Milk
Rawlins,Wyo
V-$70+

USWY15
Semi-Rare
Double Diamond
Duncan,Wy.
V-$100+

USMS01
Rare
Mt.State Rifle
West Va.
V-100+

USMS01a
Rare
Mt. State Pistol
West Va.
V-$100+

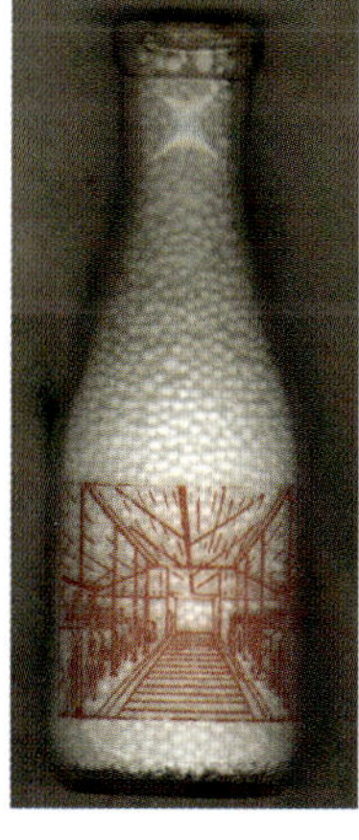

USMS03
Uncommon
Hospital Dairy

V-$50+

USMS04
Uncommon
Dresslers Dairy
Pittsburg,Pa.
V-$50

USMS05
Semi-Rare
Albers Milling
Calf Manna
V-$50+

USMS05a
Semi-Rare
Cloverleaf
Salt Lake City.
V-100+

USMS06
Uncommon
Single Milkbottle
Carrier
V-$50

USMS07
Uncommon
Aristocrat Dairy

V-$50

USMS07a
Uncommon
Foremost Dairies

V-$50

RE0053
Uncommon
Southern Daires

V-$50

USMS11
Uncommon
Polar Milk Cooler
Milkbottle Cover
V-$50+

USMS12
Uncommon
National D Stores

V-$30

USMS13
Uncommon
Independent
Grocer
V-$30

USMS14
Uncommon
White Front Dairy

V-$30

USMS15
REPRO

V-$00

Alwines Dairy

Johnstown,Pa.

Alwine's Dairy
Johnstown,Pa.
Dairy Buildings
Divco Milktruck
Set of babybottles
1/2 pint,pint and Quart
1 of 3 pyro milkbottles from
Pa. with Pennsylvania
spelled out.

Hand Milk Bottle Filler
Dairy & Creamery Equip.Co.
Kansas City,Mo.

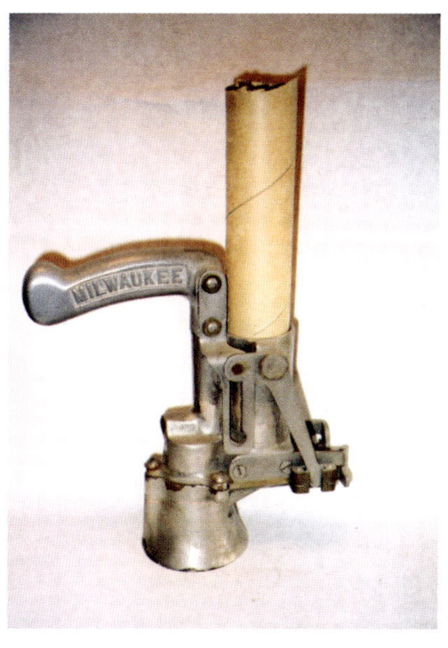

Hand Capper
Milwaukee

1. Frigidaire Meter Miser
2. Dandy Milk Bottle Top
3. tin cover
4. Sanitary Milk Bottle Cover glass
5. Sanitary Milk Bottle Cover Clear glass
6. Pour Well Milk Bottle Top
7. tin Bottle cover with Handle

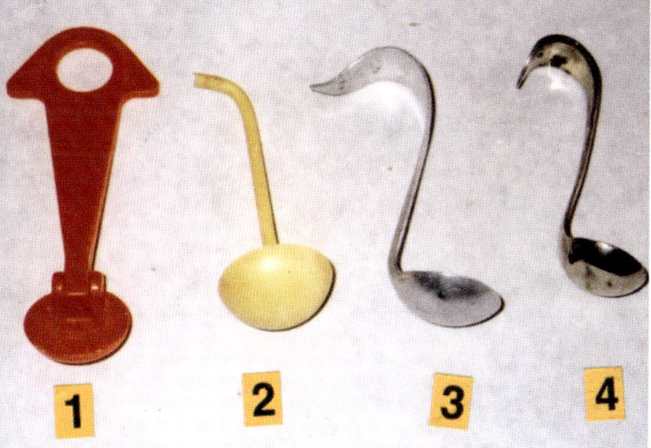

1. Modern Top Cream Separator
2. Cream top milkbottle plug
3. regular Cream top Spoon
4. smaller Cream top Spoon for newer square cream tops

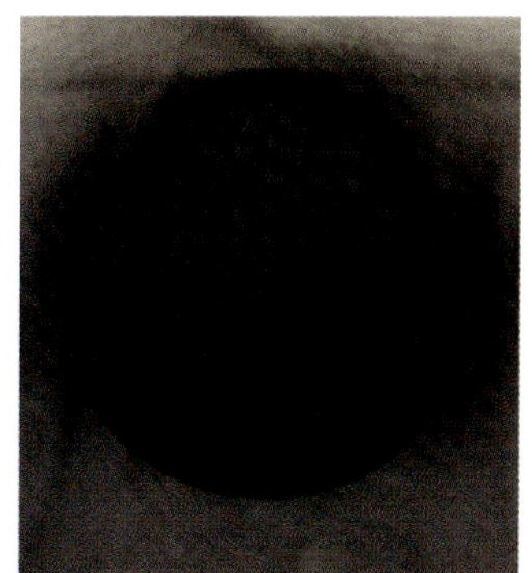

An Original Slug Plate insert
H.E.Taylor
Mansfield City

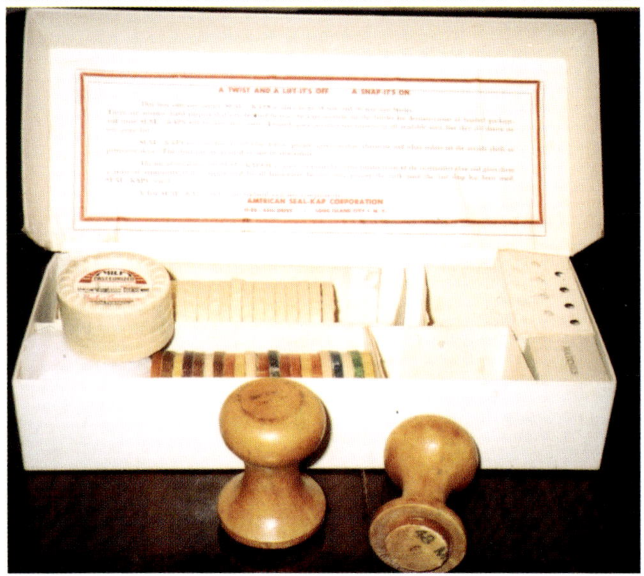

Seal Kap Salesman Sample Kit-hand cappers

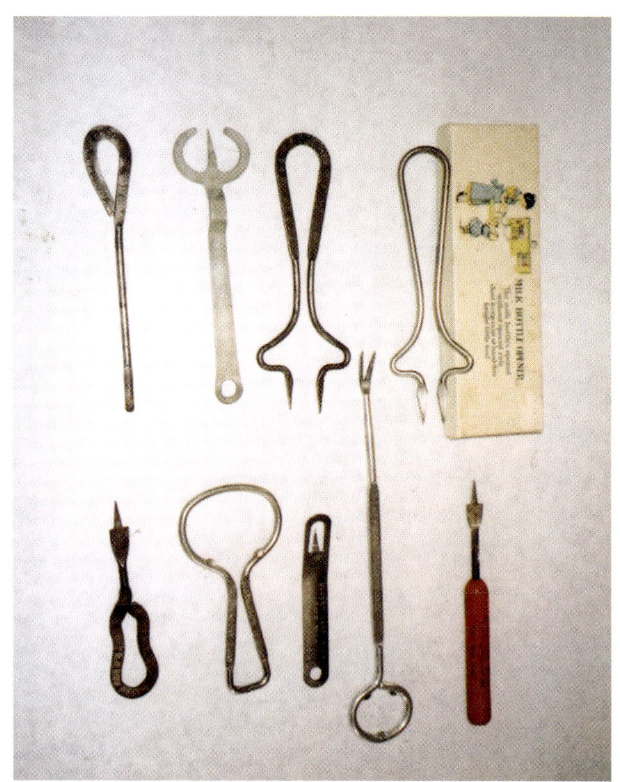

Milkbottle cap removers

Hagan dairy Supply Co. Greensboro,N.C. Milk bottle cap Supplies

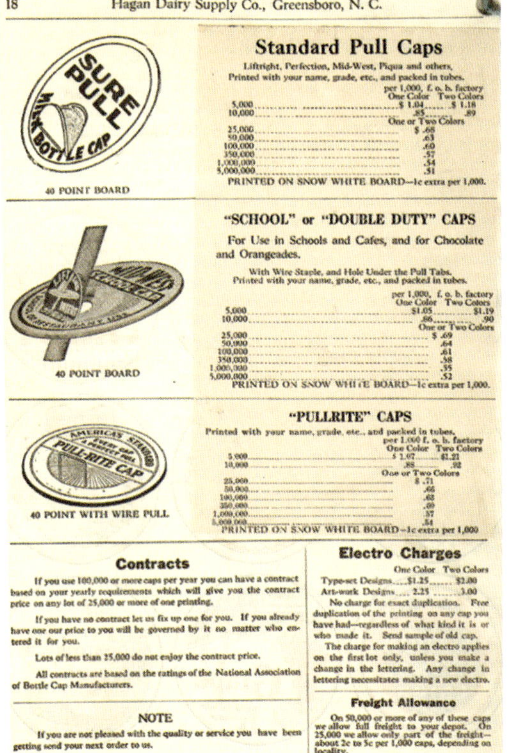

18 Hagan Dairy Supply Co., Greensboro, N. C.

Standard Pull Caps

Liftright, Perfection, Mid-West, Piqua and others, Printed with your name, grade, etc., and packed in tubes.

	per 1,000, f. o. b. factory One Color	Two Colors
5,000	$ 1.04	$ 1.18
10,000	.85	.89
	One or Two Colors	
25,000	$ .66	
50,000	.63	
100,000	.60	
350,000	.57	
1,000,000	.54	
5,000,000	.51	

PRINTED ON SNOW WHITE BOARD—1c extra per 1,000.

40 POINT BOARD

"SCHOOL" or "DOUBLE DUTY" CAPS

For Use in Schools and Cafes, and for Chocolate and Orangeades.

With Wire Staple, and Hole Under the Pull Tabs. Printed with your name, grade, etc., and packed in tubes.

	per 1,000, f. o. b. factory One Color	Two Colors
5,000	$1.05	$1.19
10,000	.86	.90
	One or Two Colors	
25,000	$ .69	
50,000	.64	
100,000	.61	
350,000	.58	
1,000,000	.55	
5,000,000	.52	

PRINTED ON SNOW WHITE BOARD—1c extra per 1,000.

40 POINT BOARD

"PULLRITE" CAPS

Printed with your name, grade, etc., and packed in tubes.

	per 1,000 f. o. b. factory One Color	Two Colors
5,000	$ 1.07	$1.21
10,000	.88	.92
	One or Two Colors	
25,000	$ .71	
50,000	.66	
100,000	.63	
350,000	.60	
1,000,000	.57	
5,000,000	.54	

PRINTED ON SNOW WHITE BOARD—1c extra per 1,000

40 POINT WITH WIRE PULL

Contracts

If you use 100,000 or more caps per year you can have a contract based on your yearly requirements which will give you the contract price on any lot of 25,000 or more of one printing.

If you have no contract let us fix up one for you. If you already have one our price to you will be governed by it no matter who entered it for you.

Lots of less than 25,000 do not enjoy the contract price.

All contracts are based on the ratings of the National Association of Bottle Cap Manufacturers.

NOTE

If you are not pleased with the quality or service you have been getting send your next order to us.

Electro Charges

	One Color	Two Colors
Type-set Designs	$1.25	$2.00
Art-work Designs	2.25	3.00

No charge for exact duplication. Free duplication of the printing on any cap you have had—regardless of what kind it is or who made it. Send sample of old cap.

The charge for making an electro applies on the first lot only, unless you make a change in the lettering. Any change in lettering necessitates making a new electro.

Freight Allowance

On 50,000 or more of any of these caps we allow full freight to your depot. On 25,000 we allow only part of the freight—about 2c to 5c per 1,000 caps, depending on locality.

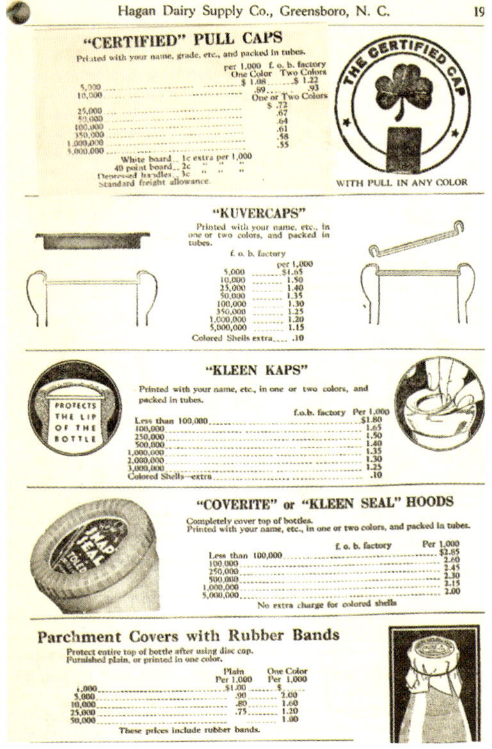

Hagan Dairy Supply Co., Greensboro, N. C. 19

"CERTIFIED" PULL CAPS

Printed with your name, grade, etc., and packed in tubes.

	per 1,000 f. o. b. factory One Color	Two Colors
5,000	$ 1.08	$ 1.22
10,000	.89	.93
	One or Two Colors	
25,000	$ .72	
50,000	.67	
100,000	.64	
350,000	.61	
1,000,000	.58	
5,000,000	.55	

White board 1c extra per 1,000
40 point board 2c " " "
Depressed handles 3c " " "
Standard freight allowance.

WITH PULL IN ANY COLOR

"KUVERCAPS"

Printed with your name, etc., in one or two colors, and packed in tubes.

f. o. b. factory	per 1,000
5,000	$1.65
10,000	1.50
25,000	1.40
50,000	1.35
100,000	1.30
350,000	1.25
1,000,000	1.20
5,000,000	1.15
Colored Shells extra	.10

"KLEEN KAPS"

Printed with your name, etc., in one or two colors, and packed in tubes.

f.o.b. factory	Per 1,000
Less than 100,000	$1.80
100,000	1.65
250,000	1.50
500,000	1.40
1,000,000	1.35
2,000,000	1.30
3,000,000	1.25
Colored Shells—extra	.10

"COVERITE" or "KLEEN SEAL" HOODS

Completely cover top of bottles.
Printed with your name, etc., in one or two colors, and packed in tubes.

f. o. b. factory	Per 1,000
Less than 100,000	$2.85
100,000	2.60
250,000	2.45
500,000	2.30
1,000,000	2.15
5,000,000	2.00

No extra charge for colored shells

Parchment Covers with Rubber Bands

Protect entire top of bottle after using disc cap.
Furnished plain, or printed in one color.

	Plain Per 1,000	One Color Per 1,000
1,000	$1.00	$
5,000	.90	2.00
10,000	.80	1.60
25,000	.75	1.20
50,000		1.00

These prices include rubber bands.

MID-WEST Improved PULL CAPS
SPECIAL HAND LETTERED DESIGNS
956 Mackensen's SANITARY DAIRY GUERNSEY Raw MILK GRADE
957 Marshall's GRADE A PASTEURIZED MILK
958 PASTEURIZED GUERNSEY DAIRY COMPANY GENERAL PURPOSE CREAM
959 HEAVY CREAM Purity Dairy FREEHOLD, N.J.
960 WILLOW PERFECTLY PASTEURIZED MILK THURSDAY
961 JOHNSTOWN SANITARY PASTEURIZED MILK HOMOGENIZED DAIRY CO.
962 Rockford DAIRIES, INC. HEAVY CREAM PASTEURIZED
963 3 Brothers DAIRY GRADE A Raw MILK PHONE 112
964 CAMILLA DAIRY FARM GRADE A WHOLE RAW CREAM
965 MOORE Lancaster, Pa. GRADE A PASTEURIZED MILK T.B. TESTED
966 Madsen Dairy SKIM MILK
967 PHONE 4059W Willowbrook DAIRY WARREN, O. PASTEURIZED-WHOLE MILK 3.6% B.F. OR MORE
Mid-West Bottle Cap Co., Belvidere, Ill.
[1]

MID-WEST Improved PULL CAPS
SPECIAL HAND LETTERED DESIGNS
896 ALFADALE DAIRY T.E. GULLINGS RAW MILK MOORHEAD, MINN.
897 CITY MILK CO. GRADE A CHOCOLATE MILK
898 CEDAR RAPIDS LEACOX'S RAW Guernsey MILK GRADE
899 PASTEURIZED Lake View Dairy SHERIDAN 8027 SELECTED MILK
900 Piasta DAIRY PERFECTLY PASTEURIZED MILK
901 DAIRYLAND FARMS CO-OPERATIVE ASS'N. pasteurized GOOD MORNING MILK
902 HOMESTEAD FARM DAIRY BANGS TESTED HERD MILK RAW DES MOINES, IOWA
903 THE CONNEAUT CREAMERY CO. CREAM 20% B.F. OR MORE PERFECTLY PASTEURIZED
904 T.B. TESTED SYLVAN VIEW DAIRY PASTEURIZED
905 HARMONY DAIRY PURE PASTEURIZED WHOLE MILK
906 Baker-Hubbell PEORIA ILL. HOMOGENIZED MILK PASTEURIZED
907 GRADE A JERSEY-GUERNSEY MILK SWANER FARMS DAIRY
Mid-West Bottle Cap Co., Belvidere, Ill.

MID-WEST Improved PULL CAPS
SPECIAL HAND LETTERED DESIGNS
968 OBERLIESEN BROS. DAIRY PASTEURIZED MILK MT. CLEMENS, MICH.
969 AMES DAIRY PASTEURIZED MILK
970 DONNAN'S DAIRY CLINTON, ILL. Natural MILK
971 Liberty CREAMERY CO. MILK PASTEURIZED
972 ST. CLAIR MILK FARM Guernsey COFFEE CREAM GRADE A
973 HAWKINS DAIRY FAIRMONT, W.VA. PASTEURIZED CHOCOLATE MILK
974 Kleinheinz PERFECTLY PASTEURIZED CREAM
975 MANCHESTER, CONN. SHADY GLEN DAIRY FARM John Rieg MILK PASTEURIZED WEDNESDAY
976 QUINN'S MILK PRODUCTS CO. GRADE PASTEURIZED MILK
977 Producer's BURLINGTON, IOWA GRADE A Pasteurized MILK
978 J.H. Ketter DAIRY GUERNSEY MILK & CREAM MINERAL POINT, WIS.
979 JERSEY MILK PASTEURIZED SHADY GROVE DAIRY CHICOPEE FALLS

MID-WEST Improved PULL CAPS
SPECIAL HAND LETTERED DESIGNS
980 Weiker's BUTTERMILK LA CROSSE, WIS.
981 Capitol Inc. DAIRIES GRAPE PUNCH
982 Gedeon's 25% CREAM
983 HEARD'S DAIRY PHONE 8451 Raw MILK ASHLAND, ORE.
984 PASTEURIZED GUZIK'S DAIRY WHIPPING CREAM 35% B.F. OR MORE
985 ALEXA'S DAIRY phone 5-8031 CREAM LANSING, MICHIGAN
986 CENTRAL CITY DAIRY TAYLOR BROS. SELMA, ALA. GRADE A RAW MILK
987 LIBERTYVILLE HOME DAIRY Genuine GUERNSEY PASTEURIZED WHIPPING CREAM
988 Bickley's QUALITY MT. VERNON, ILL. Jersey MILK
989 MOCKSVILLE, N.C. TWINBROOK FARM RAW GUERNSEY GRADE A MILK
990 Benoit's DAIRY HEAVY CREAM INDIAN ORCHARD
991 Day DAIRY CREAM PASTEURIZED
Mid-West Bottle Cap Co., Belvidere, Ill.

BLUE BONNET DAIRIES
DEMOPOLIS ALABAMA
PH 33
CULTURED
BUTTERMILK
PASTEURIZED
GRADE A PASTEURIZED MILK
BELL'S
DAIRY
KODIAK, ALASKA
ARKANSAS TUBERCULOSIS SANATORIUM
GRADE
A
WHOLE MILK
TUBERCULIN TESTED
OUR MILK TOPS THEM ALL
WICKENBURG ARIZONA
WICKENBURG DAIRY
GRADE A MILK
PASTEURIZED
Gholson's
GRADE
A
PASTEURIZED
HOMOGENIZED MILK
LOS ANIMAS, COLORADO
LEWES DAIRY
SAFE A MILK
PASTEURIZED
PHONE
3121
LEWES, DELAWARE
PRODUCED IN FLORIDA
PASTEURIZED MILK
GOLDEN GUERNSEY
DINSMORE DAIRY CO.
ALPINE DAIRY
LITHONIA GEORGIA
GRADE A RAW MILK
FROM ACCREDITED HERD
HONOKAA DAIRY FARM
HONOKAA, HAWAII
GRADE A RAW
MILK
SHADDUCKS DAIRY
COEUR D'ALENE, IDAHO
A PASTEURIZED PRODUCT
Deer Creek
CRY. CO.
GRADE A
PASTEURIZED
MILK
ATCHISON, KANSAS
FOR YOUR SAFETY AND PROTECTION
ROBERT CRAIG
JERSEY
REG. U.S. PAT. OFF.
CREAMLINE MILK
GRADE A RAW
HAZEL, KENTUCKY
CLOVER LEAF
DAIRY PRODUCTS
GRADE A MILK
PASTEURIZED
PHONE
5232
MONROE, LOUISIANA
GRADE A RAW MILK
GOLDEN GUERNSEY
ROCKVILLE MARYLAND
SYCAMORE FARMS DAIRY
Johnston's
VITAMIN D GRADE A
PASTEURIZED
CHOCOLATE MILK
M'COMB DAIRY PRODUCTS COMPANY
M'COMB, MISSISSIPPI
St. Louis
Dairy Co.
REG. U.S. PATENT OFFICE
Grade A
ST. LOUIS. MISSOURI
MILK
PASTEURIZED THURSDAY
HAREBO DAIRY
LICENSED
DAIRY
MILK
GLASGOW, MONTANA
PASTEURIZER'S PERMIT NO. 1
MILK
PASTEURIZED AT
ALLIANCE
NEBRASKA
BY THE
FAIRMONT CREAMERY CO.
MINDEN BUTTER MFG. CO.
MINDEN NEVADA
Windmill
BRAND
PASTEURIZED MARKET
MILK
MOUNTAINAIR
Mountainair DAIRY
GRADE A
PASTEURIZED
MILK
NEW MEXICO

Index

I would like to thank all the artists who worked at the milkbottle manufacturing factories who gave us such beautiful art work on milkbottles. Udderly Spendid tries to save this art work in a book form for history

All art work pictured is the property of the artist or company who they worked for and is pictured here for the information of the milkbottle collector and is reproduced here under that courtesy.

Bibliography

The Milk Plant Monthly--many issues
John Pearce & Co. Dairy Supplies
Super Milk Bottle the Lamb Glass Co
Thatcher Manuf. Co Glass Containers
Milk Bottles Lockport Glass Co
Thatcher Manu. Co. stock offering
The Milk Dealer--many issues
Hagan Dairy supply Co.

Please forgive me if I missed your name under those who sent photos or who sent photos and I could not fit them into the book. I have thousands of photos and could not use them all. Thank you again for the tremendous support of my books.

I would like to thank Susan Ochoa who helped set up the book on the computer and put in endless hours helping in all areas of the making of the book. I could never have finished on time which out her help.

I would also like to thank my wife--Maxine who has continually supported my hobby collecting milkbottles and authoring my books. She provides the support in checking for spelling, grammer and layout. Thank you Maxine, for without your support, I could never have completed this or any of my other books.

John and Maxine Tutton Norman Patton Ralph DeVillars

Printed by Berryville graphics Berryville,Va 2003